LIVING WITH PLANTS

Living with Plants

Hamlyn

London · New York · Sydney · Toronto

First published in 1982 by The Hamlyn Publishing Group Limited
London · New York · Sydney · Toronto
Astronaut House, Feltham, Middlesex, England

Copyright ©The Hamlyn Publishing Group Limited 1982

Filmset in England by Tameside Filmsetting Ltd,
Ashton-under-Lyne, Lancashire in Monophoto Garamond

Printed in Spain

ISBN 0 600 30526 0

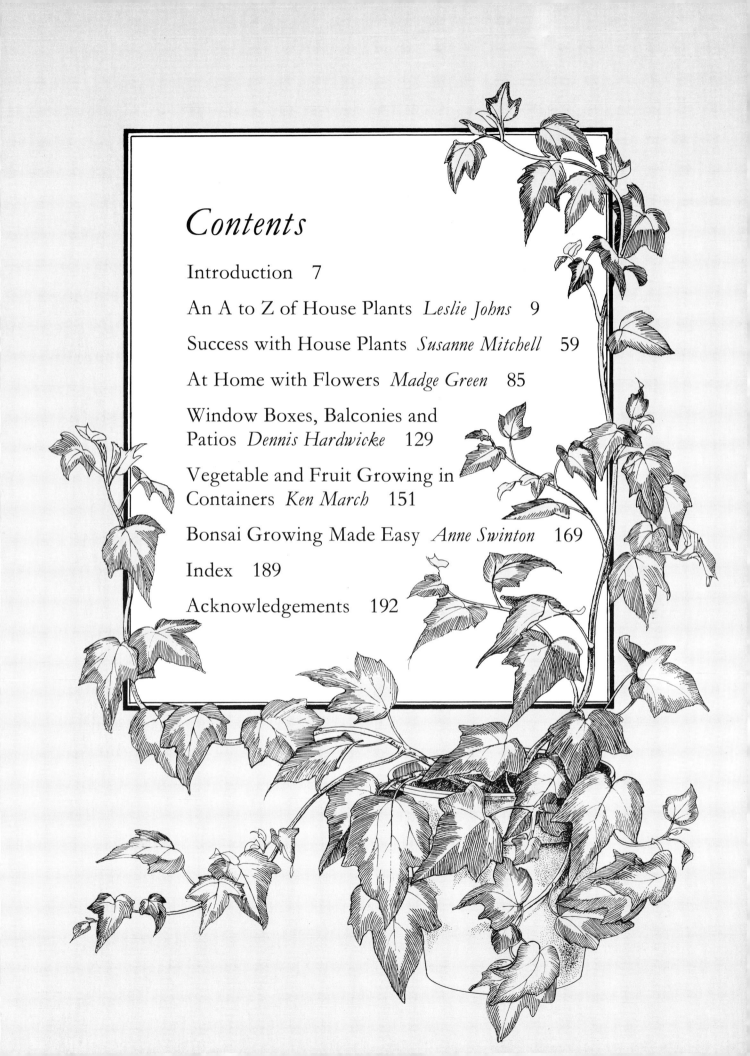

Contents

Introduction

THE PLEASURE which comes from being surrounded by plants and watching them grow and flower is something which is well known to every gardener. From the appearance of the first fresh green shoots of the snowdrops and crocuses in early spring through the opulence of the fruit blossoms and massed flowers of late spring and summer to the wonderful tints of autumn, the garden is never without some excitement. Even in winter, the evergreens and delicately flowering cherries or jasmines are there to cheer us along.

Many people, however, do not have gardens and must look for the charms of the changing seasons in a more confined area. This book, *Living with Plants*, has been put together with these people especially in mind, although it can be enjoyed by anyone interested in growing plants. It sets out to show how even the smallest space outdoors, such as a window ledge, can be used as a garden in miniature, and the scope offered in the home itself for surrounding ourselves with plants and flowers – real and artificial – is exploited to the full. But even more than this, within these pages will be found many ideas and suggestions for both beautifying the home, and enjoying and having the fun of growing an amazingly wide range of plants.

House plants are usually the first introduction many of us have to the trials and joys of growing plants indoors. To cater for this fairly recent innovation to the gardening field, nurserymen have been steadily increasing the choice of plants which can be used within the home over the last thirty years. Some species, although beautiful, have proved too unreliable and expensive and have been dropped from cultivation, but each year sees more and more unusual and colourful varieties being introduced to our homes. For many people, how to care for all these, often exotic, plants can prove a slight source of worry, but as a general rule as long as they are not over- or under-watered and have an adequate source of light and warmth most plants will grow well.

The 'A to Z' section (pages 9 to 57) which opens the book has been specially put together as an at-a-glance guide both to identification and the most important aspects of each individual plant's cultivation requirements. This gives details of any particular idiosyncrasy and indicates how much water is required, when to feed and repot and in what sort of temperature the plant is happiest. The plants described have been chosen as being representative of the ones most widely available and popular to grow.

Following on from this descriptive section is 'Success with House Plants' (pages 59 to 84), in which there is much pertinent advice on all the general aspects of house plant care including the selection and care of them as well as methods of propagation and dealing with pests and diseases.

A well-grown house plant is, in itself, a thing of beauty but its effect as a well chosen ornament is partly dependent on how it is displayed. Single plants dotted around the room on any convenient surface do not look as good as a group of plants arranged either on a tray of gravel or actually planted together in a large container. Try to suit the plant to the space available and if one of your prize specimens does become too large for its surroundings then maybe the time has come to donate it to a nursery or give it to someone with larger premises.

Many house plants fall into related groups and it could make an added interest to collect one of these groups. Those especially recommended are ferns, bromeliads, the various peperomias or pileas, African violets and begonias.

From house plants to flower arrangement is but a short step; in fact, both are related as the aim of each is to use flowers and plants to their greatest ornamental effect. 'At Home with Flowers' (pages 85 to 128) takes a very imaginative look at flower arranging in several different types of home such as a town house, a country cottage, a house by the sea and a flat or bedsitter. The ideas and arrangements are suggested by each type of location and make use of the material which is most likely to be easily available but, of course, a great number of the ideas can be used in any location. Here are so many ideas, written about so enthusiastically, that you will be encouraged to look for an interesting or unusual container to set off a few flowers and leaves even if you have never considered yourself to be a flower arranger.

Have you thought, for example, about using the lovely silk flowers, now so widely available, to make long-term displays in winter or when conditions are against the use of fresh flowers and they are expensive to buy? Or looked at the possibilities of making tiny

7

arrangements under four inches high with accessories chosen from the doll's house? Arranging flowers for the table or to welcome guests are also little touches which make the home come alive with colour and friendliness. The important thing to remember is not to worry about rules but simply to enjoy the flowers and leaves for their own sake and to allow your imagination to run away with you.

Moving on now to the surroundings of the home, which is perhaps some highrise apartment where there is only a window ledge or balcony or a small paved area, such as is often found outside a town house, in which to create a garden. 'Window Boxes, Balconies and Patios' (pages 129 to 150) sets out to show the reader how to use flowering and foliage plants of all kinds to their greatest effect. By using window boxes, hanging baskets and planters of all kinds it is perfectly possible to have a year-round display of colour and interest with which to lift a monotonous skyline or brighten a dingy basement. The results of such efforts can be a delight to passers-by, too, for just occasionally when walking along a street and glancing into a basement area or up at a window box filled with bright flowering bulbs or brilliant summer annuals one is momentarily transported from the city street.

On the practical side there is advice, too, on various ways of growing and training plants, including shrubs, roses and climbing plants and an especially useful section on maintaining a variety of herbs at close quarters to the kitchen.

'Vegetable and Fruit Growing in Containers' (pages 151 to 168) is a 'fun' section which is also highly practical. Given here in a most readable way are instructions for growing a wide range of vegetables, and even some fruits, both indoors on the kitchen windowsill and outside in whatever space is available. By spreading the crops into hanging baskets or the ever-useful growing bags it is even possible to have a mini-allotment with an assortment of salad crops available for summer eating – one novelty suggested is the growing of potatoes in a plastic dustbin! Some of the other crops described, such as mustard and cress

and bean sprouts, are so easy and quick that they provide ideal entertainment for children, as well as giving them an opportunity to see how plants grow.

The last part of the book, 'Bonsai Growing Made Easy' (pages 169 to 188), includes a fascinating and informative account of the cultivation techniques required in order to enable a beginner to grow successfully an exquisite miniature tree. These trees are rightly considered to be living works of art and are very beautiful. The deciduous kinds, in particular, are a source of continual delight in spring as each day they open more leaves and many of them also exhibit the most brilliant autumn colour.

Some of the trees illustrated in this book are extremely old, for example the hornbeam on the title page and the juniper on page 182, and, whilst caring for these is something very few people can aspire to, it is well within most people's scope to grow a very charming little tree in a small proportion of that time. It is important to remember, however, that bonsai of our native hardy trees, such as horsechestnut, hornbeam and beech, cannot be kept satisfactorily indoors for long periods. They are in no way house plants and for the most part of their lives must live outside, although they are not demanding on space – a series of shelves on a balcony will provide a home for a number of plants. The trees can be brought indoors for intervals of a few days at a time and enjoyed at close quarters before being returned to the cooler and lighter conditions outdoors. However, there is a way round this requirement for those who wish to grow bonsai entirely in the house and this is to choose tropical and warm climate trees which would not survive out of doors anyway. But whatever type of tree is chosen, growing bonsai is likely to become an enthralling and captivating hobby.

Living with Plants is a very wide-ranging book which has been prepared by a team of horticulturists in the hope that it will be of interest and provide a source of pleasure and encouragement to all who would like to use and grow plants and flowers in and around the home.

METRIC CONVERSION TABLE

Imperial	Metric	Imperial	Metric	Imperial	Metric	Imperial	Metric
½ in	1 cm	4 in	10 cm	9 in	23 cm	3 ft	1 m
1 in	2·5 cm	5 in	13 cm	10 in	25 cm	5 ft	1·5 m
1½ in	4 cm	6 in	15 cm	11 in	28 cm	10 ft	3 m
2 in	5 cm	7 in	18 cm	1 ft	30 cm		
3 in	8 cm	8 in	20 cm	2 ft	60 cm		

An A to Z of House Plants

The popularity of growing plants in the home is
increasing all the time, even among those people who
profess no interest in gardening. In response to
this demand the variety of suitable plants
available seems to be wider than ever. There really is a
plant for every situation and to suit every taste.

Achimenes hybrid

Adiantum

Achimenes

Common name Hot Water Plant; if rhizomes are plunged into hot water they are said to begin to grow more readily.
General information Tender plants with short-lived flowers, five-lobed on slim tubes, red, pink, white, blue.
Temperature No extremes of heat or cold, 16–24°C (60–75°F).
Position Good light, even sunlight for brief periods.
Watering As soon as rhizomes start into growth keep the soil constantly moist, though never sodden. After flowering reduce water gradually until quite dry.
Care Remove some growing points to promote bushy appearance and where necessary support or stake long, trailing stems. Use an equal part peat and perlite compost with added lime. Repot annually following propagation hints below, planting rhizomes just below soil surface in the loose mixture.
Propagation Allow rhizomes to dry off completely in a frost-free place after flowering. In early spring separate them, plunge briefly in hot water (not vital) and plant in fresh moist compost. Seed can be sown at this time or plants propagated from stem cuttings in spring or early summer. Use a light, sharply drained soil-based compost, kept always moist.

Adiantum

Common name Maidenhair Fern, several popular varieties.
General information Beautiful, delicate ferns with fronds up to 16 in long divided into many fan-shaped pinnae and growing on slim, generally black leaf stalks, the 'maiden hairs'.
Temperature 10–24°C (50–75°F), preferably about 18°C (65°F).
Position In good, strong light but never direct sun.
Watering Never allow adiantums to dry out but do not keep them too wet. Water well, then allow upper soil to dry out.
Care A peat-based compost suits these ferns, allowing the wiry rhizomes to spread just beneath soil surface. Feed lightly but regularly. When temperatures rise increase humidity by standing plants on trays of wet pebbles or by spraying with water on occasions. Roots will eventually fill the pot; repot or divide when these show above the soil surface.
Propagation Remove root ball from pot and divide into sections, each with a good piece of rhizome and one or more fronds. Pot each section separately in a moist, peat-based compost, making sure in the early stages that this is kept only just moist. Too dry will kill the immature plant, too wet will lead to rotting of the rhizomes.

Aechmea rhodocyanea

Aechmea rhodocyanea

Common names Urn Plant, Greek Vase Plant.
General information An easy-to-grow, rewarding, epiphytic bromeliad with 4-in wide, 18-in long, spine-edged leaves, pale green dusted with grey, growing from a central cup or urn which should be kept filled with water. From this cup rises a single flower stalk bearing a large, prickly pink inflorescence and between the many bracts of this appear tiny blue and pink, short-lived flowers. The inflorescence lives for some months and then the plant begins to die while one or more offsets appear growing at the base of the urn.
Temperature Normal living conditions, about 16–20°C (60–68°F).
Position Bright light, even direct sunlight.
Watering One of the easiest of all house plants because the only thing to remember is to keep the central cup filled with water at all times. Water sometimes trickles down to the compost. Add liquid feed to the water when necessary.
Care Repotting will not be required. Instead use offsets to replace old plants which will not flower again.
Propagation Allow offsets to reach manageable size, then cut each away from the parent with a share of the meagre roots. Pot in rich, light compost and keep in light shade at first.

Aglaeonema
'Silver Queen'

Aglaeonema 'Silver Queen'

Common name Differs according to species or varieties.
General information Leaves of this attractive foliage plant are about 12 in long and 5 in wide, spear-shaped, tough, greyish-green with silver stripes and blotches, growing on short stems from a central thicker stem or trunk.
Temperature 18–20°C (65–68°F) would be ideal.
Position Light shade, never in full sun even briefly.
Watering Make sure the root ball is uniformly moist and then leave until the surface is dry before watering again.
Care Plants enjoy humidity, so if your rooms are dry stand pots on a tray of wet pebbles or plunge into a cache-pot. Feed monthly except during winter. Aglaeonemas are sometimes attacked by mealy bug, so spray liberally if this is seen. Repot annually while young, older plants less frequently.
Propagation This is normally by the division of a root clump in spring, potting each section in a moist mixture of peat and coarse sand or perlite. A heated propagating case is helpful but not essential. Plants can also be air layered or a basal shoot bearing some roots and one or two leaves can be detached and planted in the same open soil mixture.

Ananus

Common name Pineapple.
General information The pineapple which produces our fruit, *Ananus comosus*, is both too large and too unspectacular to be worth growing indoors, but there are other forms, smaller and more decorative. *A. bracteatus* 'Striatus' is probably the best known of these, with long, savagely toothed leaves striped green and gold with a background hint of pink. The spectacular pink flower, followed by the small, decorative but inedible fruit, seldom develops under normal home culture but some nurserymen sell plants in this mature stage.
Temperature High, preferably about 20°C (68°F) with humidity.
Position In a south-facing window, even during summer.
Watering Water thoroughly and then allow compost almost to dry.
Care Repotting is seldom necessary, for roots are small, but if carried out use a peat- or soil-based compost with good drainage. Feed fortnightly throughout the entire year. Beware sharp leaf edges and perilous points.
Propagation By offsets. With a sharp knife cut away an offset about 6 in long at the base of the main plant and root in a peat-sand mixture in propagating case or plastic bag.

Anthurium scherzerianum

Common names Flamingo Flower, Piggy Tail Plant.
General information Grown mainly for the striking, unusual inflorescences, consisting of a gleaming, almost waxen spathe, usually a vivid scarlet, from which grows the often curling spadix which holds the many tiny flowers.
Temperature Warm, 18–24°C (65–75°F) normally.
Position Plants do not like direct sunlight but should be placed where the light is softened, perhaps by a net curtain.
Watering Soil mixtures should be kept well moistened at all times during the growing season, but in winter only sufficient water is needed to keep the roots from drying out.
Care Plants seem to grow best in a peat-based compost so long as a regular feeding programme is instituted. Each spring plants should be moved into pots just one size larger. Humidity is essential to successful culture, so plants should stand on trays of wet pebbles, in cache-pots filled with moist peat, or should be sprayed with water on occasions.
Propagation Overcrowded and matted clumps of roots can be gently pulled apart in spring, making sure each piece has both leaves and roots. Pot in a peaty soil, keep warm and humid.

Ananas bracteatus 'Striatus'

Anthurium scherzerianum

Aphelandra squarrosa
'Lousiae'

Aphelandra squarrosa

Common names Zebra plant, Saffron Spike.
General information A striking and attractive plant because of the dark green, spear-shaped leaves bearing white stripes along the main veins and the yellow-orange, short-lived flowers appearing in a long-lived cockscomb of bracts. A difficult plant to keep attractive for more than a season.
Temperature Fairly high, 18–24°C (65–75°F) while growing.
Position Always in good light but never direct sun.
Watering Roots should always be kept wet; not sodden but more moist than is normal for most house plants.
Care Aphelandras are greedy plants and in addition to being kept moist at the roots at all times they require a rich compost and weekly feeding. After the flowers have faded and the longer-lived bracts have begun to look tired, it is helpful to let the plant rest by slightly reducing the amount of water it receives, cutting out the feeds and slightly reducing the temperature. Then in spring cut back the plant to the lowest pair of leaves and repot in a rich soil-based compost.
Propagation Insert 3-in tip cuttings in rich compost, preferably in a propagator, otherwise in a sealed plastic bag.

Araucaria excelsa

Common name Norfolk Island Pine.
General information A real conifer, which will grow to more than 165 ft in the Antipodes, yet indoors is unlikely to reach 6 ft. It is a slow grower, tough and easy, unspectacular but graceful, particularly pleasing in spring when the branch tips produce their fresh, soft green needles.
Temperature Accommodating, between 7–24°C (45–75°F).
Position Surprisingly, perhaps, araucarias should be kept out of direct sun, though never in too shady a spot.
Watering Plenty of water in summer, much less during winter.
Care This is normally a tough plant that makes few demands on the owner, yet this does not mean it can be neglected. Dry roots will make it droop and die and too little light will result in needles dropping. Because of the slow rate of growth repotting will be necessary only once every three or four years, using a rich, soil-based compost.
Propagation By seed, but impossible without special equipment.

Araucaria excelsa

Ardisia crispa

Common name Coral Berry.
General information This slow grower will reach about 3 ft in height as an upright shrub and is popular mainly for its long-lasting bright red berries which are preceded by small, star-shaped, pale pink or white flowers.
Temperature Fairly cool, preferably between 10–16°C (50–60°F). Extra humidity is necessary if warmer.
Position Good light is essential, even direct sunlight for brief periods each day so long as this is not too strong.
Watering Keep the roots always well moistened during the growing period of spring and summer, use less in winter.
Care Never try to hurry the normal slow growth of ardisias. Feed fortnightly. Repot annually into a pot just one size larger. Do this in spring and use a rich and well drained soil-based compost that will hold water.
Propagation Seed is both difficult to obtain and unsatisfactory because of the slow growth rate. Heel cuttings from laterals can be potted in a peat and sand mixture, preferably in a propagator with bottom heat, otherwise enclosed in plastic.

Ardisia crispa

Asparagus

Common names Asparagus Fern, Maidenhair Fern.
General information There are several of these 'ferns' of which *A. setaceus* (*A. plumosus*) is a popular example. *A. asparagoides* is smilax, *A. densiflorus* has a number of varieties producing 'Sprengeri' and foxtail fern, and *A. setaceus* has both dwarf and vigorous forms.
Temperature Normal room temperatures are suitable for all.
Position Give plants good light but not direct sun.
Watering Keep soil well moistened at all times during the growing season and dryer, but never dry, during winters.
Care Plenty of water and regular feeding will keep asparagus plants happy and growing well. Repot plants every spring, using a rich soil mixture. Roots become thick and easily fill pots, so leave space. Soft green fronds drop in sun. Plants can look charming in an indoor hanging basket, some to grow upwards, others to trail, making a lacy green ball.
Propagation In spring divide the probably matted root ball into as many portions as are required, using a sharp knife. Seed is easy to germinate but plants are slow growing at first.

Asparagus setaceus

Aspidistra lurida

Aspidistra lurida

Common name Cast Iron Plant.
General information An easy-to-grow plant, though slow. It makes few demands and will grow where other house plants die, but it repays the basic essentials of normal plant care. A variegated form with creamy-yellow stripes is sometimes seen and this requires good light to retain leaf colour.
Temperature Anything from 5–24°C (41–75°F) will suit.
Position Out of direct sunlight. Plants will grow in quite shady positions but will do better in good steady light.
Watering Do not overdo it. Keep the root ball just moist at all times, allowing the top inch or two to become dry to the touch before next applying water.
Care To get good, glossy leaves make sure your aspidistra stands in good light, perhaps directly in a north window. Clean the leaves regularly using plain water – no leaf gloss preparations. In the growing season give regular fortnightly liquid feeds. Plants do best if ignored, so repot only when grossly overcrowded or top-dress with fresh compost.
Propagation Divide overgrown plants in spring. Cut away pieces of the rhizome which carry at least two good leaves and pot these in a well drained, soil-based medium, keeping this just moist and giving no food until growing well.

Asplenium nidus

Common name Bird's Nest Fern.
General information Glossy green fronds, as long as 3 ft when treated well, grow upwards and outwards from a central rosette. The fronds uncurl gradually from the base of the rosette and are easily damaged when small, though tough later.
Temperature Do not permit winter temperatures to fall below about 16°C (60°F) or rise above about 26°C (80°F) in summer.
Position Keep out of direct sun but in good, strong light.
Watering During spring and summer make sure that the compost is kept constantly moist and never allowed to dry out. In winter give only enough water to prevent the soil drying out.
Care Mature fronds are large enough to hold dust, so wipe them over with a moist sponge once a month or so. Feed plants monthly. They can be left to grow in a small pot until this is filled with the wiry roots, when they should be repotted in a peat, leafmould and perlite compost.
Propagation The bird's nest fern can only be propagated from the spores gathered together in little cases on the underside of some fronds. Collection and sowing of these spores is a task best kept for the enthusiast or the specialist.

Asplenium nidus

13

Azalea indica

Azalea

Common name Azalea. Sometimes known as *Azalea indica*, but more correctly as *Rhododendron simsii*.

General information Plants grown indoors are invariably hybrids grown to flower at special times. Flowers are in several hues of red, white, sometimes bi-coloured. Life of plants indoors is usually brief, although with care they can be kept from year to year to flower at natural times.

Temperature Keep out of all danger of frosts but in as cool a position in the house as possible.

Position Out of direct sun but otherwise in good light.

Watering Roots must never be allowed to dry out, so water thoroughly and frequently, using rain- or lime-free water.

Care Give additional humidity by plunging pot in a moist peat-filled cache-pot or standing on a tray of wet pebbles. Give light feeds fortnightly when growing well. Remember that plants have been grown under artificial conditions and that roots have been trimmed, so treat as a temporary plant.

Propagation Take 2-in tip cuttings in spring and plant in an equal perlite and peat mixture, preferably using a propagating case or enclosing in a sealed plastic bag.

Begonia 'Lucerna'

Common name Spotted Angel-wing Begonia.

General information A large, bushy, fibrous-rooted begonia, strong, vigorous, growing as tall as 6 ft, almost always in flower, with attractive white-spotted green leaves, red beneath, long green stems turning brown, flowers pink to red.

Temperature Normal room temperatures are ideal, but give added humidity if winter air is too hot and dry.

Position Good light is necessary so place where the sun will rest on the plants for an hour or two each day.

Watering Water carefully even in summer, allowing the soil to dry out a little between applications. Give less in winter.

Care These plants will grow large, so make sure the pot is stable. It will help to plunge it in a peat-filled cache-pot which will also provide added humidity. Vigorous growth necessitates moving on to a larger pot each spring. Use a rich soil mixture and feed plants regularly when in growth.

Propagation Cut 4-in shoots in early summer, trim ends and plant in a peat and perlite mixture, preferably after dipping in hormone rooting powder. A propagating case will ensure success, but pots can be placed inside a sealed plastic bag. Keep in good light and water carefully until growth is seen.

Begonia 'Lucerna'

Begonia masoniana

Common name Iron Cross Begonia.

General information A rhizomatous begonia with characteristically heart-shaped, lop-sided leaves, this time crinkled and almost rough to the touch and bearing the chocolate-red iron cross pattern. Easy to grow, easy to propagate.

Temperature Normal living-room temperatures · suit this begonia, but if warmer, give a little added humidity.

Position In good light. So long as there is humidity even an hour or two of direct sun each day will do little harm.

Watering Do not allow these plants to be too moist. Water thoroughly in spring and summer but let the soil dry out before watering again. In winter keep the compost just moist.

Care Repot annually in spring in a shallow pot or pan, using a peat-based compost left quite loose around the roots. Apply fertilizer regularly throughout their growing period. When plants are over-large merely topdress with fresh soil or discard and replace with an easily propagated young plant.

Propagation Divide a strong rhizome into 2–3 in sections each bearing good roots and plant each in a moist peat and perlite mixture. Use a propagating case or sealed plastic bag.

Begonia masoniana

Begonia rex

Begonia × tuberhybrida
'Roy Hartley'

Begonia rex

Common name Painted Leaf Begonia.
General information Deservedly one of the most popular of all house plants because they are easy to grow and come in the widest possible range of colours and patterns, greens, reds, pinks, purples and silvers.
Temperature Normal room temperatures are suitable.
Position Good, strong light helps keep colours bright but direct sun should be avoided except for brief periods.
Watering The rex begonias are fairly tolerant and so long as neither drought nor flood is overdone they will flourish.
Care Use a rich and well drained soil-based compost for the rex begonias. Repot annually or keep dwarf by retaining the roots in the same, small pot. Feed fortnightly when growing actively. When plants are too large for repotting topdress with fresh compost when necessary.
Propagation Take a good, healthy leaf and cut through the main veins in several places. Pin this slashed leaf onto a flat bed of moist peat and perlite in a propagating case or plastic bag and new plants will grow from the cut areas.

Begonia x *tuberhybrida*

Common name None.
General information There are many large-flowered tuberous begonias which can be bedded out in summer or grown indoors, a race of beautiful, comparatively new hybrids.
Temperature Normal room temperatures, but if above about 20°C (68°F) raise the humidity level a little.
Position Good strong light but no direct sun.
Watering Water well when plants are growing and flowering, allow to dry out a little between applications.
Care Feed regularly when in full growth and flower. These large-flowered hybrids sometimes outgrow their pots during a single season and need potting on. When leaves begin to yellow in autumn reduce and finally stop watering. In early spring remove and clean tubers and plant, concave side up, pressed down on a pan or pot of moist peat. Plant out and pot on as growth is made by the young plants.
Propagation Examine dried tubers in spring and cut each into two or more pieces each bearing a growing tip. Before planting and treating as a complete tuber, dust cut sides gently with sulphur as a preventive against stem or root rot.

Beloperone guttata

Common name Shrimp Plant.
General information The name is derived from the shrimp-like bracts at the end of each flower stalk, reddish-brown and overlapping like shrimp scales. Tiny white flowers between the bracts are insignificant and last but briefly, while the bracts can live much longer and appear almost all year.
Temperature Normal home heat of about 18°C (65°F) suits.
Position Must be in good, strong light but not where sun is likely to alight for more than a few minutes a day.
Watering Although the root ball must never be allowed to dry out, water must drain through it and leave the soil surface dry to the touch before the next soaking.
Care Shrimp plants can become sparse and leggy, so pinch out growing tips when young to encourage bushy growth. Repot each spring using a soil-based compost with added peat and feed fortnightly when growing strongly.
Propagation Take tip cuttings about 3 in long and insert in an equal soil and perlite mixture in pots which should go into a propagating case or a sealed plastic bag. To get a bushy appearance use three or four cuttings to a single pot.

Beloperone guttata

15

Billbergia nutans

Common names Queen's Tears, Friendship Plant.
General information An easy-to-grow bromeliad with long, narrow, arching leaves and flower stalks bearing long-lived pink bracts from which emerge the little blue, pink, green and yellow flowers. Several species of billbergia are available but *B. nutans* is probably the best known.
Temperature Normal living temperatures suit these plants.
Position Strong light essential, preferably including several hours of direct sun to get good flower and leaf colour.
Watering Some plants make a characteristic bromeliad cup in the centre of the leaves and where this is so it should be kept filled with water. Otherwise keep the soil just moist, allowing it to dry out slightly between applications.
Care Potting compost should be rich, porous and well drained and an equal proportion of peat and leafmould is suggested as suitable. Roots are not extensive so plants will grow in a small pot and will need moving on only when obviously necessary. Feed fortnightly in the cup or on soil when watering.
Propagation Cut offsets from the parent when almost mature with as much root as possible and pot in almost dry compost.

Billbergia nutans

Bougainvillea

Common name Paper Flower.
General information This is not an easy plant to grow indoors except under conservatory conditions. It is a climber producing long-lasting coloured bracts and little creamy flowers, highly spectacular when well grown.
Temperature Normal living-room temperatures are suitable in summer and a little cooler than normal in winter when resting.
Position Good light is essential and several hours of sun are necessary to get the flowering processes working well.
Watering In summer ample water is required although plants should almost dry out between applications. Reduce in winter.
Care In winter bougainvilleas usually lose their leaves but this is a normal process and so long as watering is reduced new growth should soon appear. Plants should be kept almost dry during the winter rest period. Feed only during the summer and move plants into larger pots in spring.
Propagation A propagating case, high temperatures and humidity, good light and plenty of time are necessary to propagate bougainvilleas, so this is best left to the experts. Cuttings in a sealed plastic bag in a warm place might succeed.

Caladium

Common names Angel Wings, Elephant Ears.
General information This tuberous-rooted plant has the most delicate and beautiful foliage of any house plant, irregularly heart-shaped, sometimes quite large, so thin as to be almost translucent, white, green, pink in splashes and spots, with the main veins usually in deeper colours. Unfortunately it is impossible to keep indoors for long periods.
Temperature Not less than 18°C (65°F) with high humidity.
Position In good light but never any direct sun.
Watering While in strong growth keep the soil always moist but as the leaves dry and shrivel reduce until almost dry.
Care Keep out of all draughts, hot or cold. Plants only grow for about six months, during which period they need a regular feed every two weeks. When the foliage dies down reduce watering until almost dry and keep warm and dark. Pot in fresh compost in late spring and give added warmth to induce growth, then increase humidity by standing the pot on a tray of pebbles which are kept constantly wet.
Propagation Small tubers will be found attached to the parent and if removed and potted they will grow gradually.

Bougainvillea glabra

Caladium

Calathea

Common name Peacock Plant.

General information The common name is applied to another species, *C. makoyana*, although *C. insignis*, like other species and varieties, has similar light and dark green spear-shaped leaves, purple underneath. They are not easy plants to grow.

Temperature No lower than 16°C (60°F) and always with added humidity to the extent of a daily misting spray of rain water.

Position Keep in light shade.

Watering Try to maintain the compost in a moist state just short of being wet when the plant is growing well in spring and summer, but reduce this quantity in winter.

Care Calatheas like an acid growing medium so use a peat-based compost, and water only with rainwater. Feed plants regularly while growing strongly and repot each spring in a compost strengthened with added fertilizer.

Propagation By division. Before new growth appears in spring knock the plant from its pot and divide the clumps, each new group having a fair share of roots. Keep in a propagating case or in plastic bags until new growth is seen.

Calathea insignis

Calceolaria

Common names Pouch Flower, Slipper Flower.

General information Temporary flowering plants with blooms in the form of a pouch or slipper, vividly coloured with reds, oranges and yellows in spots, blotches and streaks. The large, shield-shaped leaves grow beneath the flowers.

Temperature If possible, keep plants in the coolest part of the houses as too high temperatures will shorten their flowering life.

Position Keep in good light but never in direct sun.

Watering Give plenty of water. Do not let plants paddle, but keep the soil just short of this mark. If the soil dries the plant will quickly droop and may never recover.

Care Keep plants in humid conditions if possible and feed regularly and frequently, using weak doses rather than fewer stronger applications. Watch carefully for attack by aphids or greenfly and take immediate remedial action if this happens.

Propagation By seed sown in early summer to flower during the following year. Throughout growth conditions should be cool rather than warm and seedlings should gradually be moved on to larger pots as they develop.

Calcolaria × herbeohybrida

Callistemon citrinus

Common name Bottle Brush.

General information The common name is due to the shape of the petal-less flowers, the 4-in long bristles being made up of a series of red stamens. *C. citrinus* is a shrub which will grow to more than 6 ft tall, but can be kept smaller by regular pruning after the flowers fade.

Temperature Normal room temperatures are suitable when the plant is growing well, with a much cooler winter rest period.

Position Direct sunlight every day is necessary to get good flowers. Place plants outdoors in full sun when flowering has been completed and bring indoors only when frosts threaten.

Watering Keep soil moist while growing well, dryer in winter.

Care Use a soil-based compost and feed plants regularly while growing well. Repot each spring or topdress with new soil if maximum pot size has been reached. Plants react well to pruning, preferably after flowering to ensure later blooms.

Propagation Plants can be grown from seed but it is easier and quicker to take 4-in cuttings from non-flowering shoots and plant in a peat and perlite mixture in warmth.

Callistemon citrinus

Camellia japonica 'Tricolor'

Campanula isophylla 'Alba'

Common name Italian Bellflower.
General information This is the white form of the normally blue *C. isophylla*, an easy flowering trailer which demands cool conditions and good light. It grows attractively indoors in a hanging basket if this is kept well watered.
Temperature When growing well and in flower they will accept about 18°C (65°F) if given extra humidity. In winter cool conditions are necessary, preferably about 5–10°C (40–50°F).
Position These flowering plants must have really good light, even an hour or so of direct sun each day if not too strong.
Watering While growing well the plant roots must be kept moist at all times. In winter keep roots barely damp.
Care Repot in early spring using a soil-based compost and feed plants regularly. Pinch out fading flowers to encourage further blooms and when flowering has ended the trails should be cut back almost to soil level to give plants their rest.
Propagation Tip cuttings, 2 in long, can be taken in spring and inserted in an equal peat and perlite mixture protected in a sealed plastic bag. If cuttings are dipped in a hormone rooting powder this will hasten rooting and stop sap bleeding.

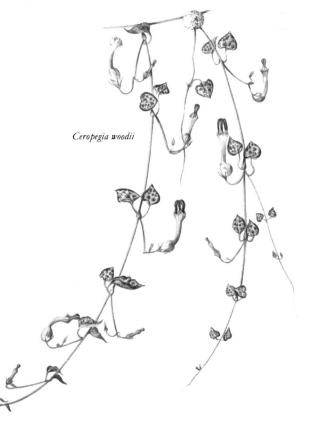

Ceropegia woodii

Camellia

Common name None.
General information Flowering shrubs of the tea family, better outdoors in sheltered positions than in the home, where they must be kept cool and humid. White, pink, red and bi-coloured flowers bloom in late winter and early spring.
Temperature If temperatures exceed about 16°C (60°F) plants will not flower and it is best to aim for 10°C (50°F).
Position Good, bright light, even brief sunlight in winter.
Watering Plenty of water so that the compost is kept quite moist during the growing period. After flowering, almost dry.
Care A daily spray will help camellias, but as lime haters they must be given only rain-water. For the same reason they should be grown in a lime-free compost. Keep an eye on your plants and when it appears necessary repot in spring. When maximum pot size has been reached, topdress with fresh soil. In summer plants are best placed outdoors in a place safe from strong winds and not subjected to too long periods in direct sun. When outdoors make sure pots are watered regularly and sufficiently for they dry out very quickly.
Propagation Best left to the nurseryman grower.

Campanula isophylla 'Alba'

Ceropegia woodii

Common name Hearts Entangled.
General information A succulent oddity with long trailing stems sparsely spaced with small heart-shaped leaves and little tubular flowers, both grey-green with a little purple. This plant is best grown suspended in a window where it will get full light and the trails can hang down for 3 ft or more.
Temperature Normal room temperatures are quite suitable.
Position Where light is really good. A darker situation will result in fewer leaves and flowers, poorer coloration.
Watering This plant is a succulent and requires very little water, just moist in summer and nearly dry in winter.
Care Just as a ceropegia needs little water, so does it require little food; once a month will be ample under most conditions. Pinching out the trail tips will result in thicker growth. Repot each spring until large, using a well drained compost made up of a soil-based compost with the addition of an equal part of perlite or sharp sand.
Propagation In spring or summer take one of the tubers produced on the trails and place this on a perlite or sand layer over normal compost. Keep almost dry until rooted.

Chlorophytum comosum

Chrysanthemum

Common name None.
General information Potted chrysanthemums for indoor culture are today the products of science, produced all the year round by giving artificial days, artificial nights and dwarfing chemicals. Uniform in size and appearance they will last about six weeks in a cool place in the home and can then be planted out in the garden to flower according to season.
Temperature Fairly cool, about 12–18°C (55–65°F).
Position Good light essential, but no direct sun.
Watering Keep the root ball moist at all times, which may mean watering at least once a day during hot summer days.
Care Because these must be regarded as temporary plants they will not require feeding or repotting. Choose carefully when buying, however, making sure plants are clean, pest-free, with a moist root ball and crisp leaves. Make sure the flower buds are showing colour, for if too tightly closed they may fail to open when brought into home conditions. When flowering indoors has finished the plants can go out into the garden where they will grow taller and flower in late summer.
Propagation Plants are cheap, plentiful and excellent, so buy.

Cineraria

Chlorophytum comosum

Common names Spider Plant, Ribbon Plant.
General information A popular and easy plant with long, ribbon-like leaves striped green and cream arching from a central point from which also rise creamy stems bearing tiny white flowers followed by miniature plants, including roots. There are several similar varieties of *C. comosum*.
Temperature Normal room temperatures are suitable.
Position To retain good foliage colour plants should have good light, even including some direct sun for brief periods.
Watering Enough water during the growing period to keep the compost uniformly moist at all times. Give less in winter.
Care Grow this plant in a soil-based compost as it is greedy. Feed frequently, even in winter, with dilute fertilizer. Brown tips to leaves show that the fleshy roots are starved or thirsty. Repot when necessary.
Propagation Easiest method is to pin one of the baby plantlets onto the surface of a pot of suitable soil. When growth is seen the stem can be cut. Alternatively, remove a plantlet and rest the roots in water or on the soil of a separate pot.

Chrysanthemum

Cineraria

Common name Cineraria; correctly, *Senecio cruentus*.
General information Late winter- and spring-flowering plants with daisy-like blooms (blue, red, mauve, purple, white). Generally bought in flower, kept until the flowers have finished, about two months, and then discarded.
Temperature Cool, no higher than about 10°C (50°F).
Position In good light but out of any direct sun.
Watering Soil should never be allowed to dry out but should never be too wet, so use an open, well drained compost.
Care As it is sometimes difficult to keep the plants as cool as is best for them, added humidity should be provided by standing pots on trays of wet pebbles or plunging each pot in a cache-pot full of moist peat. Cinerarias attract aphids, so spray at once if these are seen or take preventive measures by watering the soil with a weak systemic pesticide. The plants are short lived so no fertilizer will be necessary.
Propagation Sow seed on a suitable seed compost in spring and pot on seedlings when large enough to handle. Keep temperatures low, provide light shade and airy conditions.

19

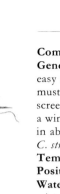

Cissus antarctica

Cissus antarctica

Common name Kangaroo Vine.
General information A popular foliage climbing plant that is easy to grow and tolerant in its demands. Not self-clinging, it must be tied or clipped to a support and will make an attractive screen as well as an accent plant for a corner or to grow around a window or doorway. The pointed toothed green leaves grow in abundance on short brown stalks. Less frequently seen are *C. striata*, *C. discolor* and *C. sicyoides*.
Temperature Normal room temperatures are suitable.
Position Good light but no direct sun except briefly.
Watering Keep soil just moist during growing period but in winter allow it almost to dry out between applications.
Care Some degree of humidity is advisable for the kangaroo vine, otherwise attack by red spider mite is likely. Repot annually in a rich, soil-based compost until too large, then topdress.
Propagation In spring take tip cuttings about 4 in long, remove lower leaves, dip the ends in hormone rooting powder and insert several to a small pot in a peat and perlite mixture.

Citrus mitis

Common name Calamondin Orange.
General information A miniature orange tree which bears scented white flowers and then small green fruits gradually turning orange, not normally edible. Flowers and fruits can grow simultaneously, even on surprisingly small plants.
Temperature Normal room temperatures, neither too high nor low.
Position In good light, including direct sun, particularly in winter. Plants can be grown out of doors in summer.
Watering Thoroughly in summer, less frequently in winter, adding a potash-rich fertilizer when in flower or fruit.
Care Give added humidity where rooms are dry. Repot annually using a rich, soil-based compost. Cut back growing tips occasionally and prune long shoots rigorously in spring.
Propagation Stem cuttings about 4 in long, dipped in hormone rooting powder and planted in pots of a peat and perlite mixture, will root easily in propagating case or plastic bag.

Clivia miniata

Common name Kaffir Lily.
General information A large flowering plant with thick, dark green, attractive, strap-like leaves growing from a central point from which in early spring one or more flower stalks rise to produce up to a dozen trumpet-shaped flowers, usually orange-red, sometimes more yellow, long lived.
Temperature Normal room temperatures when growing and in flower. A winter rest at just below 10°C (50°F) is important.
Position Really good light, even weak sunlight, so a place in a west- or east-facing window would be highly suitable.
Watering Plenty in spring and summer but almost dry in winter.
Care Fleshy roots quickly fill pots, so repot when noticed, using a soil-based compost which should be firmed around the roots. Remember that clivias enjoy being in a pot that looks too small. Remove seed pods after the flowers have faded.
Propagation By offsets. Remove these very carefully with a sharp knife and replant separate offsets with root and leaves in a peat and perlite mixture. Keep warm and in good light, but propagating case or plastic bag are not normally necessary.

Citrus mitis

Clivia miniata

Cocos weddelliana

Coffea arabica

Cocos weddelliana

Common name Coconut Palm.
General information *Cocos weddelliana*, or more correctly *Microcoelum weddellianum*, is a relative of the coconut palm, not the species itself. It is a dainty little palm, sometimes difficult to grow for long indoors, where it will reach 4 ft with fronds on short stalks fanning out to about 8 in wide. No main trunk and no flowers are the normal expectation of plants grown indoors, even under excellent care.
Temperature Between about 16 and 26°C (60–80°F).
Position Good bright light but no sunlight.
Watering Keep the soil just moist at all times, increasing humidity when warm and slightly decreasing water when cold.
Care Keep plants in small pots unless the basic root begins to show above the soil-based, well drained compost. Fronds will brown in dry air, so make sure humidity is sufficient. Feed only occasionally during the growing period, no more than once a month. No flowers appear on indoor grown plants.
Propagation Commercial growers propagate by seed, a lengthy and difficult business best left to these experts.

Codiaeum

Common name Croton.
General information Small shrubs, up to 3 ft tall with brilliantly and variously coloured foliage in different shapes, outlines and sizes. Practically all crotons are forms of *Codiaeum variegatum pictum*. Plants were once very difficult to grow indoors, but new types last much longer.
Temperature Normal room temperatures, but not too low.
Position For good leaf colour and to ret 'n leaves it is necessary to have good light, even some direct sunlight.
Watering In spring and summer keep the soil thoroughly moist, almost wet, but give much less during the winter rest period.
Care For added humidity stand pots on trays of wet pebbles which will help prevent attack by red spider mite. Repot annually using a well drained, soil-based compost. Give regular feeds during spring and summer but not in winter. To stop bleeding of latex use water or powdered charcoal.
Propagation Take 6-in tip cuttings in early spring and place in a peat and perlite mixture in a sealed plastic bag or a propagating case in good light for about a month.

Coffea arabica

Common name Coffee Plant.
General information The genuine coffee, for fruits and coffee beans can actually be grown indoors. Really a foliage shrub with shining green leaves, it will produce pretty, scented flowers when mature and these develop into the fruits. Plants will grow to more than 3 ft to make a bushy shrub.
Temperature Keep warm, not less than about 16°C (60°F), and try to keep this steady rather than subject to variations.
Position Light shade, never direct sunlight.
Watering When in growth the soil should be kept thoroughly moist at all times, though not wet. In winter keep almost dry.
Care Use a well drained soil-based compost to avoid water-logging and although regular fortnightly feeding is recommended, repotting annually is also wise, preferably in early spring. Cold is a danger, as is dry air. A light misting with clean rainwater at least once a week will prove helpful, even in winter if rooms are warm and the air consequently dry.
Propagation Not easy. Seed must be fresh, sown ½ in deep with bottom heat of 24°C (75°F) in a propagating case. Alternatively take 4-in cuttings, dip the ends in rooting powder and plant in seed compost in a warm propagating case.

Codiaeum variegatum pictum

Coleus blumei

Columnea

Common name None.
General information A lovely, flowering, trailing plant with small, chunky green leaves and vivid scarlet tubular flowers which will last as long as a month under favourable circumstances. So long as humid conditions can be provided columneas can look magnificent in hanging baskets, their heavily flowered stems trailing gracefully down more than 3 ft.
Temperature High, not less than 18°C (65°F) at all times.
Position Good, bright light but no direct sunlight.
Watering It is important that columneas do not get too much water but give a light feed at each watering. Try to use water at room temperature, for cold water on the leaves, either from can or spray, can result in ugly brown spots.
Care These plants are epiphytic in nature, so keep the soil-based potting compost sharply drained. Repot when necessary.
Propagation By tip cuttings. Take 3–4 in cuttings in spring or summer and insert in almost dry peat or vermiculite. No extra heat is required, room temperature will suit and the cuttings should be maintained in a light situation.

Coleus

Common name Flame Nettle.
General information Perennials normally grown as annuals for the beauty and variability of the foliage. Small spikes of flowers are usually nipped out as insignificant and to promote bushy growth. Coleus are easily grown from seed in a mixture of vivid colours, but named hybrids of this species are equally simple to grow from cuttings.
Temperature Fairly warm, best at 16°C (60°F) or above.
Position Must have really good light, even including direct sun for several hours of the day.
Watering Soil must be kept really moist at all times.
Care The soft and sappy growth of coleus must be preserved by plenty of warmth, plenty of light, plenty of moisture and plenty of food. If plants are allowed to become dry they will droop quickly. Repot frequently as seen to be necessary, using a rich, well drained, soil-based compost. Extra humidity will help discourage attack by red spider mite.
Propagation Sow seed in a rich compost in late winter in a temperature of about 18°C (65°F). Pot on as necessary. Take cuttings of best plants through the year and overwinter some.

Cordyline terminalis

Common name Flaming Dragon Tree.
General information Best known example is *C. terminalis*, but there are several other less dramatically coloured species. This one has spear-shaped leaves, 12 in or longer and some 3–4 in wide, growing from a central stem, bright red at first and toning down with age to green, copper and red. *C.t.* 'Rededge' is popular, perhaps a little easier than others and a little smaller, but like others difficult to grow for long.
Temperature Normal room temperatures will be suitable.
Position Good light but no direct sun at any time.
Watering Plenty during spring and summer, less in winter.
Care Feed regularly when in full growth and try to use rain-water when moistening the soil-based compost. Repot each spring until the largest pot size is reached, then topdress.
Propagation Cordylines can be grown from seed sown 1 in deep in a peat and perlite mixture in spring and placed in a warm propagating case or plastic bag. The growing tip can also be used as a cutting as can 2-in sections of the main stem containing a dormant bud. Growth is slow.

Columnea gloriosa
'Purpurea'

Cordyline terminalis

Crassula portulacea

Cryptanthus

Common name Earth Star.

General information A genus of bromeliads which are both easy to grow and highly decorative. Generally small, with 3–4 in spear-shaped leaves, sometimes waved, they hug the soil surface with many variations of leaf pattern and colour – green, brown, cream, grey, pink. *C. bromelioides* is unusual in tending to grow upwards instead of hugging the soil, and although perhaps the most beautiful, it is also one of the more difficult. Others include *C. acaulis*, *C. bivittatus*.

Temperature Normal warm room temperatures, preferably humid.

Position Good light including some direct sun each day.

Watering Keep the soil only just moist, preferably giving a little water and then allowing the soil almost to dry out.

Care Use a soil-based compost with extra peat but repot very seldom and feed only two or three times during the growing season.

Propagation *C. bromelioides* differs from other species by producing plantlets on stolons, whereas the others grow offsets. Both plantlets and offsets should be removed and planted in a peat and perlite mixture, almost dry, placed in a propagating case or sealed in a plastic bag.

Crassula portulacea

Common name Jade Plant.

General information One of a considerable range of succulents, large and small, simple and complex, with showy or insignificant flowers, but all having opposite leaves on each side of the stem. *C. portulacea* (also known as *C. argentea*) will grow to 3 ft or more, with chunky green leaves and pale pink flowers. There are several types, some variegated, and other popular species of crassula include *C. arborescens*, *C. lycopodioides* and *C. lactea*.

Temperature Normal room temperatures are generally suitable but keep cool, not above 13°C (55°F) during winter.

Position Light must be good, including some sun.

Watering While growing well moisten the soil as necessary but allow it nearly to dry out between waterings.

Care Feed regularly when growing well and repot in a sharply drained soil-based compost every two or three years.

Propagation Stem cuttings some 2–3 in long inserted in a peat and perlite mixture in spring will root without any special facilities in a warm, well lit room.

Cuphea ignea

Common name Cigar Flower.

General information The little flowers on this plant are the obvious reason for the common name: they have long, tubular, cigar-shaped flowers which end in a white or grey band similar to the ash. These flowers appear continuously throughout spring and summer almost into winter. *C. platycentra* is also known as *C. ignea* and there is a variegated form.

Temperature Normal room temperatures are suitable.

Position In bright light, even including several hours a day of direct sun except on the hottest summer days.

Watering Give average doses, enough to moisten thoroughly the root ball, which should be allowed almost to dry out before the next dose. In winter the plant should be kept almost dry.

Care Repot once or perhaps even twice a year in spring or summer using a good soil-based compost. Regular fortnightly feeding while growing well will keep plants decorative.

Propagation Take tip cuttings about 2 in long in late summer, insert in a peat and perlite mixture and envelope in a sealed plastic bag or place in a propagating case.

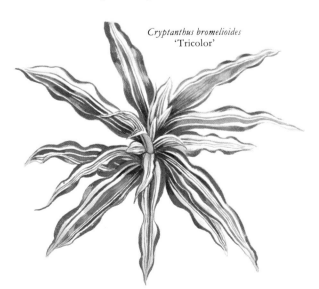

Cryptanthus bromelioides
'Tricolor'

Cuphea ignea

Cyclamen hybrid

Cyclamen

Common name None.
General information A well known tuberous-rooted flowering plant largely popular for Christmas decoration. Plants usually last only a few weeks in the home because of hot, dry conditions, but if kept in a cool, airy situation they can last as long as six months constantly in flower. Some cyclamen foliage is beautiful, silver flecked or banded.
Temperature Try to keep plants in rooms which are not too warm or stuffy, preferably at between 13–18°C (55–65°F).
Position Light should be good but keep out of direct sun.
Watering The potting compost should be kept moist, almost wet, at all times, but the tubers themselves should not be watered, so water from below, which gives added humidity.
Care Use a well drained, soil-based compost with a little added peat. Feed moderately. When flowers fade, pluck the entire flower stalk from the tuber with a short, sharp tug.
Propagation Plants are plentiful, inexpensive, good, so buy. You can flower plants each year by drying off the tuber when it is finished, then repotting it in fresh compost in autumn.

Cyperus

Common name Umbrella Plant.
General information The common name arises from the leaf-like bracts held at the tops of long stalks, which radiate like the spokes of an umbrella and which are surmounted by a tiny spray of flowers like those of grasses. As a bog plant, cyperus is one of the very few house plants which can, with profit, stand in water at all times. *C. diffusus* is also known as *C. albostriatus* and grows to some 15 in. Other species, *C. alternifolius* and *C. papyrus*, reach 3 ft.
Temperature Normal room temperatures are suitable.
Position Plants will take full sun if getting enough water.
Watering Although most species of cyperus need to paddle, *C. diffusus* is a little less tolerant and the roots should be kept moist at all times but never dripping wet.
Care Use a rich, firm, soil-based compost which will retain moisture and repot frequently when the fast growing roots fill the pot. Try to keep the atmosphere humid by spraying the plants and feed lightly during the summer months only.
Propagation By division. A mature plant is a tangle of roots, cut these into sections, each bearing good top and bottom growth.

Cyperus diffusus

Davallia canariensis

Common name Deer's (Hare's, Rabbit's, Squirrel's) Foot Fern.
General information A fairly tolerant and easy indoor fern distinguished mainly by the rhizomes that cover the pot surface and are themselves covered with hairs like fur, a rusty brown sometimes going grey. From these arise green stalks bearing the large triangular lacy green fronds.
Temperature Normal room temperatures are suitable.
Position Best in light shade. No sun at any time.
Watering Water the soil until the root ball is uniformly moist and then leave until almost dry before watering again.
Care Davallias are more tolerant of dry air than most ferns, but added humidity will always be welcomed. If they get too cool some fronds may brown. Use a peat-based compost. Regular fortnightly feeding will be appreciated. Plants look attractive in hanging baskets, but make sure they do not dry off. They usually need an annual repotting.
Propagation Cut sections of rhizome each bearing two or more fronds and pin or weight these into a peat and perlite mixture. Place in a propagating case or seal in a plastic bag.

Davallia canariensis

Dieffenbachia exotica

Common name Dumb Cane.

General information The name comes from the poisonous sap, which causes pain and swelling if it gets into the mouth, so carefully wash hands if sap-soiled. Foliage plants with soft large green leaves flecked or spotted with cream or lighter green. Other species are *D. picta*, *D. bausei*, *D. amoena* and *D. maculata*, differing mainly in coloration.

Temperature Plants like to be both warm, certainly no lower than about 16°C (60°F), and in a humid environment.

Position Good bright light in spring and summer but full sun only in the darkest days of winter.

Watering Sufficient to moisten the root ball thoroughly, then leave until the soil surface is dry to the touch.

Care Try to use a rich, but well drained, soil-based compost for dieffenbachias and give a regular fortnightly feed when plants are growing vigorously. Repot each spring if necessary, otherwise every two years or so.

Propagation From tip cuttings 3–6 in long, dipped in rooting powder, planted in peat and perlite mixture in warmth.

Dieffenbachia exotica

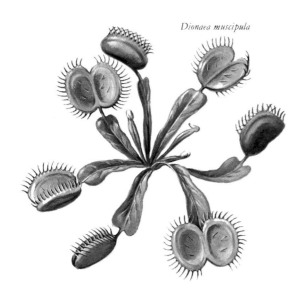

Dionaea muscipula

Dionaea muscipula

Common name Venus Fly Trap.

General information A curiosity plant rather than decorative. Very difficult to grow indoors except in an enclosed bowl or terrarium where both temperature and humidity can be maintained at high levels. The interest lies in the trap-like leaves which swiftly close on any insect unwary enough to investigate the opened and inviting interior.

Temperature Warm at all times, not below about 18°C (65°F).

Position In good light, even brief direct sun so long as the plant is enclosed and in a humid atmosphere.

Watering The growing medium should be almost dripping wet at all times, accompanied by almost saturation humidity.

Care Dionaeas grow best in sphagnum moss with some added peat, both of which must be very wet at all times. Humidity is so vital that an enclosed atmosphere is essential. As these plants are grown for curiosity not decor, they can profitably be treated as expendable and grown in a water-filled saucer by a sunny window for just a few days.

Propagation Generally bought as a partially grown bulb in sphagnum moss. Ensure good condition before buying.

Dizygotheca elegantissima

Common name False Aralia.

General information An elegant little tree with its long, slender, toothed leaflets, pinkish red at first, then light green, dark green and almost black. Plants will grow to 6 ft or so if conditions are suitable, but as time passes the lower leaflets drop to reveal an unattractive naked stem. Plants appeal to mealy bugs, so beware of these creatures and treat them at the first sign.

Temperature On the high side, not less than about 16°C (60°F).

Position In good light but never in direct sun.

Watering Careful here, remembering that the slim leaves cannot transpire much moisture. So keep soil barely moist.

Care If a dizygotheca likes its position in the home and is watered carefully it can live for a year or more and be elegantly decorative during the whole of this time, but as a rule it is somewhat temperamental and has a brief life. Plants like a soil-based compost and feeding fortnightly during spring and summer, not at all during the winter rest.

Propagation Plants can be grown from seed sown in heat in spring, but are better bought as immature youngsters.

25

Dizygotheca elegantissima

Dracaena concinna

Common name None.

General information One of the easier dracaenas to grow because it will tolerate lower temperatures. The most attractive form of *D. marginata* is 'Tricolor' or *D. concinna*, which has long slim leaves striped green, cream and pink. Plants tend to lose their lower leaves as they grow, gradually revealing a long, slim lower trunk topped with a spray of foliage, giving an effect almost like that of a palm tree.

Temperature Normal room temperatures are best but plants will tolerate a drop to about 10°C (50°F) for brief periods so long as the soil is kept fairly dry at this time.

Position Good light is necessary to maintain the foliage colour, but sunlight should only be tolerated in winter.

Watering Try to keep plants very slightly on the dry side.

Care Each spring move a dracaena plant into a larger pot, using a rich, soil-based potting compost. Feed fortnightly when plants are growing well. They will grow to ceiling height without trouble but will lose most lower leaves.

Propagation By tip cuttings as with *D. deremensis*, or by pieces of stem cut into lengths of about 2 in and potted, right way up, in a peat and perlite mixture with some warmth.

Dracaena
concinna

Dracaena
deremensis

Dracaena deremensis

Common name None.

General information One of several decorative foliage plants mainly with long, spear-like leaves radiating from a central stem. The most popular forms of *D. deremensis* are 'Bausei' and 'Warneckii', which have respectively a central white stripe down the leaves and two white stripes. Plants will grow more than 3 ft tall, with a spread of about 12 in. Not an easy plant to grow for long periods.

Temperature Keep warm, preferably about 18–24°C (65–75°F).

Position Keep in a situation where there is good light.

Watering So long as drainage is good, water thoroughly while plants are growing strongly, but give less in the winter rest.

Care To give of their best plants must be kept warm and in humid conditions. Light but regular feeding in summer will help and annual repotting in a soil-based compost is advised. Plants will drop their lower leaves if too cold for long.

Propagation By tip cuttings about 3–6 in long in spring or early summer, planted in a peat and perlite mixture and placed in a propagating case or a sealed plastic bag.

Echeveria glauca

Common name None.

General information One of a large family of easy-to-grow succulents, forming a rosette of chunky, grey-green leaves from which arise stalks bearing a number of red flowers. The leaves appear to have a bloom and if plants have been grown outdoors in summer in good light there may be hints of subtle red and purple in the foliage.

Temperature Normal room temperatures will be suitable but in summer plants are best kept outdoors in the better light.

Position In good light, including direct sun even in summer.

Watering Keep these plants almost dry during their period of growth and even drier when resting. Keep water off leaves.

Care Never forget that these plants are succulents and need dry conditions to give of their best. Too little light and they lose their attractive tight rosette shape. Use a well drained soil-based compost, repot annually and feed regularly. Watch for attack by mealy bugs and treat as advised.

Propagation From offsets which are freely formed. Remove carefully, trim lower leaves and insert in well drained compost.

26

Echeveria glauca

Epiphyllum

Common name Orchid cactus.

General information A cactus hybrid grown entirely for the size, beauty and colour of its flowers, which grow from the long, chunky green stems, bluntly saw-toothed and sprawling unless staked. The flowers are showy but soft and with a vivid life of only two or three days.

Temperature Try to keep plants warm at all times.

Position Find a lightly shaded spot in the garden in summer and equally, indoors keep them near a lightly shaded window.

Watering In spring and summer give plenty of water, sufficient to keep the root ball thoroughly moist. After plants have flowered reduce the water and allow an almost dry rest period.

Care These are easy plants to grow but worthy of some care. Give high humidity including a daily spray. Feed until in flower. Repot annually in spring in a mixture of one part lime-free sharp sand or perlite to three of peat.

Propagation Take cuttings about 6 in long, allow to dry for a day and then insert in a slightly moistened compost like that used for mature plants. Rooting is a quick process.

Ephiphyllum
hybrid

Episcia cupreata

Common name Flame Violet.

General information There are several species and many hybrids of this attractive genus, all having beautiful foliage and flowers. *E. cupreata* varies considerably, some forms having smooth leaves, some rough, with colours changing from several hues of green through copper and brown almost to purple. Flowers are mainly red and yellow. Stolons growing from the central stem reach out and root into the soil so that its surface is quickly covered with a mat of leaves.

Temperature High, with high humidity. Plants should not be grown in under about 18°C (65°F) and a good average would be about 24°C (75°F) with equally high humidity.

Position Bright light including direct sun for an hour or two each day. Failing this use artificial light for periods.

Watering Keep compost always wet but do not allow plants to paddle. If temperature is low reduce amounts of water.

Care As well as watering copiously, feed frequently, but with dilute doses. Use wide, shallow pots to allow plants to spread and a compost of equal parts of sphagnum moss, peat and perlite. Repot only when apparently necessary.

Propagation Remove ready-rooted stolons and pot up.

Episcia cupreata
'Silver Queen'

Erica

Common name Heather.

General information Of the several hundred species and varieties of heathers none are really suited to home growing except for short periods, for they all like cooler, moister, more airy conditions than can be provided indoors except in special areas. The best species for indoors are *E. hyemalis* and *E. gracilis*. Both of these have a number of varieties. Even these should be kept cool and treated as temporary.

Temperature Try to keep plants in the 7–10°C (45–50°F) range and give as much humidity as possible, even spraying them daily.

Position Plants must have good light but no direct sun.

Watering Use rainwater or lime-free water and keep the roots moist at all times without letting them become waterlogged.

Care There is little one can do for indoor ericas other than keep temperatures low, humidity high and use water without any lime content. Plants do not require feeding and they will not normally need repotting from their peat-based compost.

Propagation Tip cuttings will sometimes succeed, but a propagating case is normally necessary. Best buy good plants.

*Erica
hyemalis*

Eucalyptus
gunnii

Euonymus japonicus

Common name None.

General information A woody shrub that will grow to more than 3 ft indoors and taller in the garden. The variegated forms of *E. japonicus* are the most popular indoors and *E.j.* 'Aureus' has oval green leaves with a bright yellow centre. To maintain the attractive leaf colour it needs bright light indoors but fairly cool temperatures.

Temperature Preferably cool, about 10–16°C (50–60°F).

Position Good light but no sun in summer. In winter give full sun as available but keep out of hot rooms.

Watering Keep the roots just moist during summer and little more than dry during the plant's rest period of winter.

Care Plants sometimes suffer from mildew so spray with a fungicide once or twice a year. Feed when actively growing and repot annually. Use a soil-based compost.

Propagation Take 3-in tip cuttings in spring or summer, dip in rooting powder and plant in a peat and perlite mixture.

Euphorbia milii

Eucalyptus

Common name Gum Tree.

General information Eucalyptus trees and shrubs grow large and quickly, so they cannot be considered as permanent house plants but rather as temporary residents. They are easy and attractive in a quiet way. *E. gunnii* and *E. globulus* are the most popular for indoors and can be grown from seedlings until they are 6 ft or so when they should go into a sheltered spot in the garden. The grey-green almost circular leaves carry a white powder and change into a longer shape when they mature out of doors. Plants may need staking to stay upright.

Temperature Normal room temperatures are suitable.

Position To grow well and to develop strong leaf colour plants must have bright light, including full sun as available.

Watering Water thoroughly but let the top half of the soil dry out before watering again. In winter if the temperature falls below about 10°C (50°F) reduce the watering rate.

Care Use a rich soil-based compost and feed regularly when plants grow well. Be sure to pot on as new growth is made.

Propagation Sow seeds in a seed compost and place in a warm propagating case in good light. Pot as soon as ready.

Euonymus japonicus
'Aureus'

Euphorbia milii

Common name Crown of Thorns.

General information This flowering shrub with vicious thorns is one of the huge family of euphorbias. Flowers are the tiny yellow centres surrounded by the more spectacular though still smart scarlet or yellow bracts. Plants will grow to 6 ft or so. Spines are really sharp and the plant bleeds an irritating latex, so best keep children away. The small green leaves fall after a few months and are not replaced so bare stems appear, but plants can 'flower' continuously.

Temperature Warm, dry rooms suit this plant. Leaves tend to drop when temperatures fall further than is liked.

Position Place where plants will always get maximum sun.

Watering Keep moist while growing well but allow to dry between waterings. When resting or if cool reduce watering rate.

Care Use a very sharply drained, soil-based compost and repot every second year early in the spring. Feed fortnightly in summer unless flowering continuously, then monthly all year.

Propagation Avoiding thorns, take 4-in tip cuttings. Stop latex bleeding by spraying plant and dipping cuttings in water. Plant in peat and perlite mixture in warmth, no sun.

Euphorbia pulcherrima

Common name Poinsettia.

General information New hybrids of this Christmas plant have made it much easier and long lasting for the home, but this has been achieved by artificial daylight and darkness with chemical dwarfing. Today this winter-flowering shrub is small, about 1–2 ft in height, with soft green leaves and tiny yellow flowers like berries surrounded by white, pink or scarlet bracts.

Temperature Normal room temperatures are suitable.

Position In as good light as possible out of full sun.

Watering Go carefully. Watch the plant and when the leaves begin to droop water copiously and continue this way.

Care Make a compost of half rich leafmould and half perlite and insert added drainage at the base of the pot. Repot annually if intending to flower the plant for a successive year, normally a difficult operation.

Propagation The original plant can be cut down, given a period of rest and then started into growth again, or it is possible to take cuttings, but artificial shading and dwarfing make this a task too demanding for the average home grower.

Euphorbia
pulcherrima

Exacum affine

Common name German Violet.

General information A small, flowering perennial plant grown indoors as an annual, with lavender-blue flowers in profusion and shiny green leaves. Although a delicate plant in appearance it will last a surprisingly long time indoors in constant flower so long as the fading flowers are removed regularly and some humidity is provided.

Temperature Normal room temperatures are suitable but in high summer it will be helpful to stand pots on trays of wet gravel or plunge them in cache-pots filled with moist peat to provide the extra humidity that will be required.

Position Where there is good light but no direct sun.

Watering Keep the root ball moist at all times.

Care These plants are so colourful and attractive, so easy to grow, that it is worth raising or buying a succession. Grow them in a rich, soil-based compost and feed at regular fortnightly intervals while in flower and growing well.

Propagation Seeds should be sown in a seed compost in slight warmth in autumn to be over-wintered in warmth and potted up in late spring, when new sowings can also be made.

Exacum affine

x Fatshedera lizei

Common name None.

General information This is that most rare of plants, a bigeneric hybrid; a cross between two species of differing genera, a fatsia and an ivy. The result is nearer in appearance to the fatsia than to the ivy, for the green leaves are smaller versions of the palmate fatsia. The fatshedera will not climb by itself and unless there is space for it to sprawl or crawl it should be trained up a cane, where it will make a splendid, dignified and striking specimen. There is a variegated form with white marks on the foliage.

Temperature Normal room temperatures are suitable.

Position Bright light is not essential except for 'Variegata'.

Watering Keep the root ball just moist but no more and allow it to dry out a little between waterings.

Care This is an easy plant to grow, using a soil-based compost with added peat and feeding fortnightly during spring and summer. Move plants into the next size pot each spring to obtain upright growth and glossy foliage.

Propagation Tip cuttings about 4 in long will root quickly in a peat and perlite mixture in a propagating case.

× Fatshedera lizei

29

Fatsia japonica
'Variegata'

Fatsia japonica

Common name Aralia.
General information An easy and quick-growing shrub that does well both in the home and in the garden. Its main attraction is the foliage, consisting of large, leathery green leaves 12 in or more wide, deeply divided into seven, eight or nine lobes. Groups of little white flowers appear on outdoor plants but not on those grown indoors. There are one or two variegated forms with cream veins or edges.
Temperature Like many outdoor plants fatsias like it cool and should not be grown in a temperature of more than about 16°C (60°F), and even lower during the rest period of winter.
Position The better the light the stronger the plant and even short periods of sunlight will do no harm, longer in winter.
Watering The root ball should be moist at all times, although in winter it may be permitted to dry out a little.
Care Plants as potentially large as this need a good, rich compost and a regular feeding programme. Smaller, younger plants should be potted on each spring until large enough.
Propagation Take 2–3-in stem cuttings, dip the ends in rooting powder and plant in a peat and perlite mixture in warmth.

Ficus benjamina

Common name Weeping Fig.
General information One of the most graceful of the useful and popular ficus or fig family. A small tree with 2–3 in leaves, branching and drooping. It will grow to more than 6 ft but is usually most suitable for the home at no more than half this height, preferably in a plant colony together with others selected to contrast or complement.
Temperature An adaptable plant that tolerates most conditions.
Position Good light or where there is a little light shade.
Watering Not too much. Water well then allow almost to dry.
Care Repot in spring only when evidently necessary, using a soil-based compost. Give regular fortnightly feeds while growing strongly, not at all while resting in winter.
Propagation Best by air layering. At about 10 in from the top of the plant remove a ½ in circle of bark on the main stem, sprinkle with hormone powder, bind on a bandage of moist sphagnum moss and seal this effectively top and bottom inside plastic sheeting. When roots appear cut away new growth.

Ficus deltoidea

Common name Mistletoe Fig.
General information An unusual member of the fig family in that it produces small and inedible fruits, more like tiny figs than mistletoe berries, thoughout the whole year. Given favourable conditions it will grow to 6 ft or so but in home situations it seldom reaches more than about 2 ft. It is also known as *F. diversifolia*.
Temperature Normal room temperatures are suitable.
Position Light shade is more favourable than dark, but this little ficus will adapt to most positions in the home.
Watering As with most ficus, over-watering should be avoided. Best to water thoroughly and then allow roots almost to dry.
Care The leaves of this ficus are thick and tough, but although they may not benefit directly, the little berries enjoy an occasional spray with tepid rainwater, which both plumps them up and keeps them clean of dust. Use a soil-based potting compost and repot in spring only when this appears to be necessary, for a small pot is generally preferred. Pinching out growing tips will result in a thick, bushy plant.
Propagation Tip cuttings about 2 in long will root in a moist peat and perlite mixture in warmth and humidity.

Ficus benjamina

Ficus deltoidea

Ficus elastica
'Robusta'

Ficus lyrata

Ficus elastica

Common name Rubber Plant.
General information Undoubtedly this is the best known of the many ficus plants grown indoors and there are today several hybrids which present new forms and new colours as well as new strength, ease of handling and longevity. All have the single stem or tree-like habit and all have large leaves, usually shiny and green but some almost black and others agreeably variegated with gold, cream, grey or red.
Temperature Normal room temperatures will be suitable.
Position Tolerant of shade but will grow better in light.
Watering Water thoroughly, making sure the whole of the compost is uniformly moist, and then leave until almost dry before repeating the process. Keep dryer in winter.
Care Use a well drained but rich potting compost and repot in spring when plants fail to absorb water or when the roots become visible. Feed fortnightly when growing well. The large leaves become dusty so clean them gently.
Propagation Use the air layering process.

Ficus lyrata

Common name Fiddle Leaf Fig.
General information The shape of the large, glossy and slightly crinkled leaves is the reason for the common name. This is the largest and most stately of the indoor figs and the size alone is a reason why it is rather more difficult to keep in a decorative condition in the home.
Temperature Higher than normal, with 21°C (70°F) as the aim and only a few degrees lower as the absolute minimum.
Position In good light with occasional brief sun in winter.
Watering Moisten root ball then allow almost to dry.
Care The fiddle leaf fig has thick, strong roots that quickly fill a pot, necessitating regular and frequent moves to larger containers until the plant becomes almost impossible in the home. Use a rich, well drained soil-based compost and feed regularly. When too large, merely top dress with fresh soil.
Propagation Use the air layering technique.

Ficus pumila

Common name Creeping Fig.
General information This fig is completely different from those we have seen so far, for it is a creeping plant on wiry, black stems with 1 in soft green leaves. It is not difficult to grow if one can provide the warmth and high humidity it requires to maintain leaf colour and new growth.
Temperature Try to allow a minimum of 18°C (65°F), but the plant will only grow more slowly if temperatures are lower.
Position Light must be good at all times but no sun.
Watering The creeping fig must never be allowed to become dry at the roots or the leaves will fall almost immediately.
Care A peat-based compost will hold sufficient moisture to keep the plant in good health, but it should not be allowed to become wet. Feed regularly and repot only when obviously necessary, for plants like to be snug in their pots.
Propagation Tip cuttings, some even bearing immature roots, can easily be removed and potted in a moist peat and perlite mixture in propagating case or plastic bag in warmth and light.

31

Ficus pumila

Ficus radicans variegata

Common name None.
General information This is similar in some respects to the creeping fig just mentioned. The leaves are roughly twice the size here but more important is the fact that F. *radicans* (more correctly known as F. *sagittata*) is much more difficult to grow in the home because it demands greater degrees of warmth and humidity than are available except under the controlled conditions of a terrarium.
Temperature Plants may live, but will not flourish in temperatures lower than about 18°C (65°F).
Position Light shade is necessary, never bright light or sun.
Watering The leaves of F. *radicans* are almost papery to the touch, which suggests that the plant should not be kept too wet at the roots and that moisture should be provided by air.
Care This creeper should be grown in a peat-based compost, fed regularly while growing well and moved to a larger pot only when roots appear at soil surface or through drainage hole.
Propagation Like F. *pumila*, F. *radicans* will produce aerial roots, so tip cuttings can quickly become established.

Ficus radicans
'Variegata'

Fittonia verschaffeltii

Fuchsia

Common name Lady's Eardrops.
General information Popular and familiar flowering shrubs with several forms and many varieties, some of which will bloom for several months in the home with moderate care. It is important that plants settle in happily, so young plants should be brought into the hot, dry air of the home in spring before flower buds have appeared so that they can get used to the atmosphere and the treatment before coming into flower.
Temperature Try to keep plants no warmer than 16°C (60°F).
Position Bright light including sunlight is essential.
Watering Keep soil well moistened during spring and summer but reduce watering rate in autumn until soil is almost dry.
Care To keep plants flowering well they must be fed rather more than most other plants, beginning in spring and ending with the winter rest period. Use a soil-based potting compost and move young plants to a larger pot in spring.
Propagation From tip cuttings taken in spring or autumn. These should be about 3–4 in long and inserted in a peat and perlite mixture in warmth in a propagating case.

Fittonia verschaffeltii

Common name Snakeskin Plant.
General information It is the delicate tracery of red or silver veins on the brown-green leaves that is responsible for the common name of this beautiful but difficult plant. It must have constant warmth, high humidity and good light, all requirements difficult to provide in the home except with the aid of a terrarium or bottle garden.
Temperature Preferably a steady 18°C (65°F) at all times.
Position In bright light but never direct sunlight nor where there is any possibility that artificial light will burn.
Watering A thoroughly moist compost is necessary together with high humidity, which means plunging the pot in moist peat, standing it on wet pebbles or giving light sprays of water.
Care A terrarium or bottle garden will give the enclosed and humid atmosphere necessary to these plants. It also helps to use a peat-based potting compost and give a fortnightly feed. Repotting will not normally be necessary.
Propagation Tip cuttings will root in a peat and perlite mixture in warmth and humidity. Or you can layer plants by pinning growing tips down to root in the soil of a nearby pot.

Fuchsia hybrid

Gardenia jasminoides

Common name Cape Jasmine.
General information A slow-growing flowering shrub with glossy green foliage and strongly scented double or semi-double blooms. It must grow in lime-free compost, be watered with rainwater and be maintained at a steady temperature of 17°C (63°F) if the flower buds are to be retained on the plant and open into flower. Plants grown indoors will remain comparatively small, seldom more than about 1–2 ft.
Temperature Try to maintain a constant 17°C (63°F) always.
Position Gardenias must have bright light but no sun.
Watering Use tepid rainwater and thoroughly moisten the root ball but allow this to dry out a little before the next watering. In winter leave a little longer between waterings.
Care Use a lime-free, peat-based compost and move plants to a larger pot only when roots appear at the surface of the soil or growing through the drainage hole. Feed during the normal flowering period but remember never to introduce any lime.
Propagation Take 3-in tip cuttings in spring, dip in rooting powder and plant in a slightly moist peat- or lime-free soil-based compost in a warm propagating case or sealed plastic bag.

Gardenia jasminoides

Gloxinia

Common name Gloxinia.
General information Correctly *Sinningia speciosa*, the florists' gloxinia is a hybrid with many forms, grown mainly for the colour and velvet texture of its brilliant blooms. The large leaves serve as a carpet for the vivid flowers of red, white or purple, trumpet shaped, large and striking, which appear in summer, the plant growing from a large tuber.
Temperature Between 18 and 24°C (65–75°F) with added humidity.
Position Place plants where light will be strong for the major part of the day but where no sun will strike them.
Watering Keep plants moist at all times but never wet at the roots. A light mist over is helpful, but droplets should not be allowed to lie on the foliage or flowers.
Care Use a mixture of half peat and half perlite to hold moisture yet provide efficient drainage. Feed frequently with doses of dilute fertilizer. Repotting as such is unnecessary.
Propagation Seed can be sown in spring in a temperature of about 16°C (60°F) and seedlings potted on. Cuttings also root easily. After flowering the soil should gradually be dried out and the tubers potted in fresh compost in spring.

Gloxinia

Grevillea robusta

Common name Silk Oak.
General information A quick-growing evergreen tree with pinnate leaves that appear almost like fern fronds. It will grow to 6 ft indoors in two or three years, retaining its silky foliage and making no special demands. It can go outdoors in the summer, where it will enjoy the generally better light it will find there, but it must come in again before there is any danger of frosts.
Temperature Normal room temperatures will be suitable, but added humidity will be required when above about 18°C (65°F).
Position Stand your plant where it will get good light but no sun in summer and the best light including sun in winter.
Watering Make the root ball uniformly moist and then allow it to dry slightly before watering again. Keep drier in winter.
Care Regular feeding will be necessary to keep the grevillea growing at its normal rapid rate, so repotting will also be required regularly, using a lime-free compost. As plants quickly outgrow allocated space, have seedlings coming along.
Propagation Sow seeds in a peat-based seed compost in spring and raise in a warm propagating case in good light without sun.

33

Grevillea robusta

Gynura sarmentosa

Hedera
canariensis

Gynura sarmentosa

Common name Purple Velvet Plant.
General information A trailing plant noted for the fine purple hairs covering the foliage, dramatic or barely visible depending on the way the light falls. Small orange flowers are produced in spring or summer but these are best removed before they open as they smell unpleasant. *G. sarmentosa*, the best known species, needs pinching out to keep it bushy. Keep it for only one or two years and replace annually with easily rooted cuttings for best results.
Temperature Normal room temperatures are suitable.
Position Good light is essential to maintain both colour and bushy habit, so place where some sun is available.
Watering Keep the soil only just moist at all times but see that there is added humidity by plunging the pot or standing it on a tray covered with sand or pebbles kept moist.
Care Keep drops of water off foliage to avoid brown spots.
Propagation Take tip cuttings about 3–4 in long in spring in a peat and perlite mixture, warmth and in good light. Pot in rich, well drained soil-based compost when of a convenient size, preferably several to a pot.

Hedera helix 'Adam'

Common name None.
General information This is one of the many varieties or cultivars of *H. helix*, the English or Common ivy, with smaller leaves and a somewhat more bushy habit of growth. The 1½–2 in leaves are basically green with a grey and cream marking or marbling, thick and bushy so long as the trails are kept pinched back and there is good light. 'Adam' can be grown as a climber, trailer or equally as a bush.
Temperature Normal room temperatures are suitable.
Position Good light at all times, including some direct sun.
Watering Make sure the root ball is uniformly moist and then leave it until nearly dry before watering again, but make sure that humidity is high enough to keep red spider mite away.
Care Ivies benefit from a brief rest period in winter, so if possible remove them to a cool room, reduce watering and do not feed for a month or so. Repot or topdress with fresh soil when bringing back into warmth and they will repay you.
Propagation Easiest method is to place tips with lower leaves removed in a glass of water. When roots are strong, pot up.

Hedera canariensis

Common name Canary Island Ivy.
General information Perhaps the most popular of the ivies, from a genus with few species but innumerable varieties. The Canary Island ivy has green leaves variegated with grey and gold patches and margins, a climber which must normally be helped up a cane with clips or ties but capable of putting out root hairs onto a moist surface and pulling itself upwards. It is also known as *H.c.* 'Gloire de Marengo'.
Temperature Normal room temperatures are suitable and plants will accept cooler conditions without objection.
Position This variegated ivy should have bright light in order to maintain its leaf colour and stay compact rather than elongated and with comparatively few leaves.
Watering Keep the soil just moist, never dry, never wet.
Care Feed regularly, less in winter than in summer and try to maintain a humid atmosphere. Repot in spring if necessary, using a rich, soil-based compost.
Propagation Tip cuttings will root easily in a peat and perlite mixture or even in plain water. Alternatively, take a shoot and layer a portion near the tip into a nearby pot.

Hedera helix 'Adam'

34

Helxine soleirolii

Heptapleurum arboricola

Helxine soleirolii

Common names Mind-your-own-business, Baby's Tears.
General information A curious but endearing little creeping plant with neat, almost round, tiny green leaves and pinkish stems that covers a pot surface and creeps over the edge to spread over any nearby moist surface. Apart from being grown alone, it is excellent as a carpet at the feet of taller plants which might otherwise grow from a naked soil.
Temperature Normal room temperatures are suitable.
Position Good light is required to keep the leaf colour bright, but plants should be kept away from direct sun.
Watering Never allow the soil to become dry, but go rather to the other extreme and keep it almost on the wet side.
Care Plants grow and spread easily to make a carpet where this is required or where it will add to the general effect. Light and frequent applications of liquid fertilizer keep growth lush. There is no need to repot or move on.
Propagation The little trails root as they creep across any moist surface, so it will be seen that to raise some new plants merely pull off a few pieces and push them into a pot of wet compost where they will quickly make roots.

Hibiscus rosa-sinensis

Common name Rose of China.
General information A quick-growing and potentially large flowering shrub with beautiful but short-lived blooms, single or double, in red, pink, orange, yellow or white and sometimes with multicoloured foliage. The species generally found indoors is *H. rosa-sinensis*, which has several varieties. Because the plant will outgrow any indoor situation it is necessary to cut it back to shape and size. This is usually done in early spring and the shrub comes to no harm if it is pruned almost to soil level in this process.
Temperature Normal room temperatures are suitable during growth and flowering, but when the flowers cease it is best to reduce watering and keep the plant in a temperature of about 13°C (55°F) for a couple of months, when the foliage will be shed and the shrub will rest and gain strength.
Position Light must be good and strong, including some sun.
Watering In spring and summer water thoroughly and then allow to dry out slightly. In winter reduce watering rates.
Care Repot annually in a soil-based compost. Give regular feeds.
Propagation Take 3–4-in tip cuttings in spring and plant in a half-peat, half-perlite mixture in a warm propagating case.

Heptapleurum arboricola

Common name Parasol Plant.
General information A fast growing foliage plant that will grow to 6 ft in a couple of years but can be kept shorter and bushy by pinching out the growing points. The main attraction is in the leaves, growing on a stalk up to 12 in long, divided into seven or more leaflets, each radiating outwards on a short stalk like parasol spokes.
Temperature Keep fairly warm, maintaining a minimum temperature of 16°C (60°F) at all times, winter and summer.
Position Plants must be in good light and need several hours of direct sun each day in order to stay stocky and compact.
Watering Make sure the root ball is moist but no more, then let it dry out slightly before watering like this again.
Care As plants seem to grow at all seasons they must be fed lightly but regularly summer and winter. Keep them in good light and move to a larger pot each spring, or topdress, using a rich, well drained, soil-based potting compost.
Propagation By tip cuttings taken in spring and inserted in a peat and perlite mixture in a propagating case at about 18–24°C (65–75°F) in good light but without direct sun.

Hibiscus rosa-sinensis
hybrid

35

Hippeastrum
hybrid

Hoya carnosa
'Variegata'

Hippeastrum

Common name Amaryllis.
General information Bulbous flowering plants which normally produce two or more huge and striking trumpet flowers in red, white or orange, sometimes streaked or margined. Bulbs are large, not inexpensive, and can be of a prepared type to flower at Christmas instead of the more normal early spring.
Temperature Normal living room warmth will bring bulbs into flower but too much heat will reduce the flowering period.
Position It is important that when plants are growing well they should receive good light, including direct sun, and when the flowers have finished good sun is essential to build strength into the plant for next year's flowering.
Watering Take it in stages. Water lightly when bulb is first planted, then give a little more and when in flower keep soil moist, continuing until autumn, then stop during winter rest.
Care Use a rich, well-drained soil-based compost, feed regularly while in flower or growing vigorously, but not in winter.
Propagation From young bulblets produced at the parental base.

Hoya carnosa 'Variegata'

Common name Wax Plant.
General information A vigorous flowering climber with many white, waxy flowers in clusters and thick, chunky leaves. The flowers are long-lasting, sometimes sweetly scented and popular in wedding bouquets. *H. carnosa* is the species usually grown indoors. Variegated forms available.
Temperature Normal room temperatures are suitable.
Position To get good flowers and strong growth it is vital that light be bright, to include some hours of direct sun.
Watering Water moderately then let soil almost dry out.
Care Use a rich soil-based compost and feed plants well while they are growing and flowering. Repot annually. Train growth so that maximum light is constantly available. Beware of attack by mealy bug, search cracks and crevices and spray. Prune to required shape and size after flowering is finished.
Propagation Take stem cuttings in spring, remove lower leaves, dip in hormone rooting powder and plant in a peat and perlite mixture in a warm, lightly shaded propagating case.

Hydrangea macrophylla
Hortensia variety

Hydrangea

Common name None.
General information A generous, attractive and popular flowering shrub for house or garden, *H. macrophylla* 'Hortensia', with huge, mop-head flowers, white, pink or red unless in an acid soil when they can be blue. Plants must be kept moist at the roots at all times, cool and in an airy situation. They are best put in the garden after flowering.
Temperature Keep plants cool, no more than 16°C (60°F).
Position In order to get good flower colour plants must be in strong light, but direct sun should always be avoided.
Watering Hydrangeas should never be allowed to dry out or permanent damage will be caused. Keep the root ball well moistened at all times, even wet when the weather is hot.
Care Hydrangeas are best treated as indoor-outdoor plants, being grown indoors to flower in spring and then put in the garden or on a patio, but if potted watering must be watched.
Propagation Cuttings taken from non-flowering shoots may grow well but equally may not flower. Best buy young plants.

Hypocyrta glabra

Common names Goldfish Plant, Clog Plant.

General information A small, spreading, flowering plant covered with tiny, glossy, chunky, dark green foliage and studded with little orange flowers, almost egg-shaped, which give it the common names. It is an easy, tolerant plant, bearing a few flowers almost all the year round, although the thick foliage alone is most attractive. Trails will grow quite long or can be cut back severely, depending on where your plant is to be displayed.

Temperature Normal room temperatures are suitable.

Position In good light but not direct sun except in winter.

Watering Keep the soil moist in summer, almost dry in winter.

Care Repot annually in spring using a peat-based compost.

Propagation Take 3–4-in cuttings in spring, remove the lower leaves, dip in a hormone rooting powder and plant in a peat and perlite mixture. Place in a warm and well-lit propagating case or into a polythene bag, sealing it to give increased humidity. When growth shows plant four to a pot.

Hypocyrta glabra

Hypoestes phyllostachya

Common name Polka Dot Plant.

General information A small, shrubby plant noted mainly for the dark green leaves liberally dotted with pale pink spots. The species grown as a house plant is *H. phyllostachya* and there are one or two varieties differing mainly in the size or colour of the spots. Plants will produce small, pale blue or purple flowers in spring but these are insignificant and detract from the general interest so are best picked off. Fairly large plants with a height and spread of more than 12 in can be grown but these tend to become leggy and thin, so it is best to concentrate on smaller, younger and brighter plants for growing as decoration in the home.

Temperature Normal room temperatures are suitable but care must be taken that these do not drop below about 13°C (55°F) or permanent harm and possible death are likely to result.

Position Strong light is essential for good leaf colour but keep plants out of direct sunlight at all times.

Watering While in growth the root ball should be thoroughly moistened and then allowed almost to dry out; give less in winter.

Care Although hypoestes plants will grow quite quickly they do not make great roots, so small pots will suit them. Use a soil-based compost and feed regularly while growing well.

Propagation Seeds germinate easily or cuttings can be taken and rooted in plain water or in the usual peat and perlite mixture in warmth in a propagating case or plastic bag.

Hypoestes
phyllostachya

Impatiens

Common name Busy Lizzie.

General information Popular, bushy, soft, almost perpetual-flowering plant in two main forms: *I. wallerana*, with green foliage and flowers in many colours, and *I. petersiana*, with reddish chocolate-bronze leaves and large red flowers. Both are fairly easy so long as plants are kept warm, in a humid atmosphere and in a pot that might appear to be too small.

Temperature Never below about 13°C (55°F) but otherwise at normal room temperatures, with added humidity when hot.

Position In order to flower well and maintain their colour plants must have strong light but not direct sun except briefly.

Watering Keep the root ball just moist at all times.

Care Repot in a soil-based potting compost only if large plants are required. Young well fed plants look best.

Propagation Pinch out growing tips in summer and place in water, planting out in rich compost when rooted.

Impatiens

Iresine herbstii

Common name Blood Leaf.
General information The vivid red leaves, the quick growth and the accommodating habit of growth are the main reasons for the popularity of this shrubby little plant, which does well in the home and during summer in the garden. Growth is soft but colour is crisp and bright. Stems sometimes become lank and attenuated, so pinch out growing tips once every month or two which will encourage strong, bushy growth.
Temperature Normal room temperatures are suitable all year.
Position Iresines must have good light, including some sun.
Watering The soil should be kept a little more than merely moist during the growing period, but can be drier in winter.
Care Provide plenty of moisture, regular feeds, added humidity and then pinch out growing shoots regularly. Repot each spring in a soil-based compost if found necessary.
Propagation Easy to propagate by pinching out a growing shoot and putting this in water. When roots are seen to be 2 in or so long, pot up in a soil-based compost.

Iresine herbstii

Jasminum polyanthum

Jasminum polyanthum

Common name Jasmine.
General information Few of the many species of jasmine can be grown successfully indoors but *J. polyanthum* is one. It is a quick growing climber with many large clumps of fragrant white flowers appearing during late winter. A further credit point is that plants will flower after only six months or so. Keep somewhat rampant growth under control and train the clinging shoots on trellis or other support.
Temperature Not too hot an atmosphere, about 16°C (60°F).
Position As with all flowering plants good light is quite essential, including some direct sunlight, though not at mid day.
Watering Give plenty of water while the plant is growing and flowering well, but rather less during the rest period.
Care This sweet and endearing flowering climber is tougher than would appear and too much coddling would do harm. Keep plants cool and in an airy situation, feed regularly while growing well, thin out and prune when necessary, give good light. Repot annually in summer unless too large, using a soil-based compost and a pot not one, but two sizes larger.
Propagation Take tip cuttings in late summer and plant in a peat and perlite mixture in a warm, well lit propagating case.

Kalanchoe blossfeldiana

Common name None.
General information This succulent plant has now become a Christmas production, appearing in full flower in the shops two months or so before its normal season. *K. blossfeldiana* is the most popular of several species and a number of cultivars have appeared, including some miniatures. The clustered flowers are mainly red, sometimes orange or yellow. Leaves are thick, chunky, almost round and can be red rimmed.
Temperature Normal room temperatures will be suitable.
Position Plants should be placed where they will get as much light, including direct sun, as is available in winter.
Watering Go easy; give enough just to moisten the soil while plants grow and flower well. Apply less after flowering.
Care This is generally treated as a temporary plant, to be enjoyed while in flower during winter and then discarded when it has lost its flowers and attractive appearance. So pay attention to watering, feed lightly and give good light.
Propagation Cuttings will root but are unlikely to flower indoors without special treatment. Best to buy young plants.

Kalanchoe blossfeldiana

38

Kentia forsteriana

Common name Parlour Palm.

General information Often known today as *Howea forsteriana* rather than kentia, this single-stemmed palm has leaf stalks growing to 2 ft or so with horizontal fronds and many leaflets arching from the central midrib. These palms are seen less frequently than before largely because they are slow growers and need some years of high temperatures to mature sufficiently to suit indoor culture, when they will take less favourable conditions and grow at a more acceptable rate.

Temperature Normal room temperatures will be suitable.

Position Preferably in good light with perhaps a little gentle sun, but will succeed in comparatively dark corners if transferred to good light occasionally for recuperation.

Watering Plenty in growing season and much less when resting.

Care These palms remain decorative with little attention so long as they are fed, kept warm and never too wet. They tend to collect dust, so spray occasionally or place on the patio in a summer shower. Repot annually if growing well.

Propagation Only by fresh seed in considerable heat.

Kentia forsteriana

Lantana camara

Laurus nobilis

Common name Bay Tree.

General information This is not really a house plant at all although it is sometimes grown indoors for brief periods mainly as a formal decorative feature where light is good. The foliage is not exceptional, the flowers are insignificant and the shape must be controlled by cruel pruning if formality is desired. Much better to grow the plant on the patio or in the herb bed where occasional leaves can be taken for cooking. *L. nobilis* is the species usually grown, a hardy shrub which will grow perfectly well in the garden although it may require some shelter and staking in strong winds.

Temperature Indoors keep the plant cool and airy.

Position Good light is essential at all times.

Watering When grown in a container it is essential that the soil does not dry out, but make sure that drainage is adequate and that plants are not allowed to sit in a puddle.

Care Try to treat plants as though they were outdoors.

Propagation Cuttings taken in autumn will root in a garden frame, or shoots may be pinned down for layering.

Lanata camara

Common name Yellow Sage.

General information This little flowering shrub will grow quite large in the wild and is kept small indoors by continuously pinching out the growing tips. The plant is popular mainly because of the globular flower heads which consist of many tubular flowers packed in circles which open from the outside to the centre, yellow, orange, pink or white. Plants are mainly sold in winter and treated as temporary, but if pruned regularly they can be decorative for years.

Temperature Normal room temperatures are suitable so long as added humidity is provided, with cooler winter conditions.

Position Plants must have bright light, including direct sun summer and winter if they are to flower as well as they can.

Watering Keep the root ball well moistened while growing well.

Care Maintain compact and floriferous growth by frequent pinching out of the growing tips, otherwise plants will tend to grow leggy. Watch out for whitefly and treat at once.

Propagation Take 3-in cuttings, dip in hormone rooting powder and plant in a peat and perlite mixture in warmth and light.

Laurus nobilis

Maranta leuconeura erythrophylla

Maranta leuconeura erythrophylla

Common name Herringbone Plant.
General information This is one of the several forms of *M. leuconeura* and is sometimes known as *M. erythroneura*. All have striking, distinctive and beautiful foliage and apart from requiring somewhat higher temperatures than usual all are fairly easy to keep in the home for long periods. The leaves of the herringbone plant have a deep green background while the central red vein is margined much lighter green and all veins are as red as the underside of the leaves. The plant has every appearance of fragility and delicacy but is in fact much tougher and stronger than its looks indicate.
Temperature Aim to keep your plant at about 18°C (65°F).
Position Some light is necessary to maintain the leaf colour but this should not be too strong or the leaves will tend to turn brown at the edges and to become papery.
Watering Keep the root ball well moistened while the plant is growing strongly, but in winter allow it almost to dry out.
Care Use a soil-based compost, feed regularly during the growing period and repot annually in early spring.
Propagation The easiest way is to divide large clumps into smaller pieces. Also take cuttings in warmth and shade.

Maranta leuconeura 'Kerchoviana'

Common names Rabbit's Foot, Prayer Plant.
General information This other maranta gets its common names from its leaf markings which are vaguely like a rabbit's tracks and from the habit of the plant to fold its leaves as if in prayer at darkness. Leaves are pale green and distinguished mainly by the darker green or almost chocolate brown blotches on either side of the main vein, which is a normal green in colour. Rabbit's foot leaves are a little more delicate than those of the herringbone plant and a little more humidity is called for to keep them in health. The plant will not grow quite so large as the first and is particularly suited to growing in terrarium or bottle garden.
Temperature Keep your plant in a warm, humid situation.
Position Choose light shade where no sun will touch the plant.
Watering The root ball should be kept just moist at all times.
Care While plants are growing well feed them regularly at fortnightly intervals. Repot into shallow containers each spring using a soil-based compost with added perlite.
Propagation Take cuttings from just above soil level and root in light shade and warmth in a propagating case.

Maranta leuconeura 'Kerchoviana'

Mimosa pudica

Mimosa pudica

Common name Sensitive Plant.
General information This is not the mimosa with fluffy yellow flowers that grows in the south of France and is sold by florists in many parts of the world, but a smaller perennial plant. *M. pudica* is usually grown as an annual and noted for the way in which its feathery leaves close up and droop when they are touched, taking several minutes to regain their previous turgid, upright and alert appearance. This strange behaviour appears to weaken the plant so should not be demonstrated too frequently. In summer little clusters of pinkish flowers appear and when these have finally faded it is best to discard the plant and start again in the next year.
Temperature Normal warm room temperatures will be suitable.
Position In spite of the delicacy of its appearance this mimosa needs bright light including direct sun to do well.
Watering Water well and then allow almost to dry out.
Care Use a soil-based compost for mimosa and use every means of providing humidity other than spraying the plant foliage.
Propagation Sow two or three seeds in a pot of barely moist seed compost and place in a propagating case in good light. Pot on young plants as soon as strong enough to handle.

Monstera deliciosa

Common name Swiss Cheese Plant.

General information This climbing vine is one of the most striking of all house plants. It has plain green leaves (there is a variegated cream and green form), whole when the plant is young and increasing in size up to 2 ft wide, slashed and holed dramatically. Easy to grow, plants will send out trails which grow around the walls of an entire room. The specific name comes from the delicious fruit, which is unlikely to appear when grown indoors in normal conditions.

Temperature Normal room temperatures are suitable.

Position Light should be good but plants should not stand in direct sunlight except during winter for short periods.

Watering Give less water to monsteras than might appear necessary. Just moisten the soil, then leave almost to dry out.

Care The thick aerial roots produced should be directed into the soil in the pot or can grow into a moss pole if this is provided as a support. Use a rich, soil-based compost, feed regularly and pot on each spring while of convenient size.

Propagation Not easy. By a tip cutting with at least two leaves, by air layering and by seed; a lengthy process.

Monstera delicosa

Neanthe bella

Neanthe bella

Common name Parlour Palm.

General information A charming miniature palm that should correctly be called *Chamaedorea elegans*. Easy to grow and small enough for a terrarium or bottle garden or graceful enough to stand on its own or to be mixed with other plants. Tiny and insignificant yellow flowers are sometimes produced on a mature plant. Growth is slow, so plants remain at a conveniently small size for years without becoming straggly.

Temperature Normal room temperatures will be suitable.

Position These little parlour palms must have good light without standing in direct sun. Too dark and they become elongated.

Watering Surprisingly, this palm needs plenty of water while growing well but much less in winter. Provide some added humidity, even spraying the plant gently in warm weather.

Care Use a rich, soil-based compost with the addition of a quarter portion of peat and feed plants while growing strongly. Repot only when the roots have visibly filled the container, handling them with great care for they are thick and brittle.

Propagation A difficult matter without special equipment, for propagation is by seed sown in constant high temperature.

Neoregelia

Common name None.

General information One of the several bromeliads which are so easy, so popular and so decorative in the house plant scene, *N. carolinae tricolor* maintains the highly convenient habit of producing a central vase at the point from which all the long, arching leaves radiate, so that if this is kept filled all other watering problems can be forgotten. The plant also has the habit of blushing a deep, fiery red in the area of this central vase when it produces its tiny, insignificant, almost submerged flowers. The leaves otherwise are striped green and gold with a hint of pink.

Temperature Normal room temperatures will be suitable.

Position Whenever plants are brightly coloured they need strong light and here an hour or two of sunlight is advised.

Watering Although the central cup should be kept filled with water at all times, the neoregelia is one of the very few bromeliads which benefit if the soil is kept just moist.

Care Feed in cup. Repotting is seldom necessary.

Propagation Detach young basal rosettes with as much root as possible, pot up and keep in warmth until growing well.

Neoregelia carolinae tricolor

41

Nephrolepis exaltata

Nephrolepis exaltata

Common name Boston Fern.
General information The Boston fern is one of the several forms of *N. exaltata* which will sometimes grow fronds as long as 6 ft, soft green, arching, divided into alternate narrow pinnae on each side of the main midrib. These rise from an underground rhizome which sends out furry runners along the soil surface carrying young plants at the tips.
Temperature Normal room temperatures will be suitable so long as these do not fall below about 10°C (50°F).
Position In good, strong light without risk of direct sun.
Watering The root ball should be kept constantly moist at all times of the year unless temperatures drop significantly, in which case water less frequently but never allow to dry out.
Care Feed this fern lightly but regularly while in growth and if it grows too large to be moved conveniently, topdress the soil with a handful of fresh, soil-based compost.
Propagation Cut off one or more strong plantlets at the end of a runner and plant up in normal potting compost.

Nerium oleander

Nerium oleander

Common name Oleander.
General information A flowering shrub which will grow quite large and is best kept indoors in winter and on the patio in summer. The long, slim, leathery leaves serve as a foil to the six or eight 1–2 in flowers grouped at the ends of the stems, single or double, usually pink or red but also available in white, yellow, orange and a reddish purple. Some oleanders are perfumed and there is a variegated form.
Temperature Normal room temperatures are suitable but it is helpful to give a winter rest period at about 11°C (52°F).
Position The production of flowers is dependent on good light, including direct sun. In summer out of doors this will mean that plants will require a great deal of water.
Watering Keep the root ball moist and allow it to dry out a little between treatments. Give a little less water during the rest period but make sure the soil is never too dry.
Care Repot annually in spring if roots have filled the container, using a soil-based compost. Feed regularly.
Propagation Tip cuttings 3–6 in long, with their lower leaves removed, will root easily in plain water or can be planted in a peat and perlite mixture in good light.

Oplismenus hirtellus 'Variegatus'

Common name Ribbon Grass.
General information Similar in some respects to and sometimes confused with tradescantia, this little grass with variegated 2 in leaves can be as attractive or as dull as you care to make it. When grown well the leaves studding the long stems will be green and white with a pink tinge that can suffuse the whole of the foliage. Small, greenish, uninteresting flowers may be produced in summer. Plants are suited to growing in hanging baskets but trails should not be allowed to grow long and straggly. Young plants root easily.
Temperature Normal room temperatures will be suitable.
Position Best in an east or west window where there is good light including direct sun when it is not overpoweringly hot.
Watering Keep the compost well watered, almost wet.
Care Grow in a rich soil-based compost and feed regularly in spring and summer. Do not keep plants too long but replace them with young and attractive successors which are easily grown.
Propagation Take 2-in tip cuttings and insert in a moist potting mixture in light and normal warmth.

Oplismenus hirtellus 'Variegatus'

Pachystachys lutea

Pachystachys lutea

Common name Lollipop Plant.
General information *Pachystachys lutea* is a small flowering shrub that grows to about 18 in, with upright, woody stems bearing dark green 6 in leaves, puckered and veined. The flowers are the real delight of this plant. These are small, white, tubular, with a brief life, but they push their way out through a series of interleaved, upright golden bracts that persist for months, constantly bearing a new flush of the less significant flowers.
Temperature Normal room temperatures, not below 16°C (60°F).
Position As bright light as possible without actual sunlight.
Watering Keep the soil in the pot only just moist at all seasons of the year, for there is no real rest period.
Care Use a soil-based compost when repotting plants annually in early spring. Feed regularly but lightly. Plants should not be allowed either to dry out nor to become starved.
Propagation Take 3-in tip cuttings in spring, remove lowest leaves, dip in hormone rooting powder and insert in a peat and perlite mixture in warmth and good light.

Passiflora caerulea

Common name Passion Flower.
General information Of the great number of species of *Passiflora* only one, *P. caerulea*, can be grown successfully as a house plant. This is a vigorous climber which can be something of an uninteresting nuisance unless it is kept cut back, pruned to size and grown under strict control. The leaves take second place to the intricate and superb flowers. In the garden fruits are produced, but not in the home.
Temperature Normal summer room temperatures will suit, but in winter, if possible, give a rest period at about 10°C (50°F).
Position Good light, including direct sun, is essential.
Watering Keep the root ball moist, almost wet, while growing well, but allow to become almost dry when resting in winter.
Care Trails should be trained to trellis, wire hoops or some other means of maintaining control. Cut back side shoots to 3 in each spring. At the same time repot, using a soil-based compost and keeping the container as small as possible.
Propagation Take 3–4 in stem cuttings in summer, dip ends in rooting powder and insert in compost in warmth.

Pandanus veitchii

Pandanus veitchii

Common name Screw Pine.
General information The long, slim leaves, striped along their length with white or cream, join the short, main stem in a spiral, which explains the popular name. The leaves are 3 ft or so long, 3 in wide and have finely- and sharply-toothed edges that can inflict a nasty cut. *P. veitchii* is the best known indoor species, but there is also a slightly smaller form, with shorter, slimmer leaves, also striped.
Temperature Normal room temperatures will be suitable.
Position Light must be bright, including some hours of sun.
Watering While the plant is actively growing keep the soil mixture well moistened, but in winter allow this almost to dry.
Care This pandanus produces aerial roots at the base of the leaves and these reach into the pot and tend to push the whole plant upwards. Allow for this when repotting or top-dressing. Feed regularly and when repotting use a rich, soil-based compost, also when covering emerging roots.
Propagation Suckers appear at the base of the plant and these should be removed and rooted in sand or perlite in warmth.

Passiflora caerulea

43

Pelargonium
(Regal)

Pelargonium

Common name Geranium.

General information An invaluable group of shrubby plants grown for their flowers and sometimes their foliage. Plants for indoors are classified as Ivy-leaved, Regal and Zonal, respectively trailing, with small clusters of flowers; shrubby, with larger, softer leaves and variously coloured flowers; taller, with leaves bearing a contrasting coloured zone or band around the centre, flowers massed in clusters. There are many hybrids, all easy to grow, and scented-leaved and miniature forms all suited to individual decorative needs.

Temperature Normal room temperatures are suitable at all times, although a cooler rest period in winter will aid plants.

Position Pelargoniums need good light, including direct sun.

Watering Never give pelargoniums too much. Keep the root ball just moist while growing and almost dry in winter.

Care Try to keep pelargonium pots small, so each spring replace roots in the same pot with fresh, soil-based compost. Feed growing plants regularly but not too richly.

Propagation Take 4-in cuttings in summer, dip in hormone rooting powder, pot in peat-perlite mixture in good light.

Pellaea rotundifolia

Common name Button Fern.

General information An unusual and decorative fern with 12-in fronds composed of a black, wiry stalk studded alternately with small, almost round leaf-like pinnae. Quite different from this is *P. viridis*, with much more fern-like foliage and a number of forms.

Temperature Normal room temperatures are suitable and if they rise too high simply provide additional humidity.

Position Keep plants in light shade, away from all sun.

Watering Try to keep the root ball constantly on the wet side of moist, although it must never be allowed to paddle.

Care Feed plants regularly with dilute liquid fertilizer, missing only a few weeks during the darker, cooler months of winter. The rhizome grows horizontally just below the surface of the soil and puts down meagre roots, so shallow pans are normally more suitable than regular pots, but make sure that drainage is adequate to allow all excess moisture to escape.

Propagation Knock the plant from its pot in spring and cut the tough and matted rhizome into convenient pieces, each having a good portion of roots and fronds. Plant these pieces in a soil- or peat-based compost according to choice.

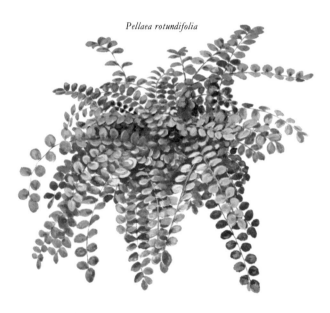

Pellaea rotundifolia

Pellionia daveauana

Common name None.

General information A low growing trailing creeper with 2-in leaves that sometimes vary in shape and colour, oblong or oval and mainly green with touches of darker green, bronze, purple or black. Useful in hanging baskets and as a ground cover. Roots grow down into the compost wherever a node touches, and as growth is swift a dense coverage of the soil or the formation of a solid ball in a hanging basket is quickly and decoratively achieved.

Temperature Normal room temperatures are suitable but make sure that the thermometer does not drop below 13°C (55°F).

Position To maintain the leaf colour it is important that pellionias should have bright light but never keep in sun.

Watering Keep the root ball well moistened at all times except when growth slows for a brief period in winter.

Care With quick and lush growth regular feeding is advised. Repotting is not normally necessary, but when required use a soil-based compost in which to root the long trails.

Propagation When plants have been layered, as described, it is a simple matter to cut away and plant a newly rooted tip.

Pellionia daveauana

44

Peperomia caperata

Peperomia caperata

Common name None.
General information This is just one of several peperomias grown as house plants. All are small, low growing and have the same tall rat-tail flower spike, white or cream and distinctive rather than attractive. *P. caperata* has small, heart-shaped leaves with miniature valleys and craters growing at the end of long, otherwise naked, pink stalks.
Temperature Normal room temperatures will be suitable so long as these are confined within a bracket of about 5°C (10°F) around 18°C (65°F). Much below this can be fatal and above will require humidity to retain the foliage.
Position Keep in light shade away from direct sun.
Watering Keep peperomias almost dry at all times of the year.
Care Use a peat-based compost and feed only seldom. If plants are over-fed or over-watered they will shed leaves, grow lank and die. Roots are meagre and shallow. Plants are best in small pots. Repot only if felt necessary.
Propagation Take 2–3-in cuttings in spring and insert in an almost dry mixture of peat and perlite in good light without sun at a temperature of about 18°C (65°F).

Peperomia magnoliifolia

Common name None.
General information The variegated form of this chunky little plant appears to have achieved greatest success. The leaves are thick, waxy, variegated light green and gold, growing on strong, pinkish stems. A young plant will grow upright but after a period the stems may droop to the horizontal and the plant then becomes a trailer. There is less likelihood of the characteristic rat-tail flower spike appearing with *P. magnoliifolia* than with other peperomias.
Temperature Normal room temperatures will be suitable, but added humidity will be advisable during hot, dry days.
Position Keep in a situation where plants get bright light and allow them to receive direct sun in winter, but briefly othertimes.
Watering In spite of the strong, fat foliage, this plant cannot stand too much water at its roots, so water lightly.
Care To maintain *P. magnoliifolia* as an upright growing plant pinch out some of the growing points occasionally. Feed only lightly and repot if necessary.
Propagation Take tip cuttings in late spring and insert in a peat and perlite mixture. Keep almost dry until rooted.

Peperomia magnoliifolia

Philodendron domesticum

Philodendron domesticum

Common name None.
General information The large philodendron family presents us with a number of house plants, some with somewhat dubious names. *P. domesticum* is also known as *P. hastatum*. The leaves are long, arrow shaped, a dark and shining green and although the plant is essentially a climber it is so heavy that a stout stake is necessary and it is seldom seen to its best effect simply because space is not generally available.
Temperature Normal room temperatures will be suitable.
Position Plants should have good, strong light but no sun.
Watering In spring and summer keep the root ball well moistened and feed regularly. Less water, no food in winter.
Care If your plant is to climb, provide a strong, heavy securely-anchored, thick moss pole. Repot only when roots fill the pot, using a rich peat and leafmould mixture.
Propagation Take 3–4 in tip cuttings in early summer, remove lower leaves and plant in a moist peat and perlite mixture in good light in a warm propagating case or plastic bag.

*Philodendron
scandens*

*Phoenix
roebelenii*

Philodendron scandens

Common name Sweetheart Plant.
General information A trailing or climbing plant with shining green heart-shaped leaves about 4–6 in long which will climb a moss pole with its aerial roots and can be trained to encircle the ceiling of an entire room. It is one of the easiest of all house plants to grow, almost impervious to insect or disease attack, not dramatic in appearance but a good background and mildly endearing plant.
Temperature Normal room temperatures will be suitable and no special provision for extra humidity is necessary until heat is quite excessive. Frosts will kill it, but low temperatures likely in homes will cause little discomfort.
Position Light or shade makes little difference except in excess and even some sun will be enjoyed for brief periods.
Watering Keep the roots only just moist at all times.
Care If fed regularly climbing philodendrons grow well in small pots. Repot only when roots have filled the container and are visible. Use an equal amount of soil- and peat-based compost.
Propagation Tip cuttings will root easily, even in plain water.

Phyllitis scolopendrium

Common name Hart's Tongue Fern.
General information P. scolopendrium is the only species of this fern that is grown indoors but there are many forms and varieties, some of which appear to be almost different plants. The fern is quite hardy and will grow in the garden if desired. The fronds grow up from the furry rhizome looking like a tightly furled question mark and gradually uncurl as they lengthen until the blades are about 12 in long, green, shining on top with spores patterned on the underside.
Temperature Normal room temperatures will be suitable.
Position Keep where there is light shade, never place in sun.
Watering Water sufficiently to moisten thoroughly the whole of the root ball and then allow almost to dry out.
Care This fern likes an alkaline soil, so use tap water rather than rain and a soil-based compost rather than peat. Repot, with rhizomes vertical, when roots fill the pot.
Propagation Knock the plant from its pot and divide the rhizome into sections each bearing healthy frond growth. Plant these sections half in, half out of the moistened potting soil in gentle shade and normal room temperature.

Phoenix roebelenii

Common name Date Palm.
General information A pretty little palm which will grow for years in the home without ever outreaching its location. The slim, arching fronds divided into many pinnae are graceful and have a slight silver sheen when mature. They grow from a central stem or crown which enlarges and thickens as time passes, yet is never obtrusive or ugly. *P. roebelenii* is a miniature form and will never produce either flowers or fruit in the home, but it can give years of decorative pleasure without taxing the skills or attentions of the grower.
Temperature Normal room temperatures will be suitable, better slightly warm than cool. Give plants a brief rest period during winter in a temperature of about 10°C (50°F).
Position Plants must have really good, bright light and will tolerate periods of direct sun except in midsummer.
Watering While plants are growing well in spring and summer keep the root ball thoroughly moistened. Give less in winter.
Care Repot in a well drained soil-based compost when roots begin to show and feed regularly while growing well. In summer give the plant an occasional overall spray with rain water.
Propagation Growing from seed is a lengthy and complex business, but the mere planting of a date stone will quickly produce a single stem which in time becomes the full palm.

*Phyllitis
scolopendrium*

Pilea cadierei 'Nana'

Common name Aluminium Plant.

General information The dwarf form of *P. cadierei*, known as 'Nana' or 'Minima', is easy and attractive, an upright grower rather than a trailer like some of the other species. It has tiny leaves only about 1 in long, which are surmounted by four regular rows of raised silver- or aluminium-coloured spots. The plant grows only to some 6 in in height.

Temperature Keep plants warm and humid, preferably never below about 16°C (60°F) with the pot on a tray of wet pebbles.

Position Light shade is best, never full sun even in winter.

Watering Try to maintain the soil at a barely moist level, letting even this dry out a little between waterings.

Care Use a peat-based compost and feed regularly when growing well. Feed regularly in spring and summer. Do not repot, but replace an old bedraggled plant with a new, young one.

Propagation In spring take 3-in cuttings, strip any lower leaves, dip ends in hormone rooting powder and plant in moist peat and perlite in warmth and light shade.

Pilea cadierei 'Nana'

Platycerium bifurcatum

Common name Stag's Horn Fern.

General information Quite unlike the general run of ferns, the platycerium has two kinds of fronds, the soft, grey-green felt or down-covered virile type that look like a stag's horns and the sterile or anchor fronds at the base which begin as a spreading green shield and then turn brown and brittle. These anchor fronds serve to secure the fern to its support tree in the wild and can be induced to take hold of a piece of wood or bark, where a plant will look more decorative.

Temperature Plants like to be warm, up to about 24°C (75°F) with plenty of humidity, but they will accept room warmth.

Position In good, strong light but not direct sun.

Watering It can be difficult to moisten the soil of a platycerium, so immerse the roots in water, leave to drain, and then replace the plant in position. Feed in water.

Care Pot-grown plants accept a peaty compost, but if growing on board or bark, wrap roots in sphagnum moss and tie on with plastic-covered wire until the roots and anchors take hold.

Propagation Very carefully break or cut off sections of the anchor bearing virile fronds and plant in peat or sphagnum moss.

Platycerium bifurcatum

Plectranthus australis

Common name Swedish Ivy.

General information A pleasant creeping or trailing plant that is so undemanding, so easy to propagate, that it has achieved greater popularity than its mere appearance would warrant. Leaves are soft, almost round, green, with a purple underside in some forms, carried on pinkish stems. Racemes of white flowers appear which are usually pinched off but can look most attractive if the plant is grown well.

Temperature Normal room temperatures will be suitable but plants will grow better if warmer and given extra humidity.

Position Light should be good and can include direct sun, particularly in cooler weather when light is also poor.

Watering Keep the root ball well moistened while plants are growing well, but reduce the watering rate slightly in winter.

Care Feed regularly during growing period and pinch out the growing tips. Use a well drained soil-based compost. Do not repot but bring on a succession of young plants.

Propagation Tip cuttings will root quickly and easily in plain water or in the growing medium without special care.

Plectranthus australis

Pleomele reflexa
'Variegata'

Plumbago auriculata

Common name Cape Leadwort.
General information This little shrub with the wonderful pale blue flowers used to be known as *P. capensis* but is now named *P. auriculata*. Branches as long as 3 ft bear at their tips bunches of pale blue flowers, as many as two dozen or so in a group, tubular and with a central darker blue stripe down the petal centres. There is a white variety.
Temperature Normal room temperatures will be suitable.
Position Strong light for this plumbago, including sunlight.
Watering Water lavishly in summer but in winter keep the root ball almost dry and reduce the temperature.
Care In spring and summer feed regularly; not at all in winter. Repot in early spring in a soil-based compost. Prune back to one-third of the mature size each spring for flower growth.
Propagation Take 3–4-in cuttings in late spring or early summer and insert in an equal peat and perlite mixture in warmth and full light in propagating case or plastic bag.

Primula malacoides

Pleomele

Common name Song of India.
General information Correctly known as *Dracaena reflexa* 'Variegata' this plant has clusters of sharply pointed leaves growing on thick stems, the tips of which lean away from the vertical. The leaves of the variegated form start off in two tones of green, then the margins turn a golden yellow. The lower leaves drop off as the plant matures to leave a graceful and colourful upper portion.
Temperature Normal warm room temperatures are suitable and it is advisable not to grow plants in less than 13°C (55°F).
Position Because of the leaf colour give good light but no sun.
Watering Moisten the root ball well, then allow almost to dry out.
Care Feed plants regularly during the growing season. Use a soil-based compost with a little peat and repot annually in spring until plants are too large, then merely topdress.
Propagation Take 4-in cuttings, dip in hormone rooting powder and plant in a peat and perlite mixture in a warm propagating case.

Plumbago auriculata

Primula malacoides

Common name Fairy Primrose.
General information Tallest of the primulas, this grows to about 18 in, with spikes bearing pink, red, white or blue flowers at the top. Plants should be dead-headed as the flowers fade to increase the flowering period, but as a rule they are treated as temporary, to be enjoyed while in flower in late winter and spring, then discarded.
Temperature Plants should be kept cool for a long life, no higher than about 12–13°C (55°F) if possible.
Position Primulas should have good light, even some sun.
Watering The soil should be kept thoroughly moistened at all times, though never actually puddled or sodden.
Care Spray occasionally to keep up the humidity. Do not attempt to keep plants from year to year, but repot small plants in a well drained, soil-based compost to encourage swift growth.
Propagation Sow seed in autumn or early spring in boxes of seed compost at about 16°C (60°F). Move to small pots when ready, then pot on before bringing indoors from greenhouse.

Primula obconica

Primula obconica

Common name None.
General information Less tall and more heavily flowered than *P. malacoides*. The flowers come in a wider range of colours and, have a longer life when kept on the cool side. Plants can be in flower from about Christmas through to the early summer so long as faded blooms are picked off and the atmosphere is both cool and humid.
Temperature Normal cool room temperatures will be suitable.
Position In good light including some direct sun, particularly during winter when light is generally poor.
Watering Keep the roots well moistened at all times.
Care These plants can be kept for another season. Keep them in a cool, lightly shaded and airy spot during summer with just enough water to prevent wilting, possibly outdoors on patio or in garden. In autumn trim and neaten the plants and topdress with rich soil-based compost and begin watering and feeding. Some people develop rashes when handling *P. obconica*.
Propagation Follow instructions as for *P. malacoides*.

Pteris cretica

Common name Cretan Brake.
General information A pleasant and popular fern bearing light green fronds divided into up to four pinnae on wiry black stalks about 6 in long. Each pinna, slim and tapering, is about 4 in long. There is a form *P.c.* 'Albo-lineata', with white areas on each side of the pinnae.
Temperature Normal room temperatures between about 13–18°C (55–65°F) are suitable. Increase humidity if above this.
Position Keep in as good light as possible without direct sun.
Watering Maintain these ferns always on the wet side but not sodden or paddling. If temperatures fall, keep a little drier.
Care This fern can be grown in a peat- or soil-based compost. In the former feed lightly but regularly every fortnight or so, less frequently with the richer soil-based compost. Pot on in spring if roots have filled the pot, otherwise wait. Plant the rhizome just below the surface and water lightly.
Propagation Best and easiest by division. Knock the fern from its pot and with a sharp knife cut the rhizome into sections each bearing good roots and fronds. Plant each piece in good, moist compost to develop and grow.

Pteris cretica

Punica granatum

Common name Pomegranate.
General information The dwarf form, *Punica granatum* var. *nana* is the one grown indoors. It will reach about 3 ft and produce orange-red flowers in late summer. These may develop into miniature fruits, good to look at but unpleasant to eat, after which the plant tends to lose its leaves.
Temperature Normal room temperatures are suitable during the growing period but plants should be cooler while resting.
Position While growing strongly pomegranates should have good light including some hours of direct sun each day.
Watering Give plenty of water and keep the root ball moist while growing well, in winter water rarely and sparingly.
Care Give separate summer and winter treatment. Feed regularly. Plants flower best in small pots, so repot in spring in a soil-based compost no more than once every two years.
Propagation In summer take 2–3-in cuttings with a heel, dip in hormone rooting powder and plant in moist peat and perlite in light and warmth in a propagating case.

Punica granatum
var. *nana*

Rhoeo spathacea

Common name Boat Lily.

General information R. *spathacea*, often known as R. *discolor*, is generally grown in its variegated form, with yellow stripes down the 10 in dark green leaves with the reddish-purple undersides. These leaves spring from a short, stumpy central stem and in the axils appear the little boat-shaped bracts which hold the short-lived small white flowers.

Temperature Keep warm, never below 16°C (60°F). Dry air is fatal, so give extra humidity.

Position Light should be good without any direct sunlight.

Watering When growing and flowering, rhoeos should be kept moist at the roots. In winter try to keep them almost dry.

Care Feed regularly during active growth. Repot each spring in either soil or peat-based compost using shallow pots.

Propagation Offsets produced after flowering around the base of the plant can be used for propagation. Tear them gently from the main plant making sure they have good roots and top growth. Plant in a moist peat and perlite mixture.

Rhoeo spathacea

Rhoicissus rhomboidea

Rhoicissus rhomboidea

Common name Grape Ivy.

General information This invaluable plant has saw-edged leaves grouped in threes, dark green with a furry brown undersides. It is a natural climber with short tendrils forked at the ends. It grows quickly and makes a fine and dense screen or a thick pole of foliage when grown up a vertical support. There are several cultivars only slightly different from the type plant. One of the best of all foliage plants.

Temperature The grape ivy will take warmth or cold in its stride. It will not tolerate frost and tends to suffer from red spider mite if conditions are too hot and dry.

Position Preferably in good light without direct sun.

Watering Make sure the entire root ball is well moistened at each watering, then leave until beginning to dry before watering again. Keep much drier during the winter months.

Care Feed plants regularly while in growth. Repot each year in spring using a rich, soil-based compost. Spray daily in hot weather or when air is warm and dry in centrally-heated homes in winter.

Propagation Tip cuttings will root in spring, but easier to layer a portion of stem in a separate pot and then cut away.

Saintpaulia

Common name African Violet.

General information Although there are many species of *Saintpaulia*, those we grow in our homes are almost exclusively cultivars of S. *ionantha*. These little plants produce double or single flowers of blue, pink, red, purple and white, which can be carried almost throughout the year.

Temperature Must be warm, preferably between 18–24°C (65–75°F).

Position In good, strong light but no direct sun. African violets grow particularly well under artificial light.

Watering Give only enough water to moisten the compost lightly and allow it almost to dry out before watering again.

Care Feed regularly but with very weak solutions. Keep saintpaulias in small pots and repot at any time of year only when obviously overdue, using a peat and perlite mixture.

Propagation Saintpaulias are easy to propagate by leaf cuttings. Remove a strong and healthy leaf next to the main stem and plant in a moist peat and perlite mixture in a propagating case or plastic bag at about 18–24°C (65–75°F).

50

Saintpaulia hybrid

Sansevieria trifasciata
'Laurentii'

Sansevieria trifasciata

Common name Mother-in-law's Tongue.
General information A semi-succulent plant with long, thick, tough, spear-shaped leaves growing vertically in a tight rosette. Foliage marbled in tones of green and with a bright yellow edge in the case of the most popular, *S. trifasciata* 'Laurentii'. Plants will grow to more than 3 ft tall and will live for years, sometimes producing small, hidden, scented flowers. There are other species and cultivars, all easy to grow.
Temperature Sansevierias like warmth, 21°C (70°F) or so, but will grow well indoors in considerably cooler temperatures.
Position In good light, including some hours of direct sun.
Watering Careful here; water just enough to moisten the whole of the root ball and then allow the soil to dry almost completely before watering again. Water even less in winter.
Care Feed once a month in summer with a dilute fertilizer. When the pot is filled with roots, repot in a soil-based compost with added perlite and ensure good drainage.
Propagation Sansevierias produce offsets beside the parent plant. Cut these away with good roots and top growth and plant in a peat and perlite mixture.

Sansevieria t. 'Golden Hahnii'

Common name None.
General information Another quite different sansevieria which is achieving popularity as more appear on the market. This plant grows in a little rosette, only a few inches high, with wider leaves bearing a broader band of gold on the margins. It is again easy to grow, long-lived and rewarding. Although a form of *S. trifasciata*, it is completely different.
Temperature Plants will grow in normal warm room temperatures but will develop more quickly if a little warmer.
Position In good, strong light, including direct sun if the essential and attractive coloration is to be preserved.
Watering All sansevierias will rot at soil level if they are kept too wet, so water only occasionally and allow to dry out.
Care Plants are slow growers and need repotting only very seldom, when the roots have obviously filled the pot. Feed lightly and seldom. Repot or topdress with soil-based compost.
Propagation Preferably by offsets. Leaves can be cut into 3–4-in portions and planted (right way up!) in a peat and perlite mixture, but the yellow band is lost this way.

Sansevieria trifasciata
'Golden Hahnii'

Saxifraga stolonifera

Common name Mother of Thousands.
General information Known for years as *S. sarmentosa*, this plant is correctly *S. stolonifera* for obvious reasons, for one of its main attractions is the appearance of the long, thread-like stolons each bearing a young and developing plant on the end. This young plant will root easily if placed on the soil surface of another pot. Leaves are almost round, dark green with silver streaks and a reddish underside.
Temperature Normal room temperatures will be suitable.
Position In good light, including a few hours of direct sun; the cool sun from east or west, not from south.
Watering Water lavishly when in growth but do not allow to paddle. Give much less water in winter when plant is resting.
Care Feed seldom and lightly. Repot using a well drained soil-based compost only if necessary; better to grow new plants.
Propagation Stolons can be pinned down on a peat-based compost to allow the little plants to root. They can then be cut away and potted up. Alternatively the tiny plants at the ends of the runners can be cut off and planted up when they will quickly send down roots and begin growing.

Saxifraga stolonifera

*Schefflera
actinophylla*

Schefflera actinophylla

Common name Umbrella Tree.
General information Still often referred to as *Brassaia*, this graceful little tree gets its common name by the way the five, six or seven leaflets at the end of the long stalk splay out like the spokes of an umbrella, each leaflet an elongated and pointed oval up to about 10 in long, light green, glossy and tough, the midrib strong and noticeable.
Temperature Normal room temperatures will be suitable.
Position Good strong light without sun is helpful towards healthy growth, but periods in light shade will be tolerated.
Watering While growing strongly apply sufficient water to moisten throughly the whole of the soil and then leave it to become almost dry before beginning again. Less in winter.
Care Feed regularly while growing well, not while resting. Use a soil-based compost and repot annually in spring until the ultimate pot size has been reached, then merely topdress.
Propagation Normally by seed with bottom warmth and extra humidity, not easy. Plants can be air layered successfully.

Schizanthus

Common name Butterfly Flower.
General information A temporary flowering plant grown for the beauty of its masses of flowers in tones of pink, purple, yellow and white, usually hybrid forms of *S. pinnatus*, often kept small and short by pinching out growing stems but plants will reach up to 3 ft or so in height, requiring support.
Temperature Keep cool to get long-lived plants, if possible, no warmer than about 10°C (50°F) in an airy atmosphere.
Position Plenty of light is essential for good flowers and direct sunlight, provided it is from east or west, is acceptable.
Watering Make sure that the compost never dries out, although equally it must never be saturated.
Care Grow in a rich, well drained soil-based compost and feed regularly. Pinch out growing tips and dead-head regularly to ensure a constant succession of flowers. Repot young plants when roots fill the pot but do not attempt to keep.
Propagation From seed sown in autumn at about 16°C (60°F). The seedlings can be moved on in spring into larger pots.

Schizanthus
hybrid

Schlumbergera

Common names Crab Cactus, Christmas Cactus, Easter Cactus.
General information A highly confused group of plants known as schlumbergeras, zygocactus and rhipsalidopsis, largely because many hybrids have appeared and the species are seldom seen in commerce. Flat, jointed stems, blunt or sharply toothed, bearing striking but short-lived flowers, mainly in hues of pink, white and purple from the tips.
Temperature Normal room temperatures will be suitable.
Position In light shade. These plants are particularly sensitive to darkness and light and artificial light at nights can delay their more normal periods of flowering.
Watering Water thoroughly from spring to autumn, much less after plants have flowered. Use rainwater if possible.
Care Repot only when the somewhat sparse roots have filled the pot, using a peat and perlite mixture for sharp drainage. Feed regularly when growing well. When flower buds appear do not move plants from original position or they may drop.
Propagation Break off several segments, leave a day or two to dry, then plant in a barely moist peat and perlite mixture.

*Schlumbergera
gaertneri*

Scindapsus aureus
'Marble Queen'

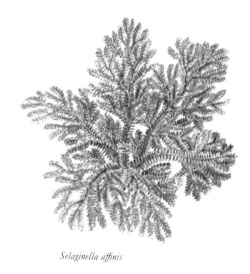

Selaginella affinis

Scindapsus

Common name None.
General information A climbing vine similar in shape to the *Philodendron scandens* with its heart-shaped leaves, but much more difficult, with larger leaves usually marbled or streaked with gold or white and thicker stems. The form usually grown in homes is *S. aureus* 'Marble Queen' or *S.a.* 'Golden Queen'. The genus is now more correctly *Epipremnum*.
Temperature Normal room temperatures should be suitable.
Position Good light is necessary to retain the variegation.
Watering Water moderately while growing well and when resting give only enough to moisten the root ball. If room temperatures are high stand pots on wet pebbles for humidity.
Care Use a rich, soil-based compost, feed regularly and repot each spring if growth is still required. When plants grow too large they can still be accommodated by cutting back.
Propagation Take 3–4-in cuttings just below a node in spring, dip in hormone rooting powder and plant in a peat and perlite mixture in a warm propagating case or plastic bag.

Senecio

Common name Cape Ivy.
General information One or two ivy-like climbers which deserve to be better known, for they grow more quickly than ivies, climb more eagerly and do not suffer in the same way from the results of hot, dry conditions that can mean death to ivies proper. *S. mikanoides*, German Ivy, is plain green, with leaves shaped like those of an ivy. *S. macroglossus* 'Variegatus' is the more popular of the two, with gold and green foliage growing from strong, pinkish-purplish stems.
Temperature Normal room temperatures will be suitable.
Position Place where plants will get bright light, including a few hours of direct sun while they are in full growth.
Watering Water carefully while the plant is growing well and allow the soil almost to dry out before watering again.
Care Feed well while plants are growing. Repot annually in a soil-based compost with added peat and perlite.
Propagation Cuttings 3–4 in long will root readily in water or in a peat and perlite mixture in bright light.

Selaginella

Common name None.
General information Tiny, endearing, moss- or fern-like plants which can form striking clumps of soft green if grown well in a moist and warm atmosphere, preferably enclosed in a terrarium or bottle garden. There are several species, some golden-green, differing mainly in the length and shape of the creeping or spreading stems or their mossy appearance.
Temperature Normal warm room temperatures will be suitable if there is sufficient humidity. Maintain humidity by spraying daily with tepid water, never cold or stems will die.
Position Keep plants in a location of light shade all year.
Watering Keep the roots always wet but never sodden.
Care Feed plants only seldom and with a much diluted form of fertilizer. Repot annually in a peat and perlite mixture and if plants spread too far cut back the trails to a more convenient size and shape in spring when repotting.
Propagation Take some of the cut trail ends about 2–3 in long and insert them only just into a peat and perlite mixture that is barely moist. Keep this warm in a propagating case or enclosed in plastic bag until rooted in a few days.

Senecio macroglossus
'Variegatus'

53

Setcreasea purpurea

Solanum

Common names Winter Cherry, Jerusalem Cherry.
General information Small, leafy shrubs bearing bright, cheerful, orange-red fruits or berries in winter. They are generally marketed for the Christmas season with berries turning colour and are seldom kept through the summer although this is quite possible given the necessary treatment. The berries are inedible but quite safe and non-poisonous. There are two species, *S. capsicastrum* and *S. pseudocapsicum*, the second of which is easier, stronger, with redder berries and with dwarf forms which still carry the larger berries.
Temperature Keep plants comparatively cool during the winter and keep humidity high, by daily spraying if necessary.
Position Allow plants to stand in direct sunlight during winter when there can be little risk of damage by burning.
Watering Always keep the soil well moistened.
Care Feed regularly while growing well. To keep for a further year repot in spring in a soil-based compost.
Propagation By seed sown in spring in some warmth and good light in a propagating case or in a sealed plastic bag.

Spathiphyllum
wallisii

Setcreasea purpurea

Common name Purple Heart.
General information Attractive trailing plants with slim, purple leaves about 4 in long and with small, fairly insignificant three-petalled flowers in summer. The foliage is covered with a fine and attractive dust or bloom which should be retained if possible by careful handling.
Temperature Normal warm living temperatures will be suitable.
Position Plenty of light is necessary to keep the colour good, so keep in a bright situation, even allowing some direct sun.
Watering Water thoroughly at all times but allow the soil mixture to dry out almost completely between waterings.
Care Plants need feeding well to keep them growing strongly, which they should do to look most attractive, but this may mean that they will have to be potted on more than once in a year, using a good, soil-based compost. Young, healthy plants are best, so do not keep them too long.
Propagation Take 3-in cuttings in spring or early summer and remove the lowest leaves before planting them in any standard potting soil-based compost which should be just moist and in a warm draught-free, well-lit position.

Solanum
capsicastrum

Spathiphyllum wallisii

Common name White Sails.
General information These stemless plants send up rolled leaves from the soil surface from the centre of which grow long stalks bearing the dramatic flowers in the form of a white, oval spathe carrying in its centre a creamy spadix. It is these flowers that give the plant its common name. There are a number of spathiphyllums, the most popular of which is probably *S.* 'Mauna Loa', a larger but less floriferous version of the more compact *S. wallisii* seen here.
Temperature Normal room temperatures will be suitable.
Position In spite of the flower, grow spathiphyllums in a lightly-shaded situation, as direct sun will damage leaves.
Watering The root ball must never be allowed to dry out completely, but should certainly never be too wet. Keep it just moist. Increase humidity by standing the pot on wet pebbles.
Care Feed lightly throughout the year and repot plants each spring in a peat- or soil-based compost with added perlite.
Propagation Knock the plant from its pot and gently tease apart sections of the rhizome, each bearing good roots and leaf stalks. Plant these sections in the same growing medium.

Stephanotis floribunda

Stephanotis floribunda

Common name Madagascar Jasmine.
General information A climbing shrub grown mainly for its clusters of creamy white, waxy, highly-scented flowers which grow in spring. The leaves are dark green, glossy and tough. Growth can be too vigorous and plants may need cutting back each year if they take too much space. It is also necessary to keep plants where temperatures and other conditions will fluctuate as little as possible or flowers may drop, as they also tend to do if plants in flower are brought indoors early.
Temperature Keep just a little on the warm side.
Position Plants should have good light but never direct sun.
Watering The root ball should be kept moist at all times, though in winter it may be allowed to dry out a little. Spray plants daily if indoor temperatures rise too high.
Care Feed regularly, not in winter. Grow in soil-based compost and repot each year until large, then topdress.
Propagation Take 3–4-in tips from non-flowering laterals, dip in hormone rooting powder and plant in a peat and perlite mixture in good light in a propagating case.

Streptocarpus

Common name Cape Primrose.
General information A range of plants, mainly hybrids, grown for their flowers, which in some cases can appear almost the whole year through. Most plants have long, spear-shaped, medium green leaves arching outwards while the flower stalks rise from their base carrying several trumpet-shaped flowers of blue, purple, white, pink, red, sometimes multi-coloured. 'Constant Nymph' is probably the best known hybrid, but more and better flowers with a wider range of colours and a longer flowering season come from the John Innes group.
Temperature Normal room temperatures will be suitable.
Position Bright light is necessary, but never direct sun.
Watering Moisten the root ball and then allow it to dry out a little before giving more water. Keep drier in winter.
Care Feed regularly while plants are growing well. Repot after the main flowering period and only when roots obviously fill the pot, using a peat and perlite mixture.
Propagation By seed sown in late winter or midsummer at about 18°C (65°F), by dividing clumps in spring or by taking leaf cuttings inserted into a peat and perlite mixture.

Streptocarpus hybrid

Syngonium

Common name Goosefoot Plant.
General information A climbing or trailing aroid with several forms, best known of which is probably *S. podophyllum* 'Emerald Gem', with dark green leaves bearing pale green veins. The common name derives from the shape of the leaf, although juvenile and mature leaves sometimes differ. The climbing stems will cling to a moss pole, a moistened board or some other suitable support. Looks good in hanging baskets.
Temperature Normal room temperatures will be suitable.
Position Bright light is required but no direct sun.
Watering Water moderately when plants are growing well and then allow to dry out a little. Less in winter.
Care Feed plants regularly when they are growing well, not while resting in winter. Use an equal parts soil and peat compost and repot each spring until large enough, then topdress. Syngoniums do not normally require very large containers.
Propagation Take tip cuttings about 3–4 in long in late spring just below a node, strip lowest leaf, dip in rooting powder and plant in good light in peat and perlite.

Syngonium podophyllum 'Emerald Gem'

55

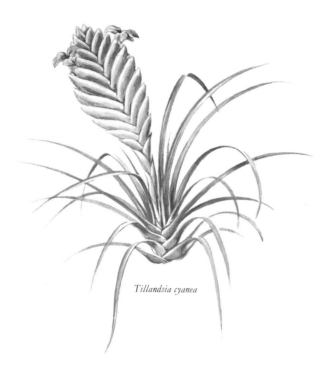

Tillandsia cyanea

Tillandsia cyanea

Common name None.
General information Another easy and attractive bromeliad, *T. cyanea* consists of a small clump of 12-in grass-like leaves growing in a rosette, dull and uninteresting, yet from the centre of this rosette rises a flower stalk carrying a pointed oval, 4–6 in long and 2 in wide, cherry-red series of interlapping bracts from which appear a succession of bright blue flowers. These last only a few days but the colourful bracts remain for two months.
Temperature Normal warm room temperatures will be suitable.
Position Place in bright light where there will be no sun.
Watering Roots are sparse, so water very lightly. Extra humidity can be provided by spraying twice weekly without watering.
Care Give a dilute feed no more than once a month and grow in an equal part of peat, soil and perlite. Repotting will not normally be necessary as both plants and roots remain small.
Propagation Gently pull offsets from the parent plant and grow in a peat and perlite mixture in a propagating case.

Tolmiea menziesii

Tolmiea menziesii

Common name Pick-a-back Plant.
General information A hardy foliage plant with little to commend it other than the habit of growing new plants on the backs of parent leaves. The foliage is a pleasant light green in colour and is covered with a fine fuzz of hairs. *T. menziesii* is the only species of the genus and is an exceptionally quick grower, so as young plants nearly always look better than old, it is an easy matter to have a constant succession of young plants coming along.
Temperature Normal room temperatures will be suitable.
Position Keep where there is good light but no direct sun.
Watering While plants are growing well keep the root ball well watered, allowing it to dry out a little between doses. Water less in winter when plants are resting and at the same time widen the intervals between waterings.
Care Give regular fortnightly feeds while plants are growing well, but none in winter. Repot only if there are no replacement plants coming along or when roots have filled the container. Use a well-drained, soil-based compost. This is one of the few house plants which is hardy outdoors.
Propagation Cut the stalk of a parent leaf with the baby plant on its back and plant in a moist mixture of peat and perlite in normal room light and no special heat.

Tradescantia

Common name Wandering Jew, Wandering Sailor.
General information This is perhaps the best known and most frequently seen of all house plants, largely perhaps because it is so easy to propagate. There are several forms, of which *T. fluminensis* 'Quicksilver' is one of the best, although all display new beauty if grown with care rather than casually.
Temperature Normal warm room temperatures will be suitable.
Position To grow well displaying the best of its leaf colour plants must have good light, including some direct sun.
Watering When plants are growing well keep the root ball moist, at other times try to keep it nearly dry.
Care Feed regularly while growing well. Use a soil-based compost with added perlite and repot only if a large plant is required, as smaller, younger plants usually look best. Pinch out growing tips to encourage thick, bushy plants.
Propagation Take 3-in tip cuttings and insert in a peat and perlite mixture or in plain water in normal room temperatures and fairly bright light. Rooting is swift.

Tradescantia fluminensis 'Quicksilver'

Vriesea splendens

Zebrina pendula

Common name Wandering Jew.
General information Zebrinas are so similar to tradescantias that they share the same common name, yet they are different in colours if not in shape. *Z. pendula* is the most popular species and it has several forms, with 'Quadricolor' probably the best. Leaves here have stripes of green, white, pink and an irridescent, shining silver, with undersides of purple, the depth of which depends on the amount of light received.
Temperature Normal warm room conditions are suitable.
Position Keep in good light at all times and even allow some sun so long as this is not in midsummer and at noon.
Watering Try to maintain the root ball in a barely moist state while the plant is growing well, just damp in winter.
Care Feed well and regularly while plants are growing, but not in winter. Use a rich, soil-based compost and repot if the roots obviously fill the container, but it is usually better to keep young plants always coming on. Pinch out tips.
Propagation Tip cuttings will root easily in a barely moist peat and perlite compost or even in plain water. Root several and keep a constant succession of vivid young plants growing.

Vriesea

Common name Flaming Sword.
General information One of the best and easiest of the bromeliads. Available in several forms and grown both for foliage and for flowers. *V. splendens* has long, dark green leaves cross-banded with chocolate, arching out from a cup-like centre from which rises the sturdy flower stalk bearing the 'sword' made up of long lasting vivid red bracts from which emerge a succession of little yellow flowers.
Temperature Normal room temperatures, high humidity.
Position Bright light and a little direct sun each day.
Watering Always keep the central cup filled with water.
Care Feed monthly with dilute fertilizer and repot in a soil-based compost with perlite only when necessary, every other year. Like most bromeliads roots of vrieseas are sparse and do little more than anchor the plants to the soil.
Propagation Normally offsets will be produced and these can be removed with good roots and foliage, and planted up.

Zygocactus

Common names Crab, Christmas or Easter Cactus.
General information *Zygocactus truncatus* is more properly *Schlumbergera truncata*, but there are so many hybrids of this family that the whole nomenclature is confused and to the average home grower there is little apparent difference between some of them. In general, the leafless flat stems are jointed and bear flamboyant flowers, usually pink, white or purple, growing from the tips and lasting only a day or two.
Temperature Normal room temperatures will be suitable.
Position Keep in a light situation but not too bright. It is sometimes found that plants growing in living rooms under artificial light at nights will flower at different times from those enjoying a natural daylength.
Care Feed regularly when growing well and repot only when roots are obviously filling the container, using a peat and perlite mixture to encourage the rather sparse roots to grow.
Propagation Snap off portions bearing several segments and plant in an almost dry compost of peat and perlite.

Zygocactus
truncatus

Zebrina pendula

Success with House Plants

House plants, gleaming with health and positioned
to display the full beauty of their form, are one of the
most effective ways of enhancing the atmosphere
of our daily surroundings. There are many
ways of displaying them, some of which entail a minimum of
attention once they are set up, as in a terrarium.

Buying house plants

The quality of a house plant at the time of purchase is important. Very few homes offer ideal conditions and all are far removed from the atmosphere of the grower's greenhouse and it is only the well-grown plant which is likely to survive and acclimatize itself.

Most people buy their plants from a local shop. Here are a few guidelines which should help you to make a successful purchase.

Avoid the shop which allows the plants to stand outside or in a draughty doorway. After the heated conditions of the grower's greenhouse such casual treatment can give the plants a setback from which they will not recover.

Avoid buying from the supermarket where the plants are put in any odd corner or over the freezer displays.

Avoid the shop where you have to hunt among a selection of plants to find one in good condition. Treat with suspicion any signs of wilting, dead and dying leaves.

Look for the shop where the plants are in a well-lighted, draught-free position.

Look for obvious signs of health in the whole collection – green, dust-free leaves and a general appearance of being well cared for.

Having chosen your plant it is wise to check it over, although if the source is a reliable one there is unlikely to be anything wrong with it. Look for yellowing or missing leaves and signs of wilting. Check for the presence of insects, looking particularly around the base of the leaves where they meet the stem. Make sure there are signs of new growth. Buy a flowering plant which has both buds and open flowers. Check the compost to see if it is dry or waterlogged – either is a good indication that the retailer has not been caring adequately for his stock.

Finally, particularly if you are buying it during the cooler months, insist that the plant is adequately packed; this is important not only for supporting the leaves but also for providing as much protection as possible from the sudden change in temperature when you leave the shop.

Caring for house plants

Unlike garden plants which can more easily fend for themselves, house plants are dependent on the conditions offered and of these the temperature, humidity and the amount of water and light given are the most important.

TEMPERATURE
The temperature of the house is set for its human rather than its possible plant occupants and rarely is it at an optimum level for the plants. These are at their most vulnerable during the winter when the greatest fluctuation in temperature is likely to occur, and this is when so many of them are adversely affected by the daytime temperature falling too low – few will be happy at less than 13°C (55°F) and many are better with a minimum of 16°C (60°F).

In their native habitat the natural pattern of temperature is such that the maximum is reached at about midday with rising temperatures in the morning and a gradually lowering of temperature to the evening and over night. However, in our homes in winter we often expect the plant to cope with a very different pattern – namely one that increases to a maximum in the evening and may often drop very low during the daytime and during the night unless a constant level is maintained by central heating. Whilst many plants can acclimatize themselves to cooler conditions it is the fluctuating temperatures which cause the most trouble.

The position chosen for the plant within the room is also important. Most will object to a draught and the sunny windowsill is only suitable for a few of the sun worshippers (see page 63) unless the effect of the sun is filtered through a net curtain. A windowsill which receives some sun during the day is a popular position and indeed is suitable for many plants provided you watch out for possible foliage scorch during the summer. There are two things to remember with plants grown in such a situation, however, one that they will need turning occasionally to keep their growth even, and two, that they will need some protection during the winter from the cold. Once the curtains are drawn on a winter's evening the temperature between curtains and window drops rapidly and the plants may well suffer frost damage, so either move them into the room of an evening or place a thick layer of newspaper between them and the glass.

The temperature also varies within the room itself and it is a good idea to move the plant around until you find a spot where it grows well, but avoid placing it next to or over a heat source.

A good air supply is also necessary if plants are to grow well – but not a draught. Try to air the room each day but do not leave plants standing in a draughty position between open door and windows.

HUMIDITY

Linked with the temperature and equally important is the humidity. This is the amount of moisture in the air; when air is fully saturated it is said to be very humid and when it is dry the humidity is low. However, the capacity of air to hold water vapour increases with the temperature and this is why the atmosphere in a well-heated room is so often too dry for human beings, let alone for the plants. It is advisable under such conditions to find some way of increasing the humidity if you are hoping to keep any of the plants which live naturally in the steamy parts of the tropics and subtropics.

Unless a humidifier is installed then the best way of coping with this problem is to increase the humidity in the vicinity of the plants. This can be done in a number of ways; try standing the pot on a layer of gravel or pebbles

A warm bathroom is an ideal setting for plants which like humidity. A terrarium makes an attractive feature

in a tray, the pebbles should be kept moist and the moisture will evaporate around the plant. Similarly, the pot can be stood on a block of wood in a container of water. Either way the level of the water should not reach the bottom of the pot.

Plunging the pots in a planter of damp peat is a very effective method for the plants with a high humidity requirement such as adiantum, fittonia, maranta and calathea and, of course, such plants can be grown most successfully in some form of terrarium where the humidity is always markedly higher than in the surrounding room.

As a supplement to these methods of treatment or if, like me, your collection is too large to be plunged in peat or stood on trays of gravel, invest in a plastic sprayer and mist the plants over

with tepid water once or twice during the day or evening when the temperature is high.

WATERING

How often do house plants need to be watered? Unfortunately there is no precise answer to this question because the amount of water required depends not only on the type of plant but also on the compost, the pot and the surrounding temperature.

Incorrect watering is, in fact, one of the commonest causes of failure. Underwatering is mostly the result of forgetfulness, while overwatering is usually mistaken kindness – the plants being indulged under the impression that they need a drink whenever their owner feels like a cup of tea!

The best way of overcoming both failings is to start a routine by checking the plants every other day or so in hot weather or a centrally-heated room, once a week is sufficient in cooler

To dry out an overwatered plant, remove from its pot and stand on newspaper

conditions. Examine the compost, when dry it has a greyish tinge, and feel about $\frac{1}{2}$ in down into the pot to make sure that it is not just the surface layer which is dry. When water is required, then fill the pot up so that the compost is moistened right the way through.

For the majority of plants it does not matter whether you water from the top or the bottom provided you give sufficient but I think it is safer to water African violets from below by filling their drip trays with water; in this way the centre of the plant is kept free from the possibility of water lodging there and causing rotting. No plant should be allowed to stand in water for more than ten minutes, so if water runs through into the drip tray and is not immediately reabsorbed it should be tipped out. Waterlogged soil means that all the oxygen spaces in the compost are filled with water and as a result the roots cannot breathe so they quite simply die and rot off.

If a plant has become very dry the compost may shrink away from the sides of the pot and it becomes difficult to get it moist again. In this instance the pot should be immersed in a container of water and left until the compost is saturated right through.

Always use the water at room temperature and try to avoid using strongly chlorinated water or water which has been chemically softened. Rain water is the very best.

Watering during holidays

Holidays present the owner of a large collection of house plants with a watering problem. The 'plantsitter' is one way of coping, but if you do persuade a neighbour to take on the task you can

Two of the methods of watering plants during holiday periods

make the job less onerous by leaving instructions on the care of each plant.

There are a number of ways of coping with smaller numbers of plants over holiday periods. A single specimen if watered well and then placed inside a large polythene bag with the top sealed will keep for a couple of weeks. It needs a light but not sunny position and the bag should be supported so that it doesn't touch the foliage.

For a larger collection, place the plants in a basin or the bath and pack them round with layers of damp newspaper. Alternatively, make a wick from some absorbent material for each pot, make sure one end is in contact with the soil in the pot and lead the other end into a container of water which is placed above the level of the pots.

If you are away frequently, then it would be well worthwhile to consider using self-watering containers or growing plants by hydroculture.

Self-watering containers There is now a wide range of very attractive self-watering plant containers which will put an end to any worries you may have about holiday watering. Such containers are also the ideal way of providing a long-lasting, low-

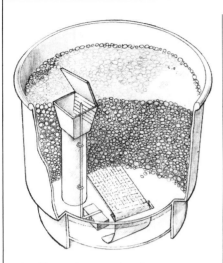

A self-watering container has a water reservoir in the base and removes much of the worry about watering

maintenance display for an office or reception area.

The containers work on the principle of capillary attraction, water being carried by means of a wick from a reservoir underneath the compost in which the plants are growing. The compost does not come into contact with the water and so does not become waterlogged. There is a water level indicator which shows when a further supply is needed. Many of the larger tubs are on castors and this greatly increases their usefulness.

Hydroculture One innovation in recent years has been the growing of house plants in water – hydroculture as it has come to be called. The plant's roots are supported in a basket of inert clay granules and this in turn fits into a larger outer container which holds a solution of fertilizer in water. An indicator shows when the water needs to be replenished and the plant's roots absorb the water and food they need from the solution in which they are suspended.

Plants growing in hydroculture are simplicity itself to look after as

their most important need – accurate watering – is easy to control. One important point, however, it is still possible to waterlog the roots and cause them to die off and when watering it is essential to let the water level indicator drop to zero and remain there for a few days between each watering. This will allow air to circulate around the roots which in turn will encourage the production of new ones.

FEEDING

Healthy houseplants need feeding but, like watering, it must be done with care and a little at a time should be the rule – too much will damage the roots. The main growing period is during spring and summer and this is the time when regular but light doses of feed are needed, many plants rest during the winter and it is better to leave these, feeding only those which continue to grow during this period.

One point of interest: plants growing in poor light should be fed very infrequently. They do much better in such a situation if not pushed into making too much growth.

There are various types of proprietary pot plant food on the market; always follow the instructions with regard to quantity and remember that dry food should be watered in and some liquid feeds will need diluting. A foliar feed is a useful way of giving a quick boost. Newly-potted plants should not need feeding for a number of months.

A word of warning here: do resist the temptation to feed a sick-looking plant, starvation is less likely to be the cause of the trouble than any of the following – too much water, too little light, too dry an atmosphere. The

symptoms of starvation show up as lack of vigour in the new growth and yellow colouration in the new leaves.

LIGHT

The main problem that arises here is that of too little light. Certainly in older houses with their smaller windows there is a tendency for the part of the room away from the window to be too dark for plants to grow well. Light is an essential requirement for plants to be able to manufacture their food from the raw ingredients of air, water and the various chemicals which they absorb through their roots and leaves.

However, the power of the sun is intensified through glass and few of the foliage plants will survive on a windowsill in direct sun. Such a position is only suitable for some of the flowering plants such as the pelargoniums and other sun lovers like coleus, codiaeum and ananas and even then you should keep an eye open for scorching of the leaves.

Try to keep the foliage plants close to the windows and leave the blinds or curtains open during the day to increase the light intensity, or supplement the natural daylight with artificial light. Plants do vary in their light requirement, for example while most foliage plants prefer diffused light, those with variegated or brightly coloured leaves need good light and many of the popular flowering house plants will not bloom if the light intensity is too low or the day-length too short.

Lack of light may not have an immediate effect on the plants but over a period of time the new growth will become drawn and spindly, the new leaves will be small and the older leaves die and drop off. The remedy is not to put the plant onto the brightest windowsill you can find but to return it to conditions of adequate light and wait. If the new growth is very spindly prune it back to encourage new buds to break.

Using artificial light Artificial light can be used to give a welcome boost to the level of light during the day and to prolong the day length into the evening. Most house plants need about twelve hours of light each day and some as much as sixteen hours. During the winter the only way of giving them light for periods as long as this is by supplementing the natural light with artificial. And this will also increase the decorative effect. The right sort of light can show up the forms of the foliage as well as the colours and gives them an intensity which is lacking when they are seen in daylight. Experiment by trying a couple of plants under an ordinary table lamp but remember that incandescent bulbs throw out a lot of heat, so the plants should never be closer than,

say, 2 ft to a 75 watt bulb. This distance should be increased to correspond with the wattage of the bulb.

Some of the most dramatic lighting effects can be achieved with spotlights; these can be angled to pick up a plant or group of plants while leaving the surrounding area in comparative gloom. I use two spotlights to highlight a plant grouping in a rather dull corner, the plants grow better for the added light and I never tire of looking at them – they have the same sort of fascination for me as a lighted aquarium.

The very best kind of artificial light for plants comes from fluorescent tubes and there are now special plant-growing tubes manufactured which give out the correct amount of red and blue light. It is, perhaps, worth knowing that red light is needed for root growth and blue light for stem and leaf growth.

Fluorescent lights do not throw out heat and can be placed much closer to the plants. Special display cases using this sort of tube can be bought or made and they are particularly useful for growing African violets which can be kept in flower for most of the year.

Daylength I have already mentioned briefly the phenomenon of daylength, this is the number of hours of daylight required by a plant before it will successfully initiate its flower buds. For example, poinsettias and chrysanthemums are what is known as short-day plants because they will only form flower buds when there is less than ten hours of daylight unsupplemented by any artificial light. This fact has been put to good use by the nurserymen who have been able to control very accurately the production of flowers in these plants by either artificially shortening the daylength (covering the plants with black polythene) or lengthening the daylength (by lighting the plants during the night).

Potting

The quality of the compost is of the first importance when potting up newly-rooted cuttings or repotting older plants. Houseplants are expected to grow in a restricted area and the medium used must make up for this – a potful of soil scooped up from the garden with a full complement of worms and soil pests is just not good enough. Choose one of the many specially-formulated soil-based or soil-less potting composts which can be bought from any nursery or garden shop.

Most of the soil-based composts are made up to the John Innes

Artificial lighting will help the growth of plants in a shady corner

OPPOSITE A stepped arrangement of shelves made to fit a windowsill can be a very effective way of showing off a display of small plants to best advantage. During the winter it is important to ensure that the plants do not get chilled behind the curtains at night, so it would be better to use a blind which can be pulled down between the window and the plants

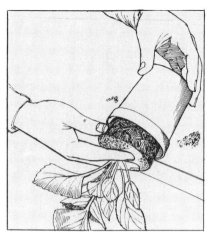

Repotting Remove the plant carefully from its pot, knocking the rim on a hard edge and supporting the top growth

Put some compost in the new pot and position the plant so that the top of the rootball is just below the rim

Fill in the space between the existing rootball and the pot with compost and firm it down gently with the fingers

formula and consist of a mixture of soil, peat and sand with added fertilizers. These composts are numbered 1, 2 and 3 and the number indicates the fertilizer content. John Innes No. 1 is used for newly-rooted cuttings and other small plants, John Innes No. 2 for repotting plants in medium-sized pots and John Innes No. 3 for the biggest of the plants.

The soil-less composts are based mostly on peat and are equally good, encouraging a good fibrous root system and needing watering rather less frequently than those based on soil. They also sometimes encourage the plants to grow too lush and then a change to a mixture of half peat and half soil is indicated.

Certain plants require special growing mediums and for these neither the John Innes nor the soil-less composts are adequate on their own. For example, a sharply-drained compost requires the addition of a portion of coarse silver sand to either the basic soil or peat compost in the proportion of 1 part sand to 3 parts compost. Similarly, a rich soil mixture should have 1 part of peat or leaf-mould added to 3 parts of the soil-based compost. Other mixes may be made up of equal proportions of peat and sand or equal amounts of peat and perlite or vermiculite.

POTS

Clay or plastic, which should you use? It doesn't make any marked difference to the plants but plastic pots tend to hold the moisture in the soil longer. New clay pots should be well soaked in water before use or they will absorb quantities of moisture from around the plant's roots.

Plastic pots are now being made in an assortment of colours, which, if they suit your furnishings, will do away with the need for pot-hiders.

REPOTTING

All plants, sooner or later, outgrow their pots and will need to be transferred to larger ones – a process known as repotting. Fast-growing plants may need repotting every four months but the majority are fairly slow growing, and for these once a year is sufficient and spring is the best time.

Plants require repotting when they become potbound, meaning that the soil ball becomes lost beneath a mass of roots. Check to see if there are any roots protruding through the drainage holes and, if necessary, knock a plant out of its pot to inspect it.

The new pot should be only an inch or two larger than the existing one. To put a plant into a much bigger pot is asking for trouble as the larger volume of compost will dry out much more slowly, it becomes difficult to control the moisture content and the roots, instead of spreading into the new compost, tend to die back. All pots used should be scrubbed clean of any old compost residues which may be harbouring pests or diseases.

The potting procedure is shown in the accompanying illustrations. Watering the plant the day before repotting facilitates its removal from the pot. The newly-potted plant should also be watered well and then allowed to dry out before it is watered again.

Some plants, such as the aspidistra, do not appreciate annual repotting and with these it is better to remove an inch or so of the compost from the surface and replace it with fresh. Top-dressing, as this is called, is also the only practical way of refreshing the compost around very large plants in big containers.

Pruning and grooming

Bedraggled, dusty specimens of plants are not decorative and keeping a collection of house plants in good condition requires time and patience. Indeed, at certain times of the year the indoor garden of any size requires almost as much attention as the outdoor one but the effort is always amply repaid because well-cared-for plants grow better and live longer.

I hold a weekly inspection of all my plants and take the opportunity to look carefully at each one for signs of insects, disease or any other marks or symptoms. Any treatment needed must be given promptly and if an insect pest is involved the plant should be isolated until a complete control is obtained.

Do not be hesitant about pruning back any plant which is making spindly, etiolated growth or is getting out of hand and sprawling around. Pinch the stems back to a convenient point immediately above a leaf. This

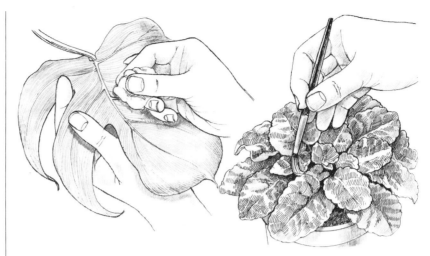

Regular cleaning of the leaves will improve the plant's appearance

will encourage fresh growth from lower down the stem.

Climbing plants must be provided with a support – a trellis, framework of canes or a single stick. Many climbers such as rhoicissus produce tendrils and can attach themselves to the support but others will need help from string or plastic-covered ties. Climbers are another group of plants which benefit from having the ends of the shoots removed periodically.

The indoor plant is subjected to much closer scrutiny than the outdoor one and a certain amount of grooming is required to retain its

attractive appearance. If the plant is a flowering one, remove the blooms as they wither, similarly, take off any dead or dying leaves – after you have checked them for the presence of any pest or disease – but there is a certain amount of leaf loss on even the healthiest of specimens. Finally keep the foliage clean, dust and dirt will clog the leaf pores and interfere with vital life processes.

With the exception of hairy-leaved plants, wipe over regularly with a soft damp cloth and wash the more leathery type of leaf once a month or so using tepid water to which a few drops of milk have been added. Use a soft cloth to apply the solution and support the underside of the leaf with the other hand while doing so. Water spots on the leaves can be removed by sponging with a weak solution of detergent (washing-up liquid) in water and then rinsing thoroughly.

There are a range of leaf cleaners and polishes on the market but I would advise you to use them with care and to test one leaf on the plant before proceeding to treat the entire plant. Certain of the ferns, such as asplenium, as well as some of the tougher plants such as the aspidistra are better

Making a moss stick for a climbing plant by lashing damp moss round a stake (see page 77)

Continued on page 70

Propagation

Many house plants are easy to propagate; the most important methods for use in the home are by cuttings of stem or leaves, by rooting plantlets or offsets, by division and by air layering.

Stem cuttings are made by removing the top 2–4 in of soft, healthy growth, trimming the end and inserting it to a depth of 1 in or so in a pot of house plant compost or even in a vessel of water. The pot can be enclosed in a plastic bag or placed in a propagator.

A plastic bag will assist the rooting of cuttings

Some soft tip cuttings will root in water

Leaves of African violets inserted in a pot of compost will eventually root and produce small plants (above)

Pin *Begonia rex* leaves onto compost and cut across the main veins. Small plants form at the cuts (above).

Leaf cuttings are taken from certain plants only, mostly African violets, *Begonia rex*, some peperomias, streptocarpus and sansevierias. Either the leaf stalk or sections of the leaf are inserted into the compost. Eventually roots form, followed by small plants which can then be potted. African violets can also be rooted in water.

Runners and offsets are produced by a number of plants notably chlorophytum, saxifraga, tolmiea and the bromeliads, and these offer a very easy method of increase b simply pegging the young plantlets into a pot of compost or removing the offset and potting it up.

Division applies to the clump-forming plants which can be broken or cut into several pieces. Each piece should retain a proportion of roots and top growth.

Air layering is a useful technique for dealing with an over-tall or leggy plant. Th technique is illustrated (right) and once roots can be seen, the plastic is removed an the plant is severed below the rooted area.

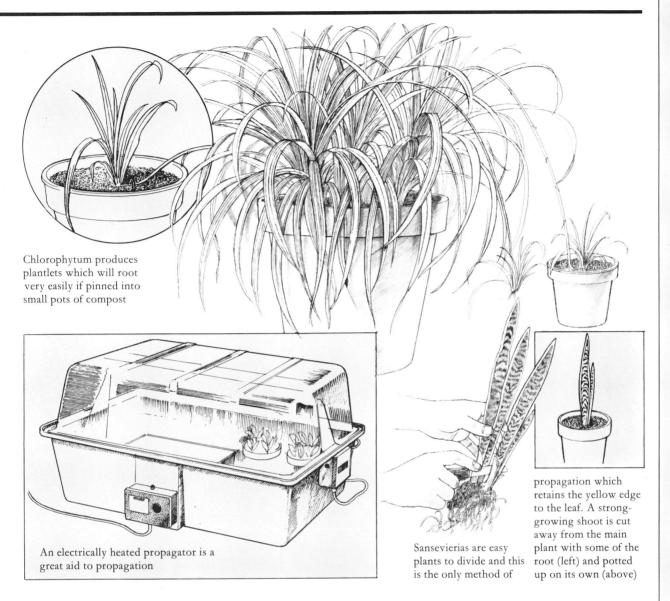

Chlorophytum produces
plantlets which will root
very easily if pinned into
small pots of compost

An electrically heated propagator is a
great aid to propagation

Sansevierias are easy
plants to divide and this
is the only method of
propagation which
retains the yellow edge
to the leaf. A strong-
growing shoot is cut
away from the main
plant with some of the
root (left) and potted
up on its own (above)

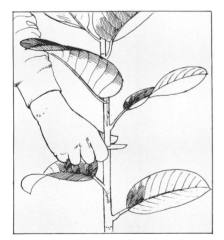

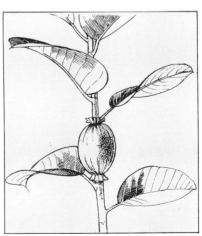

Air layering An upward cut is made into
the stem to a depth of about one-third

The inside of the cut is dusted with rooting powder and wrapped in damp moss

The mossed area is wrapped in plastic
and the ends are tied securely

without this treatment. One other point to remember when using a leaf cleaner is that it should not be applied too thickly or too often as this may block the leaf pores and cause the leaf to turn yellow and drop off.

An occasional shower bath will contribute to the well-being of all except those with hairy leaves. Put the plants in the bath and using tepid water spray them thoroughly. Allow the plants to drain before replacing them in their various positions.

The hairy-leaved plants like the African violets need dusting too

Many house plants benefit from a change of scene and should be stood in a slightly shaded spot out of doors during the summer months

but require a different method, any dust or debris on the foliage being removed with a soft paint brush or a pipecleaner. These also enjoy a steam bath. Place them on a block of wood in a basin of boiling water so that the steam can circulate around the leaves. Make sure that the base of the pot does not come into contact with the water.

Like any pet, house plants will react to the amount of attention and care they get, talk to them if you like, but do take the time to check them over regularly and keep them in good shape.

Keeping plants healthy

Unfortunately house plants can be afflicted by a range of disorders and it may require some clever diagnosis to detect the cause. It is worth stressing, however, that plants which are well cared for and regularly inspected are less likely to fall victim to such problems.

Pests

Any plant which is looking less than its best should first be inspected for the presence of pests. Look carefully on the underside of the leaves, along the stems and in the leaf axils, around the growing tips and flower buds.

In general, pests are most easily dealt with by improving the growing conditions, such as increasing the humidity, and spraying with a specially-formulated house plant insecticide. When using any chemicals, be sure to read the manufacturer's instructions carefully. Spraying plants with insecticide indoors is always a bit difficult but a new

product – Plant Pins – is especially easy and safe to use. This consists of small pieces of cardboard impregnated with insecticide which is released and taken up by the plant's roots when the cardboard pin is buried in the compost.

Many pests can also be controlled by washing the plant with water to which a few drops of washing up liquid have been added.

Aphids (greenfly) Soft, green, pear-shaped insects which attack young shoots, buds and the underside of young leaves. They suck the sap which causes the leaves to curl and fall. Growth is poor and the aphids secrete a sticky substance called honeydew which may get a black or sooty mould growing on it.
Control Wash plants in soapy water or treat with an appropriate insecticide.

Mealy bugs Small insects covered by a white, waxy coating.

They cluster in the leaf axils, on the stems and roots and weaken growth by sucking sap. They also secrete honeydew.
Control Touch each bug with a paint brush dipped in surgical or methylated spirit.

Red spider mites Not true spiders but small reddish mites which can only be seen through a hand lens. Found on the under-surface of the leaves. They suck the sap and the leaves may develop pinprick holes, become yellowish and fall off. An established colony can be detected by the presence of fine white webbing. Infected plants are stunted and may die.
Control Increase humidity around plants. Move to cooler conditions and wash foliage frequently with water. Treat with insecticide.

Scale Louse-like insects which attach themselves like limpets to stems or leaves particularly along the midribs. They suck the sap and eventually stunt the plant as well

as secreting honeydew. The mature insects protect themselves beneath a hard shell which is brown or greyish in colour.
Control Remove the insects by sponging the leaves and stems with water. Treat with an insecticide; take care on ferns.

Thrips Very active small insects which jump when disturbed. They rasp the plant tissues to extract the sap and cause deformity and streaking in the tissues. Flower buds may turn brown and fail to open.
Control Increase humidity around plants, treat with insecticide and repeat at intervals.

Whiteflies Tiny white flies which suck sap and weaken plants. Leaves become discoloured and may be coated with a sticky grey excrement. The flies can occur in large numbers and fly off in a cloud when disturbed.
Control Treat with an insecticide. Place plant in a plastic bag, seal and leave for twenty-four hours. Repeat at intervals.

Diseases

On the whole it is unlikely that diseases are the cause of major trouble. Mildew, a fungus disease, is the most usual and this appears as a furry grey covering to stems and/or leaves and results in them rotting. Remove these rotting leaves and stems, give the plant more ventilation and cut back on watering.

Other disorders

It is, in fact, more usual for plants to suffer from disorders caused by poor cultivation than from either pests or diseases. The symptoms of these disorders may affect the entire plant or show up as mark-ings or discolouration on the leaves. The following is a brief guide to the most usual symptoms and their causes. Some symptoms may be caused by a number of factors; you will have to decide which is likely to be the most appropriate one.

LEAVES

Brown tips or margins Plant is too close to a source of heat; humidity is too low; overfeeding; plant is in a draught; watering is spasmodic.

Brown spots Water splashes on leaves; sun scorch.

Brown and rotting Over-watering; sudden drop in temperature; water left lying on leaves at night.

Yellow at edges Insufficient food; natural senescence if it is the oldest leaf.

Yellow at back of plant Lack of light.

Yellowing followed by leaf fall Overwatering; draughts; lack of humidity; change in growing conditions; drop in temperature.

New leaves smaller Insufficient food; too little light or too much light.

ENTIRE PLANT

Growth slow or stationary Normal in winter. In spring or summer underfeeding or over-watering; plant may need repotting; too little light.

Growth spindly In spring and summer, lack of light or insufficient food. In winter plant too warm or moist for the amount of light available.

Wilting Too much sun; under-watering; overwatering or over-feeding – indicates root damage.

BUDS AND FLOWERS

Buds dropping Pot being moved; lack of humidity; overwatering.

Failure to flower Overfeeding – plant putting on too much growth; wrong daylength.

Many common pests can be eradicated by washing the plants in a bucket of water containing some detergent

Flowering Bulbs Indoors

In the bleak winter months there is no better way to boost morale than by anticipating spring and filling the house with bowls of flowering bulbs. For remarkably little effort you can enjoy weeks of delight from hyacinths, narcissus (daffodils), tulips and crocus.

Plan your campaign in early autumn when nurseries and garden shops offer a wide range of bulbs. Some will have been specially prepared for Christmas flowering and will be marked as such, but the ordinary sorts for growing outdoors can be forced into bloom many weeks ahead of schedule by being grown in pots. It is much better to plant each bowl or container with the same type of bulb, and even the same variety, although your inclination may be to mix the colours. Unfortunately such colour mixtures do not always flower at the same time and you are left with bowls which never look their best.

Choose the bulbs carefully, discarding any that feel soft or show signs of disease or damage on the outside. With bulbs you really do get what you pay for and the larger, fatter specimens are worth the extra few pence.

Pottery or plastic bowls, flower pots, old china soup tureens: it doesn't matter what you use as a

container but it is important to invest in specially prepared bulb fibre if the container is without drainage holes. Bulb fibre is prepared from peat and crushed shell with some charcoal to stop it going sour. Any of the soil- or peat-based composts can be used in ordinary pots.

METHOD OF PLANTING

If bulb fibre is to be the planting medium then this must be well moistened. Put a layer in the

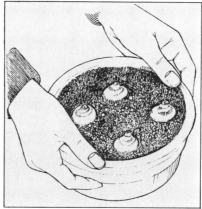

All bulbs and corms require a period in the cool and dark in order to build up their root systems

bottom of the bowl and set the bulbs about $\frac{1}{4}$ to $\frac{1}{2}$ in apart. Pack more fibre around the bulbs leaving the tops just showing and put the container in a cool dark place; not an airing cupboard, heat at this stage will stop the proper development of the flower buds. Light can also be excluded by wrapping the pots in a thick layer of newspaper and making a small hole for each one to grow through. The pot can then be put in a cool place. Leave in the dark for eight to ten weeks.

The procedure is the same for ordinary composts except that instead of soaking these before planting the bulbs, the pots are watered well afterwards. Check all containers occasionally and water if necessary.

Novelty pots If you have decided to grow some crocuses you might like to use one of the novelty crocus pots which has holes pierced in the sides. These are a little more difficult to plant up as

The bulbs are positioned about half an inch apart on a layer of moistened fibre

More fibre is packed gently around the bulbs with just the tips left showing

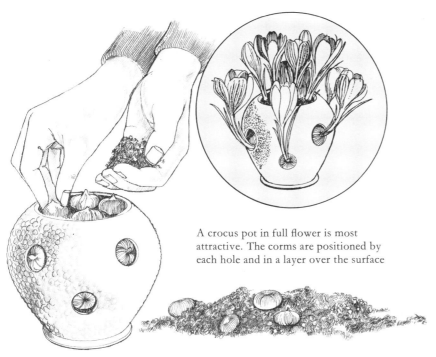

A crocus pot in full flower is most attractive. The corms are positioned by each hole and in a layer over the surface

wither or the leaves to discolour. Once you can see the flower buds then move the bulbs into full light.

Water the containers sparingly at first and then more freely as growth proceeds. There will be no need to feed, for the bulbs contain a sufficient reservoir of food. In order to prolong the life of the flowers it is better to keep the bulbs out of too much sun and to remove them from a hot room in the evening.

Staking Some of the bulbs have heavy flowers which may need supporting. Hyacinths can be staked individually using a wire or thin cane. Narcissi, which produce tall foliage as well as flower stems, do best if several canes are inserted around the edge of the pot and a string tie put round.

it is necessary to place one crocus corm by each hole in such a way that the shoot will grow through the hole. Finish the pot with a layer of corms on the top.

Daffodils Daffodil bulbs look more effective if planted in two layers in an ordinary pot. The bulbs in the second layer are positioned so that they sit between the bulbs in the lower layer. This will allow double the number of bulbs to be put into each pot.

GROWING ON

When the bulbs have put out an inch or so of growth, they should be moved into the light and allowed more heat. But this must be a gradual process of acclimatization: too sudden a move from the dark to a warm, sunny window may cause the buds to

AFTER FLOWERING

When the bulbs have finished flowering, cut the dead blooms away and put the bulbs into a cool room until the foliage dies down. Bulbs which have been forced will not bloom again indoors the following year but if planted out in the spring they will flower in the garden.

Planting daffodil bulbs in two layers results in more flowers to each pot

A large bowl of *Crocus chrysanthus* 'Saturnus' brightens up late winter

Narcissi are an even more welcome sight indoors than in the garden

Using plants to best effect

Architects nowadays are well aware of the value of plants in interior decoration. Plants provide a contrast of textures, structural forms, a softness, a source of changing dramatic shadows which are not found in inanimate objects. Add to this the fascination of bringing the garden indoors where it is possible to study in comfort the marvels and intricacies of nature, and it is small wonder that the last twenty years have seen a dramatic increase in the range of plants being grown by nurserymen for use in the home. Contrasting colours, leaf pattern, silhouettes: it is all available if you take the time and a little trouble to seek out the plants rather than to select the first one that catches your eye.

SHAPE IS IMPORTANT

Once you have identified your room conditions and seen something of the plants available, you will need to give some thought to the overall decorative effect you are aiming at. For instance, will one or two large specimens with dramatic leaf outlines be sufficient? Or are you hoping to achieve an air of opulence and luxury by incorporating containers of lush tropical plants?

For those with less ambitious tastes or less room to spare, a bowl garden or small selection of plants grouped together can be all that is needed to make a living, growing ornament.

OPPOSITE Large plants with a strong leaf shape such as the monstera can be very dramatic and should be displayed in a suitably spacious setting

SPECIMEN PLANTS

Certain plants have great architectural merit for their shapes and these are the ones to choose if you want only one or two to highlight a room or a structural feature of the house, for example an entrance hall or stairwell. However, large plants are expensive and you must be prepared for this if you want an immediate effect. Such plants can be grown from smaller, more reasonably-priced specimens if you are prepared to wait a few years. A small monstera I acquired some four years ago has now reached a height and spread of 5 ft or so and continues to put out leaves with a rapidity which is quite startling.

The type of plant which looks good on its own is the one which has strong leaf outlines and a bold shape and, of course, it helps if it is fairly fast growing; the palms unfortunately are not, but rubber trees, heptapleurum, monsteras and philodendron will grow reasonably rapidly when well treated. To fill the upper reaches quickly it is also worth trying two lovely Australian natives – the silk oak, *Grevillea robusta*, and the gum, *Eucalyptus gunnii*. Both can be grown from seed and within a year you may well have a 4-ft high specimen on your hands.

Almost without exception the plants which make good specimens are in shades of green, but as long as the foliage is kept clean (nothing is worse, to my mind, than a large dusty plant) they have the advantage that they can be used against any background.

Plants intended for floor placement need to be at least 3-ft high and they must be positioned out of the way of traffic routes and where they won't be knocked.

These specimen plants will need a good supply of compost to provide the root run necessary to anchor their bulk as well as a source of food. Large tubs and planters of many kinds are available or you may even be lucky enough to have a planter incorporated into the structure of the house. Many of these larger containers are not provided with drainage holes and care is needed in watering these as well as making sure that a thick layer of pebbles has been included below the compost to assist in drainage.

For a plant in a key position it is well worth while considering buying one grown in hydroculture (see page 63). These are simplicity itself to look after and are already in attractive containers.

DISPLAYING SMALL PLANTS

To my mind nothing does more to create a restless untidy feeling to a room than to see numerous small pots of plants dotted around looking as if they have come to rest on any available piece of furniture. Although it is more difficult to create an impact effect with small plants it can be done. Try, for example, to group them together on a table or shelves near a window. Their contrasting shapes and colours will help to show them all off to advantage and the plants themselves will show their appreciation by growing better – they really do enjoy each other's company. One easy way of creating an interesting effect is to arrange the plants on an old tea trolley. Apart from

A variety of plants arranged on the shelves of a room divider makes a very effective and attractive screen

appearance there is another advantage in that the entire arrangement can be easily moved to alternative accommodation in the room or house should the need arise.

The value of a group of small plants as a focal point of interest lies in the overall effect created by the colours and patterns incorporated in the group. Try to use the bright colours against neutral backgrounds and keep the plain foliage kinds for more vivid surroundings. For example, an arrangement of crotons or coleus and pink caladiums blended with a couple of green foliage plants will look superb against a cream or neutral background but will do nothing for a highly-coloured or patterned wallpaper.

Too many dark green plants together can have a depressing effect. Add some sparkle in the form of a variegated plant such as dieffenbachia, chlorophytum or sansevieria and your group will come to life.

In any arrangement of foliage plants it is a good idea to create a centre of interest by adding a flowering plant, either one of the seasonal kinds such as poinsettia, chrysanthemum, cyclamen or a bowl of flowering bulbs, or one of the more long-term flowerers like the African violets.

POT-HIDERS

The Victorians, who were great lovers of house plants and grew their aspidistras, ferns and palms to perfection, also produced a range of ornamental jardinières for the purpose of hiding the plant pots and protecting the furniture from water. These large glazed containers in many colours and patterns often had their own pottery stands and together made an impressive feature for the drawing room.

These jardinières can be found today in antique shops but they are expensive. However, the idea of pot-hiders to disguise the plant pot is still with us and a wide range is available in wood, pottery, plastic or metal which will blend with any style of furnishing. Other objects, too, although not especially designed with this purpose in mind, can be pressed into service – a jug, large mug, even an old teapot or copper coal scuttle and I have found wicker-work wastepaper baskets cheap and highly effective, although not so good for water catchment; line them with plastic or place a drip tray inside.

Since pot-hiders are undrained it is never a good idea to pot up the plants directly into them.

HANGING BASKETS

The trailing house plant is always one of the most useful whether it is used to soften the edge of a container or trained up a trellis to create a room divider, but in one type of container the trailer really comes into its own and this is the hanging basket. For any position in good light where a hook can be provided, hanging baskets offer the chance of having plants at a different level and viewpoint and many of the plants with a pendent habit are best when viewed from below. Choose from among the many types which can be found – pottery or basketware, plastic or metal, many of them with attractive string or rope hangers.

When it comes to the planting up remember that there may be no provision in the base for drainage, so a layer of small pebbles or broken flower pot will be needed. One of the problems of using hanging baskets indoors is that of drips and all watering will need to be done carefully. Some containers have clip-on plastic trays and these can be watered in situ. So too can the undrained containers but with these you will need to exercise care so that they do not become waterlogged. Other containers can be lifted down and placed in a sink for watering after which they will need to be thoroughly drained before they are rehung. Plants in hanging containers often need more frequent watering than their counterparts on the floor or table, warm air rises and this will cause the plants to dry out more rapidly. Many of the trailing plants grow vigorously and need pruning back to keep them bushy and encourage new growth.

Because of the problem of water drips I do not advise the planting up of the wickerwork type of basket. I have tried to make these waterproof by lining them with polythene or aluminium foil before placing the compost in position but they have never been completely successful. It is much more satisfactory simply to arrange a pot with its own drip tray inside the basket.

This philodendron is being used to frame a long mirror over the kitchen sink. Such an arrangement is not only attractive but is also a good way of making the room appear larger and lighter

If the container is large enough two or more different plants may be combined but the smaller ones look more effective when holding only plants of the same kind. There is a wide choice of suitable plants including tradescantia and zebrina, pellionia, the ivies, *Scindapsus aureus*, *Philodendron scandens*, gynura, plectranthus, chlorophytum, *Saxifraga sarmentosa*, tolmiea and the ferns – especially varieties of *Nephrolepis exaltata*. For flowering plants you might try African violets, ivy-leaved pelargoniums, episcia and pendulous begonia.

CLIMBING PLANTS

If not used in a position where their growths can hang down then the climbing and trailing plants will need some kind of support around which they can grow. A trellis is easily made from bamboo canes lashed together, and you may even like to go one step further and create a room divider by using window boxes to hold the plants and providing a system of bamboo poles up which they can grow. If this is to be placed some distance from a window then use the plants which will tolerate shade such as rhoicissus, cissus and philodendron with more non-climbing interest coming from sansevieria and a palm or fern.

The philodendron and related plants such as scindapsus and monstera are all tropical climbers which push out aerial roots from their stems. These roots are used for the absorption of moisture from the atmosphere as well as for anchoring the plant and all this group of plants will grow better if the roots are given a moist support such as a pillar of damp moss to which to cling. Such a support can be easily made from either a cylinder of fine mesh wire netting filled with damp sphagnum moss, or a stake of up to $1\frac{1}{2}$ in in diameter which has been rolled in moss. In this case the moss will have to be lashed in position with plastic string. The most important thing about these supports is to keep them continually moist otherwise they will not fulfill their function.

Some of the trailing plants can be encouraged to grow along a shelf or even a ledge in the wall. I came across one of the most effective uses of *Philodendron scandens* I have ever seen in a Danish house. The plant had been encouraged to send out several long trailing growths which were anchored to the wall of the room and made a curtain of living green. The wall was neutral in colour and the effect as dramatic as a well chosen picture.

GROUPING PLANTS IN CONTAINERS

A decorative way of grouping a number of small plants is to arrange them together in a larger container. The container can vary in size from a soup tureen to an old-fashioned washing bowl.

The corner of a wide window seat is an ideal position on which to display a collection of plants provided that it is not in full sun all day. The plants shown here are standing in a tray of moist gravel which keeps them tidy and provides humidity around them. To look its best such a display should contain a good variety of plants

Baskets are always a good counterfoil to plants but there is often a water seepage problem and it will not do to stand them directly on a piece of furniture. It is not necessary to have drainage holes in the container but if these are absent then a thick layer of broken flower pot and pebbles should be placed on the bottom to assist drainage.

There are two main ways of making up a bowl arrangement: to fill the bowl with peat and simply plunge the plants in their pots into it, or to unpot the plants and set them in compost. Of the two methods the first is the better one for the health of the plants as they do not suffer any root disturbance and it still remains possible to attend to their individual watering needs. There is also the tremendous advantage of the damp surrounding peat which adds to the humidity of the atmosphere around the plants. However, because of the restriction on placement which follows from keeping the plants in their pots, it may be difficult to achieve as attractive an overall arrangement as is possible when the bowl is actually planted up. Plants in such a grouping can be easily substituted and the rather

A mixed arrangement of plants needs variety of form and colour

temporary flowering ones included to brighten the whole effect.

With the second method involving the planting up of the bowl, there are two essentials: the first, that a good layer of drainage material is used and also some pieces of charcoal which will help to prevent stagnation, and the second that the plants used will tolerate the same amount of water. Fill the bowl with a peat-based compost or a soil-based one mixed with some extra peat and, after knocking the plants from their pots, plant them up in the compost allowing room for growth and positioning them so the shapes and colours complement each other. In each arrangement try to include some tall and short plants as well as at least one trailer; variety of shape is all important to the finished effect. After planting water well to settle the compost around the plants but from then on water with care.

Plants for the office

You have only to look into an office containing an array of plants to see the difference they make in softening the hard lines of the furniture and lending life to what is often a rather drab setting. But they must be in good condition; to spend the working day surrounded by sickly and dying specimens of rubber trees, monsteras or philodendrons does nothing to lift morale.

Success in growing plants in an office environment depends first on the willingness of someone to look after them – the odd cold cup of tea or coffee or an occasional watering when someone remembers will achieve nothing except dead plants. However, this can be solved by investing in plants growing in hydroculture or in self-watering containers (page 62).

Secondly, since most offices have fairly high temperatures and low humidity the plants must be chosen for their rugged dispositions and, on the whole, it is the plant with thick leathery leaves which survives best. Flowering plants, unless used to brighten the display in much the same way as a bunch of flowers, do not do well.

The office atmosphere does offer some advantages in that both heating and lighting are controlled and any downward fluctuation in temperature is likely to occur at the right time of day for the plant's normal growth pattern, i.e. in the evening or during the night.

Problems can arise at weekends and over holidays if the heating

Office surroundings are often much improved by the introduction of house plants. It is wise to choose the tougher kinds

and/or air conditioning are switched off and during hot weather there may well be difficulty in giving the plants sufficient water to tide them over a long weekend. Plants which are to be left in an unheated office over the weekend during the winter months should be watered with care, they stand a better chance of survival if left on the dry side for the weekend.

Maintaining an adequate level of humidity is one of the main cultural problems in growing house plants and this is likely to be the major downfall in the office. There are ways of increasing humidity (page 61) and I find that to mist the plants over a couple of times a day with tepid water using a light plastic sprayer is a tremendous help. So too is grouping the plants together – the close proximity seems to help them all.

CHOOSING THE POSITION

Before buying the plants, decide what you have room for and where they can be placed. Do you want floor-standing specimens (expensive unless the boss is footing the bill), a group of smaller plants, or even plantings in hanging containers? Now, where do you intend to put them, on a windowsill? On a piece of furniture some feet back from the window? In a dark corner? Each position must influence your choice of plant.

The sunny windowsill should be treated carefully as even the sun-loving plants such as cacti and coleus can be scorched through the glass. Similarly, the more shaded windowsill may be too cold for many plants during the winter. It is best to experiment to see how the plants respond and to watch out for signs of damage.

Another point to watch is the heat source, plants stationed near gratings in either walls or floors which continually blast out hot air will quickly suffer.

Artificial lighting, particularly if arising from fluorescent tubes, does nothing but good and will often make a dark corner tenable.

Terrariums

A terrarium is a modern development from the Victorian Wardian Case and in brief it can be described as any transparent vessel which is planted up with a selection of house plants.

The value of the Wardian case for keeping plants alive was discovered by chance by a Dr Nathaniel Ward in 1829 and the discovery was later put to use for the transportation of valuable plant specimens on long sea voyages. These original cases were glass containers into which the plants were hermetically sealed; there to remain unaffected by changes in the surrounding atmospheric conditions, and existing by means of their own recycled air since the loss of moisture by evaporation had been stopped.

The principle on which the terrarium works is in creating a microclimate which protects its occupants from draughts and sudden changes in temperature while supplying the higher level of humidity so necessary for the well-being of many of the tropical plants. Its attraction lies in the fact that it makes a natural living ornament which can be lighted for greater effect and to the benefit of the plants.

A terrarium makes a novel coffee table

CHOOSING THE CONTAINER

Terrariums can be made in any clear-walled container, small or large. A browse around a department store provides plenty of ideas from goblets, brandy glasses to vases, storage jars, old-fashioned sweet jars and finally to the carboys and aquaria which offer the most scope. Size is not necessarily all that important for the finished effect, a brandy glass

When planting up a terrarium try to achieve a natural landscape effect by altering the surface level of the compost

containing one African violet in flower can be most attractive.

Glass containers are the best as they are not so easily scratched by sand particles and will not become crazed as plastic vessels do eventually. But the plastic types will give enjoyment for a number of years if treated with care. Except for the narrow-necked bottles all the containers should be provided with some sort of cover, preferably one that can be left slightly open on very warm days.

PREPARATIONS FOR PLANTING

After making sure that the container is completely clean, put a 1-in thick layer of gravel in the bottom. This is essential to assist drainage. Next comes the soil and I prefer to use a peat-based compost to which I have added some pieces of charcoal to help in keeping it free from stagnation. At this stage the compost should be moist enough to hold together when moulded in the hand.

When using narrow-necked bottles it is much easier to get the drainage material and the compost cleanly into the container if it is poured in through a funnel made from a piece of rolled-up cardboard.

The finished effect of the terrarium is dependent on the skill with which the plants are positioned to form an interesting scene and this is helped by contouring the compost before planting up begins to create marked differences in levels which can become valleys and hills. This can be done with the aid of small tools – an ordinary spoon and fork will be all that are required for most containers but the narrow-necked bottle gardens need a special range of implements fairly easily manufactured by attaching a spoon, fork, cotton reel and razor blade to long canes.

With the larger container, it is helpful to include some small pieces of rock in the planting scheme. These should be settled into the compost to resemble natural-looking outcrops where their rugged texture will provide an interesting contrast to the foliage.

CHOOSING THE PLANTS

Slow-growing plants which enjoy a high level of humidity and will tolerate shade are the best choice unless you intend to light the terrarium artificially. Include a range of shapes and colours, some tall growing, others to creep over the soil surface.

Foliage plants

Aglaeonema, *Cordyline terminalis*, cryptanthus, dracaena, ferns – adiantum, asplenium, pteris – *Ficus pumila*, *Fittonia argyroneura*, gynura, *Hedera helix*, helxine, maranta, neanthe, palms, pellionia, peperomias and pilea.

Flowering plants

Columnea, episcia, hypocyrta, saintpaulia, streptocarpus.

Plants for bottle gardens

Ferns, fittonia, maranta, small palms, peperomia, pilea.

PLANTING UP

With the wider necked containers or aquaria I like to begin by planting the highest points in the design first. First examine each plant carefully for signs of pests or disease; any such organism introduced into the congenial atmosphere of a terrarium will increase with lightening speed and leave you no alternative but to replant with fresh material and compost after having sterilized the container.

Then knock the plant from its pot, gently shake or wash off some of the compost around its roots, scoop out a hole in the compost and position the plant, working the compost back around the roots

Continued on page 84

Ferns for the Home

Ferns, that group of plants so beloved by the Victorians, provide some of the most lovely and delicate foliage plants. Traditionally they were grown in ferneries – special conservatories shaded from the sun and kept warm and humid to encourage the soft green, lushness of the foliage to develop. Even the hardy outdoor species were grown in special fern gardens or walls in a shady part of the main garden.

Although some ferns do enjoy bright sunlight, most prefer a shady spot. The majority of the ferns commonly found in nurseries and garden centres today tolerate quite low winter temperatures, down to 7°C (45°F) and do not require extra heat between late April and late September. They will all benefit greatly, however, from a regular misting over with water and being stood in a tray of gravel or peat kept moist to create a humid microclimate around the plant. Consequently, ferns grow well in bathrooms, especially warm, steamy ones.

Some of the more tender and difficult ferns will thrive in a bottle garden or terrarium. Pteris, pellaea and aspleniums are particularly suitable for this purpose, as are the selaginellas. The latter are not ferns but resemble them and are closely related, enjoying similar cultural conditions.

This enclosed method of growing ferns was another Victorian innovation. Dr Nathanial Ward (1791–1868) created a travelling case to transport newly discovered plants back to England from foreign parts. It was found that ferns flourished in this moist close atmosphere and the Wardian case, as it came to be known, became a popular attraction in many a Victorian drawing room or conservatory.

Ferns do not produce flowers and reproduce themselves quite differently from flowering plants. The main method of reproduction is by dust-like spores produced on the undersides of the fronds where the clusters of spores often appear symmetrically arranged in brown spots or bars. The spores can be sown like seeds. Small prothalli, tiny green plates of cells, will be formed which will in turn produce new plantlets.

A simpler form of propagation is by division. A large fern can be split up to form a number of smaller plants either with a knife or, preferably, by easing the plant apart with two hand forks inserted into the rootball back to back and levered apart. Some ferns like *Asplenium bulbiferum* produce plantlets on their fronds. These can be pegged down onto moist peaty compost and separated from the parent plant only when they have formed a root system of their own.

Other ferns like *Davallia canariensis*, the hare's foot fern, will spread by rhizomes. In the case of this davallia, the rhizomes appear brown and furry, hence the common name, and are an attractive feature of the plant. To be displayed to best advantage, this plant should be raised slightly above the rim of the pot.

Nephrolepis exaltata 'Bostoniensis', the Boston fern

Adiantum raddianum is one of the maidenhair ferns

Pteris argyrea, a robust fern with large graceful fronds

Ferns are wonderfully varied in form and one can be found to suit most tastes. The trophy-like *Platycerium bifurcatum*, the stag's horn fern, looks striking on a plain wall or mounted on an attractive branch, and *Asplenium nidus*, the bird's nest fern, also has a strong architectural shape.

Another beauty of the ferns is the way in which they can be blended with other plants to their mutual advantage in a mixed arrangement. Although, per-haps, even more effective is a group planting of several different kinds of ferns. They are well suited to most styles of décor, both modern and traditional, and their shapely fronds in soft shades of green add a valuable restfulness to the atmosphere of any home.

The Fernery at Southport Botanic Gardens shows the walls on which ferns were traditionally planted

and firming lightly. Try adding pebbles and small stones to heighten the natural landscape effect. For example, a flat-bottomed valley set with small light-coloured round pebbles will resemble a river.

Planting up the narrow-necked bottle requires a different procedure – patience and practice in manoeuvring the long-handled and unwieldy tools. During the course of planting up my bottle garden I always seem to succeed in dislodging either the spoon or fork from its cane and had to fish for it with a magnet on a piece of string! Use the spoon to make the planting hole and then, starting with the tallest one, ease each plant through the neck of the bottle, manoeuvre it into position and work the soil back around the roots, tamping it into position with the cotton reel. A loop of string placed around a side shoot or leaf of the plant will assist you to drop it gently into position, after which the string can be pulled clear.

When the planting is completed, water carefully to settle the compost.

Planting up a bottle garden requires practice and patience. Try to keep the compost off the plant leaves as it is difficult to remove afterwards

CARING FOR THE TERRARIUM

Except for the narrow-necked bottles which can be left open, the terrarium should be provided with some sort of cover. However, it is important for the health of the plants that the temperature inside the container does not get too high so be prepared in very hot weather to remove the cover completely during daylight hours and to open it slightly in warm weather.

Unless provided with lights, the terrarium should be placed near a window or even on a shady windowsill but it must not be allowed to sit on a sunny windowsill as the sun will quickly cause the atmosphere inside the container to overheat.

The best way of lighting the container is to use a mixture of warm and cool fluorescent tubes suspended some 6 to 12 in above the cover. Incandescent lamps are too hot but a carefully positioned spotlight can be very effective. Should the plants become etiolated this is an indication that the light source is either insufficient or is too far away, while if the plants go brown at the leaf tips the converse is probably the case and the lights should be moved back.

Little in the way of standard house plant care is needed, occasional watering with a long-spouted can will be necessary, particularly if the weather is hot and the cover is removed but as the plants do not grow quickly or indeed is it desirable that they should do so, little or no feeding is necessary.

A certain amount of misting on the glass is normal, especially first thing in the morning, but this should disappear as the natural light increases. The formation of droplets is an indication that either the temperature is too high within the container or the outside temperature has dropped suddenly. If the drops turn to drips then you should suspect that the compost is too wet so the cover should be removed until it has had a chance to dry out a little.

A certain amount of plant pruning and grooming is necessary both to keep the plants under control and preserve the appearance of the terrarium. Trim and pinch back any plants which show signs of taking over, using the long-handled razor blade in the bottle garden, and remove dead leaves or any affected by fungus with a spike or fork attached to a cane.

Any plant which grows too large or dies will have to be changed and when doing so you should try to avoid disturbing the soil and other plant roots as much as possible. This is much more difficult to do in the bottle garden and I have always found it easier to empty and replant the garden once it starts looking tatty, which is usually after about twelve months.

One final task remains, to keep the glass clean by occasionally wiping inside and out with a sponge. A terrarium must be sparkling to look its best.

At Home with Flowers

Decorate your home with flowers in a way that will
enhance your life style. Use them to create atmosphere and
interest or to make a fuss of friends. Try to keep a year-
round display throughout the house and never be
afraid of using artificial fruits and flowers in your schemes –
they can be both sophisticated and young-at-heart.

Introduction

Flower arranging has never in its whole long and fascinating history been quite such a popular hobby as it is today. Yet perhaps fewer actual arrangements of fresh cut flowers are seen in the majority of homes, except on those occasions such as Christmas or a special dinner party – or if someone is ill! Down the ages, however, women have taken much quiet pleasure in having flowers about them indoors. So why don't we? What has gone wrong?

There are, of course, many perfectly logical reasons why we so deprive outselves of day-to-day flowers. 'They're far too expensive to buy these days,' or, 'I just don't get any time to do them, much as I would like to,' remark women who are holding down important jobs and running homes as well. 'Nobody notices my flower arrangements anyway,' declare those who have young children at home. 'I'd rather see flowers growing in the garden – they just don't last as long indoors and they make a mess,' is another comment which is often heard.

Don't be put off

There are many people who feel themselves deflated, and somehow put right off flower arranging after seeing the grand flower decorations put up at shows. 'I adore flowers but I really can't do with flower arranging – I'm no good at it,' they say, feeling that somehow when they are arranging flowers they are in some sort of strange competition with one another. And it is not uncommon to hear even an expert flower arranger admit: 'Actually, I don't have any flowers in the house at this moment. I've simply been just too busy today . . .'

One way or another, I find that women are tending to leave flowers out of their everyday lives and I believe a whole generation is in very real danger of getting right out of the way of expecting to see flowers around, in either their own homes or the homes of their friends. I, for one, think this is the very greatest shame. Why miss out on such a simple day-to-day pleasure as sweet and as lovely as a posy of flowers simply placed? Surely the sight of them, the arranging of them, the enjoyment of them is a delightful way of soothing nerves at the end of a long and busy day.

Rooms without flowers, more often than not, appear to lack a certain something which is lively and personal – the finishing touch, perhaps. So they seem indeed more like a television or stage set. The true underlying reason, when you come to think of it, is that somehow many people have come to believe – and believe deep down – that only some specific styles of flower arrangement are really acceptable.

These are the beautifully proportioned, carefully designed flowerpieces so much admired on calendars, in flower arrangement books and at shows, and which you may try your hand at in competitions where the aim is for perfection. But we should realize that people don't live at flower shows; they are something special and divorced from everyday life. Show arrangements are best thought of as exercises in flower arrangement and thus out of the ordinary. Many people who fail to admire a winning exhibit at a flower arrangement show say, 'I would never have that in my home,' and they misunderstand that home arrangements are special to themselves.

Show designs take quite a long time to plan and 'put up', and arrangers go to endless trouble to find exactly the right plant materials and accessories to achieve the small works of art which these arrangements often turn out to be. All that has its place, and is great fun. But home is something completely different. Home is a place to relax. So here the flowers, too, should look relaxed, in harmony, and never the over-arranged show-type pieces which are really far too much on their dignity in the average home. Successful home flower arrangement, to my mind, is absolutely anything which is pretty, easy on the eye, quick to achieve, satisfying, and fitting. Certainly it should never be taken too seriously!

Possibly everyone who likes flowers wants to know at some time or other how to do arrangements up to a reasonably high standard for public perusal (an eye-catching decoration for the stage at a prize-giving or parent-teacher association meeting, a fairytale pedestal for a wedding marquee, or a handsomely decorated swag for the harvest festival; that sort of thing) and it is pleasing and often very useful to know that we can turn out a competent-looking arrangement of which we can be justly proud, when the need arises. But this is not the stuff of everyday

A corner cupboard in a cottage room provides an ideal setting for a bunch of border carnations simply arranged and placed in an attractive toning wooden box

life. Never forget that a flower arrangement can also be simple, uncontrived and homely.

Time for a rethink

I believe the time has come to rethink flower arranging for the house and to see it afresh. To resolve not to get too bogged down with all the things that are written in books which are so often thought of as usual and what is expected.

In my work as a professional writer I find myself often interviewing famous people in their homes. My meeting with the late Sir Cecil Beaton was memorable for me in that it really made me look again at the way I was using flowers in my own house – and it completely changed my, then, current ideas. He had, I found, flowers casually placed in every room throughout the house – often four or five informal placements in a room – for he loved flowers and, he told me, had much enjoyed flower arranging all his life. On the day of my visit there were daffodils simply massed in an antique pewter tankard on the dining table and a home-grown spray carnation in a pretty rose-coloured glass on his desk. There were tall stems of spring blossoms in a stunning Picasso pot in the hall. Flowers and flowering and fruiting pot plants were everywhere to admire.

Thinking about the day as I drove home, it occurred to me that this was how I, too, used to have flowers, casually but everywhere in the house, before I 'took up flower arranging'. I felt how enchanting they appeared when less formally arranged and seen simply as little loves placed about to lighten and decorate the everyday.

I pass the thought on to you. Nobody need ever feel that they must apologize for not having the skill or the time to do homely flowers properly. All flowers are lovely, so with that thought all types of flower arrangement can be lovely if they suit the arranger, her home, and her lifestyle. I believe the time has come to gear down and to adapt our thinking on flowers and flower arranging so it slips in more easily with our special circumstances, and the informal friendly places that most homes are in the 1980s.

Houses are all different, and all rooms are different too. However, the rooms do not necessarily have to echo the character and age of the house, so although this part of the book is divided into ideas for homes in various situations I hope it will be of general interest wherever you happen to live; for even a house in town can have the character of one in the country. Some houses and rooms have no particularly strong character and this can be played on by creating an ever-changing impact by the way the eye is drawn to the flowers, the containers that are chosen and the way styles are created with a strong feeling of an age or an admired characteristic.

For busy women

Modern women are busy women. We all have schedules to meet; cooking and shopping to fit in; buses, trains and planes to catch, and somehow still find time for the laundry, fetching and carrying children, and getting our hair done! But if we spare not one moment in the week to relax and to refresh ourselves, what does it all avail us or our families? In the average life, which is planned to run like clockwork, flowers certainly should not add to the strain, worry and concentration. If we resolve to bring them into the forefront of our lives again it is important that they do not then become just one more tie; another job to be somehow fitted in, and to be over-perfectly accomplished.

If we are wise we will use potted flowering plants much more, and dried plant material and the beautiful silk flowers, now so readily available, whenever life is likely to be specially hectic. We could collect containers that are amusing in themselves or striking in some other way, so that they look effective when showing off only a very small amount of plant material or even standing alone. Somewhere along the way the average woman has begun to feel that a single rose in a bud vase, an informal posy popped into a cream jug or a teacup, and blooms unaffectedly disporting themselves in a fantasy decorated bowl, are somehow not 'proper' flower arranging; but, of course, they are.

Those lovely, tailored, carefully controlled flower-pieces of the fulsome 'English stately home' or show type, with their gentle geometric outlines, usually require chicken wire or foam to hold the stems in the desired position. These are fiddly to fit into the containers and are, more often than not – apart from at shows – something of a nuisance when it comes to topping up with water each day, as the intricately massed flowers drink it up so quickly. Especially if we happen to be out all day and the central heating comes on or the sun streams forth, the container dries itself out and the flowers will have flipped by night fall!

KEEP IT SIMPLE

Invariably flowers and foliage do not last as long in these stylish arrangements as in the less formal designs when no 'mechanics' are used. When doing even a small arrangement it is time-consuming to have to thread many stems down through crumpled chicken wire and into water or water-retaining foam in the attempt to create a fine design. However, if the flowers are arranged more simply, without the aid of any 'mechanics' (chicken wire or plastic foam), as they fade and drop their petals they are easily and quickly disposed of. It takes only a moment or two to whisk even a whole bunch from an unhampered container, retrieve any still-perfect blossoms and leaves, and just re-arrange the material. This is easier and, therefore, more realistic in most life-styles, than the often involved extrication required when those 'oh-so-useful floral aids' have been used.

Except for 'on show' arrangements there is really no need to do anything intricate at all. This does not mean to say that our arrangements will then all be 'samey' and dull, lacking in style and individuality. Far from it, for all houses, furnishings, and arrangers' personalities are different and so will spark off new and often very original ideas indeed.

There are many books to tell you how to do special flower arrangements for particular occasions – indeed I have written many myself – but in this book my only aim is to share the delight of the thought of flowers in every home once again; surely the most important place of all for enjoying them.

Selecting containers

When bunched flowers are to be displayed informally, containers then begin to play a particularly important role and should be selected with some care as to colour and style to suit the room. In competition work, containers have at all times to be subordinate to the plant material but at home they can assume as great an importance as the flowers themselves. Study the style and the colour of your containers and as you come to arrange your flowers choose the one which will best enhance them.

When I first began flower arranging as a serious hobby it was the aim of every arranger to get together a collection of rather grand containers which would, hopefully, include at least one antique urn, china cupid, alabaster tazza, silver tray or candlestick. These containers usually require the use of chicken wire (or flower foams) as stem supports, for with this aid it is possible even in the shallow bowl of a tazza, or the tall shape of a typical urn, to achieve soaring height and that gently flowing downward line, so lovely and so admired in the grand English traditional massed-flower style with which we have become so familiar.

SHALLOW DISHES

Thirty years ago it was very fashionable to arrange flowers in any kind of shallow dish, to produce a 'modern line' arrangement. Suitable low shapes were quite difficult to get hold of and we adapted to the style by using Denbyware cooking dishes, I remember, as pinholders first became available. These allowed simpler and more flower-frugal arrangements. It was all very innovative and allowed us to get away from the massed look encouraged by the traditionally-shaped containers. With clean-cut lines these dishes were, and are, most suitable for modern homes and town flats. You can put a pinholder towards one end and arrange flowers as if growing out of it, cutting the stems to varying lengths – the tallest

---

Flowers and conifer foliage are simply grouped in a carefully-chosen container which helps to link up successfully this rather difficult colour scheme

towards the back, the shortest near the front, with varying flower heights in between.

As during the past few years antique containers have become practically unobtainable because of their prohibitive cost, and because they are not very easy to find any more, and as shallow dishes specially made for flower arranging are usually hand-thrown and somewhat expensive, the average woman has adapted yet again for show work, cleverly finding the advantages of the hidden container. This may be a well pinholder, or equally useful is a small cooking dish, a shallow empty tin, with its rough edges hammered down, or a plastic plant-pot saucer sprayed some

An eye-catching china watering-can makes the most of this delicately-coloured arrangement of shop-bought anenomes and bits and bobs taken from house plants

quiet colour. With a pinholder inside, tall stems are supported and others keep to the positions we wish them to take.

TUSSIE-MUSSIES

In the low, close-packed tussie-mussie type posies, those truly traditional old-English styles of arranging flowers, which involve simple gatherings of wild or garden flowers in tiny vases and pots, the stems just hold themselves up and require no special aids. There is very little mess in their arranging, for any pre-arrangement preparation (such as the cutting down of their stems) can all take place out in the garden as you gather them.

If you are going to enjoy yourselves arranging flowers at home, buying the occasional container will be a most interesting part of it all; for a brand-new container always acts as a tonic, inspiring us afresh

with ideas. When you are not planning to use any mechanics at all you should bear in mind when selecting a new container that the shape of its rim and bowl can be quite important. Ask yourself whether it holds plenty of water. Will the design of the rim be helpful in supporting mechanically uncontrolled flowers well, so that they display themselves nicely? When you come to think about it you will see, for instance, that a funnel shape with a splayed-out top will support stems easily as well as allowing for a soft flow at the sides, whereas a slim tube shape will naturally suggest a stiffer and more upright design.

INTRIGUING SHAPES

There are many crisp, new and most intriguingly-shaped containers around at the moment. Young at heart and up-to-the-minute, they are a pleasure to the eye and lend themselves well to informal arrangements. On the whole, no-one can possibly pass them by without noticing them when arranged, so they make eye-catching flower decorations from the word go. Certainly their snazzy or amusing shapes should not be despised but recognized as objects of our own age and very suitable to modern homes.

Many 1920's styles of container are popular today; these are often decorated with bright painted flowers whose colours can be copied in real flowers and leaves. Victorian, Edwardian and Twenties glass can also be lovely for displaying a few stems. I find the clear and moulded glassware preferable to the heavily cut styles, and coloured glass is particularly effective so long as it matches or tones with the flowers. I like to stand an arrangement in a glass container where it catches the light. Big branches, strong stems, and large flowers need tall, heavy containers. Small, sweet posies require something more delicate, and glass can be very fitting.

HAPPY HUNTING GROUNDS

Little jugs and objects with nipped-in waists are good shapes for containers, in that they support stems attractively, and well-shaped low baskets with dishes inside them are also very well adapted to our purpose. There are plenty of good shapes available, both new and second-hand. Junk shops are not what they once were, usually calling themselves antique shops these days, but look out for junk stalls. These still can be found in country towns, while cities and even villages often have charity markets and jumble sales. By the way, if you are nervous about attending a jumble sale as a customer, get in early – as a helper!

A few antirrhinums and some heads of red-hot poker enhance the colours of the container, which in turn complements the plain wooden furniture

Pleasant shapes not necessarily designed for flowers are to be found in china shops. Watch out for pleasing little bowls and small glasses. Kitchen shops selling 'seconds' can be a good source of inexpensive ware which will be most suitable for country styles. Modern pottery of a good rough texture is interesting, and you can often order a particular shape or colour from local potteries specializing in hand-thrown ware. Whether antique, junk, or modern, containers in styles and colours to link with our own particular home furnishings should be chosen. Sometimes be brave and outgoing and select a colour which is not necessarily a soft and gentle one. Many homes will

take a sudden bright surprise colour accent in a flower arrangement and its container.

Suitable containers can, as you will no doubt soon discover, range from the finest porcelain to those with a near-sculpted look, from classic shapes to ultra-modern, from the palest of tints to the strongest 'look-at-me' colours. But if sensitively chosen to go into a particular setting we shall always like them and happily enjoy arranging in them.

Incidentally, I still use my lovely grand urns and tazza shapes but nowadays, for home, I simply cluster short-stemmed flowerheads and perhaps a few low trails of foliage or fruit in them so that they require no mechanics whatsoever in their arranging.

That natural look

To get the very best effect for your cut flowers, arrange them so that all the stems appear to spring from the same point. Criss-crossing stems which are visible usually look unnatural.

Flower foam A deep container may be packed almost to the brim with flower foam – a water-retaining material in which stems are pressed to keep them in the required position; it is sold under various trade names such as Oasis. This will support just one or two bold flower stems easily in a simple design. A small block of foam can be held in place in a shallow container by means of Oasis tape (a special sticky tape sold by flower clubs), which is taken right round the container and the foam. For larger designs, bring the Oasis higher up the container.

Chicken wire Other mechanics for holding flowers in more intricate, massed arrangements include chicken wire. If you wish to use this buy the cheapest 2-in gauge mesh. Use a piece crushed into a loose ball and pushed into the container to make a dome just higher than the rim.

Pinholders Although these days I personally more often than not dispense altogether with chicken wire and flower foams for homely arrangements, I really would not be without my set of medium- to large-size pinholders or my well pinholders. I find that

Mechanics in the form of chicken wire is employed to hold a massed arrangement of bright bold flowers in the deep bowl of this fishy container

with their aid I can, when I feel like it, create even quite large designs – big enough for my home, anyway – fairly quickly. The trick is to choose a pinholder which is really big enough, so that it can accommodate the required number of stems with ease. Of course, when just a few slim stems are to be arranged a smaller pinholder will do; this is something to decide for yourself as you come to start your arrangement.

Well pinholders are a truly marvellous invention, excellent for 'quickie' flower arranging. They are pinholders built into small round containers and are quite easy to hide under such things as the flowers, leaves, stones or bits of driftwood that we may be using. For even at home, I feel any mechanics should remain a beautiful mystery between the flowers and the arranger. Though perhaps it is rude to peer too closely, there is nothing visually appealing about either the pins of a pinholder or the mesh of chicken wire.

INFORMAL ARRANGEMENTS

There are, I think, two main methods of arranging flowers very informally, although you will be able to develop these for yourself. Arrange the bunch, posy fashion, in your hand, cut straight across the stems at the bottom and place them as they are into your water-filled container. Alternatively, the flowers and leaves may be inserted individually and their criss-crossing stems hidden under water will hold one another up. Women have arranged flowers this way down the centuries, and these decorations will, I feel sure, see us right through to this century's close.

AIM FOR A SILHOUETTE

However, to prevent too much of a grannified effect or 'I really don't much care how these flowers look', try to concentrate just a little on getting some feeling of a pleasing silhouette. This is quite important. Achieve it by cutting down any stem which sticks out just too far beyond its fellows or pokes out to one side so that there is a feeling of imbalance. Though informal, the outline can be shapely, just like a well-balanced growing plant or tree.

When choosing flowers and leaves, aim for some variety, with pointed shapes such as twigs, sprays, or buds, and round shapes such as open flowers and bold leaves, plus shapes and sizes midway between the two for filling in the design.

It may be helpful, as with the tailored show-type flowerpiece (or fruit or foliage designs), to try to see

Three stems of orange lilies gladden the day, their stems are pressed into the moss-like house plant selaginella growing on the old flower foam which fills the container

covering or supporting the stems. Arrangements made up entirely of foliage, or a mixture of foliage and fruits or berries, have very much of a part to play in today's home decoration, for they should last a long time.

When arranging without any form of stem support, and you feel you need a little extra height at the centre or the back, it is reasonably easy to cut longer stems in the first place for this position. Alternatively you can cut other stems down to a variety of different heights and when the design is almost complete, ease up one or more of the central stems. In tight little knot arrangements, both taller and shorter stems are supported in position by a kind of mutual wedging.

In these simply-contrived decorations, don't set yourself impossible tasks, trying to take flowers just too far out at the sides or over-high in a very low container so that the stems topple over! For such designs you really do need chicken wire or floral foam as support. By the way, in a design of only a few flowers an odd number of blooms, rather than an even number, seems to look best.

Conditioning plant material

Even country people can be heard to say, 'I don't have cut flowers indoors – they just don't seem to last very well, and I would rather have them in the garden.' I like flowers in the garden, too. But, no matter how many times one may dash up the border to stand gazing at the lovely growing blooms it is not until one or two of them are brought indoors that one is able to spend more than a short minute or two really looking at them and into them, appreciating them close up.

Certainly at some times of year it is an advantage to bring the flowers in; during autumn and winter, for instance, when frosts lurk bent on destruction, and even in the summer when long days of rain have bedraggled them.

But at any time of year, with a little pre-arrangement care, the life of cut flowers can be extended considerably so that they will last about as long as flowers growing out of doors. Obviously flowers in bud will last longer than those which have been out for a few days already, especially when bees have been working over them. So pick buds and newly-opened blooms whenever possible and select your time of day for gathering. In the cool of the morning or evening, or after light rain are just about the best times.

Pick straight into a bucket or jug of water. This really does make sense, for blooms which go straight

your container and the arrangement with an imaginary line running straight down the middle. To look well, the plant material should sit easily and look visually balanced either side of the line. This sounds complex, but in practice means that, say, nine very large flowers in a dark colour on one side will look over-heavy in relation to nine very pale-coloured blooms on the opposite side. Swap them around a little to achieve that feeling of balance.

When picking or choosing flowers and leaves, bear the colour of a container in mind if you can, and also the room in which it will stand. Try not to mix the sizes of the blooms too much. An arrangement made up of a number of little flowers will be spoiled if one or two over-large ones are added. Three or four very tiny flowers or leaves added to a decoration made up, say, of full-size peonies will look somewhat unstable.

An arrangement of all one kind of flower is always attractive, particularly so when supported by their own or some complementary leaves. Foliage is important to most designs. You can make a neat frill of suitably coloured leaves to set off a low bunchy style, which looks very Victorian. Leaves also look well appearing here and there at regular intervals among the flowerheads, or in the larger designs

into water do not have time to draw in air, which so often causes air locks in their stems. This is usually the reason why roses and other flowers droop their heads so pathetically, soon after gathering.

Scrape and split open hard woody stems. Remove the thorns from roses, and the foliage from lilac and any leaves which would be under water in the arrangement. I do all this in the garden as I gather them to save mess indoors. Place woody stems straight into shallow hot water, or give them a warm water drink as soon as you get them indoors.

Cool and dark Both wild and garden plants certainly appreciate a long drink in a deep bucket of water and being left in a dark, cool place for a few hours, preferably overnight, before being arranged. But this may well be utterly impracticable. However, if you have picked them straight into water you have the advantage that you can usually arrange most things at once. Sometimes when I do this and am to be out of the house for the day I put the completed arrangement into my downstairs cloakroom, which is cool and darkish and never gets the sun, to await my return, rather than leaving it in a room which will warm up as it catches any sunlight.

Although cut flowers look lovely in a window if it is very sunny it is not the best part of the room to choose. The cooler cut flowers and leaves can be kept, the better it is for them, and it is worth remembering, too, that preserved flowers will fade in bright sunlight. A position out of draughts is also desirable for fresh blooms and leaves.

The Country Cottage

An oak-beamed cottage set deep in quiet countryside, with hollyhocks clustering close around the door and a cosy welcoming world inside of softly lit oil lamps, the glow of old pine, gentle flower-sprigged wallpapers and faded sepia photographs, is indeed home to some lucky people. Many of us revel in feeling nostalgic and millions who live far from country meadows set with wild flowers so admire the calming look reminiscent of country life that they bring it to town, suggesting by their home's interior the little country house set in its garden.

Cleverly they win an impression of the country, indoors at least, with pine, or white-painted wrought iron furniture, shaded lighting, lace-edged pillows, tiny flowery fabrics, country-weave carpets and granny's set of old copper measuring jugs ranged along the window ledge with the Staffordshire pottery. The effect is usually very successful and quite charming, and makes a perfect natural setting for flowers and plants.

It is as important in a country setting as in a more sophisticated town one to mix and match, tone and blend colours, and when it comes to choosing containers and flowers, to relate them generally to the style of the room. For best results in any given setting, practise really looking at flowers and plants afresh with a flower arranger's eye, summing up their character and working in ways which are aware of all their exciting possibilities.

Flowers have characters

Different flowers really do have different characters! Though they may have been bought, expensively bunched, out of season from a smart shop, such flowers as larkspur, lily-of-the-valley, wallflowers, violets, daisies, daffodils, daisy-eyed chrysanthemums, snapdragons, and certainly all grasses always have a fresh just-up-from-the-country look which is associated in most people's minds with country lanes and well-stocked cottage gardens. Lilies, carnations, orchids and long-stemmed roses have more of an upstage look though they may indeed have been grown in a country garden.

So for this situation try to choose flowers and leaves with a country-girl character; chive flowers, primroses, old-fashioned roses are ever a good link-up. It doesn't matter one jot, of course, if you happen to have only a gift bunch of six straight-stemmed gladioli to arrange today. With their built-in look of high life, formality, and town living it may at first seem just more difficult to place them in a country cottage. You can take them down a peg or two, as it were, by the manner in which you present them, arranging them in simpler, more country-like ways than might be used in more splendid or clearly more modern surroundings.

Try cutting each gladiolus stem into sections (just immediately over the flowers) to make three or four

A glowing arrangement of three stems of gladioli cut down and impaled on a pinholder in a low glass bowl which catches and reflects the light

short stems from the original one. This is economical and it will allow you to make a number of low posy-type designs which can slip most comfortably into the country surroundings. The container to hold them could be a little bowl or a small dish with a pinholder in it.

You can, however, from time to time, gain impact and extra zip by the surprise of a slightly formal arrangement of grand-looking flowers, such as lilies, in a simple setting.

It is obviously most useful to have at least a few suitable things available for picking, growing just

outside the door. No matter how small the garden, and even if you have no garden other than a window box or a few tubs, if you are selective in what you grow there will always be the odd few leaves and flowers for gathering at all times of the year.

Foliage, often so very difficult to get in town, always has a lovely, just-gathered, countryfied look. Think of sprays of beech, trails of ivy, fine curly honeysuckle, sprigged lavender and ferns, of course. These all clearly speak of the country.

Whether surroundings are truly rural or only attempting to suggest the appeal of the country scene, the rural look can be emphasized by selecting country-style containers for both flower and plant displays. Flowers and potted plants disposed together in baskets of every kind have a most delightful harmony. Cane, osier and reed are always sympathetic in displaying plant materials and when placed on the light-reflecting surface of old, softly gleaming wood most plant material looks happily at home. Little pill bottles will hold water for supporting a few cut flower stems among growing foliage plants.

WILD FLOWERS

A few of these brought home with care, bunched in the hand and arranged as they are straight into little containers such as jugs, wooden bowls and boxes (with hidden water-holders inside), or in any simple homely container, look well. I have even seen wild flowers disporting themselves in an upturned straw hat complete with ribbons!

It is important when picking wild flowers to gather them with the conservation of our wild heritage in mind. But no-one, I think, could object to us taking the occasional posy of buttercups, a few stalks of Queen Anne's lace, or sprays of wild rose and haw-thorn berry, for these are still common. If possible, pick wild flowers in bud or close to opening, and put them straight into plastic bags – dampened very lightly inside and caught up at the top – so that they come to no harm on the journey home. Once home, if the flowers have flagged at all, put their stem ends into a drink of very warm water and this should revive them quite quickly.

Sculptured seedheads are ever useful to flower arrangers and at summer's end will be naturally

A few wild flowers and some foliage make a dainty grouping well-suited to this informal and unusual container studded with many pebbles and shells

preserved on the plant so that they can be arranged at once when you get them home (out of water if you wish).

COUNTRY FOLIAGE

It will not be too much of a problem to find foliage if you live in the country or on the edge of town. Both wild and cultivated foliage is invaluable to the flower arranger, for complete designs can be made with leaves alone and they have a vital part to play in any flower or fruit arrangement, acting as foil, backing, and textural contrast.

Plain, clean-cut, well shaped, unpatterned or regularly patterned leaves growing in sprays, clusters, or as shapely individuals are particularly useful. Pointed shapes such as trails of ivy, beech, fern, and iris are good as outline material, carrying the eye naturally inwards towards the heart of a design, which might be dramatized with a few plain, more dominant-looking leaves such as hosta, bergenia, or single geranium or ivy leaves inserted one at a time.

Cut foliage straight into water, if you can, after splitting thick stem ends and removing lower leaves. With foliage it really *is* worthwhile carrying a jug or bucket of water with you, down the garden path. Indoors give a deep drink (overnight if time allows) before arranging, for leaves can be tricky. When cutting foliage in the wild, pick frugally and with an eye to not spoiling the tree or bush and do not take more than you actually need, then get it home as quickly as possible. Stand the stem ends for half an hour or so in a shallow drink of boiling water, and when this has cooled fill up with cold and leave them to soak until you are ready to begin the arrangement. Foliage arrangements last best in deep containers with a good surface expanse of water. Even when arranging informally don't overpack the design.

When gathering select a few sprays with a downward habit of growth and some with a more upright manner, for a natural-looking decoration. More often than not a strong and confident-looking container, which seems properly at home with sturdy leaves, best displays such a rural bunch, though more delicate designs can be achieved with some leaves and the Victorians and Edwardians often arranged fine ferns in glass, which can be very pretty.

EVEN FUNGI

These are not to everyone's liking, but should you come across a handsome group of fungi on a woodland walk as the year turns towards autumn, a few may be gathered and carried home for inclusion in 'flower' arrangements, using a shallow bowl or dish to display them. All look particularly well when arranged with 'country' plant material like moss, ivy, blackberry flowers and berries, rosehips, haws, moorland heathers, lichened branches and any wild flower skeleton heads.

The material does not have to be wild but to harmonize with fungi it ought to have something of a wild look about it. Sometimes small fungi will have started to colonize a fallen tree stump, and it may be possible to break off some interesting bits of bark which include the fungi.

Carry delicate fungi home on a bit of moss or on newspaper, or a box with a lid may be useful if you have a long car journey.

Unfortunately some of the more colourful fungi, the white-spotted red fly agaric, for example, are certainly poisonous and I would not entertain any fungi at home where there are young children about. Many fungi and common garden plants are poisonous in one way or another, and the automatic washing of hands after any flower arranging is obviously advisable.

Some fungi, such as the so-called bracket fungus and oyster fungus, can be found on old logs and branches throughout the year, often with the brackets arranged in decorative tiers. Their corky growths can be gently prised away from the wood and will dry very easily. They can be kept for years, though it is best to soak them in a solution of domestic bleach and water overnight on reaching home to kill any lingering bugs. Then they can be dried out of doors on a sunny, windy day. After this they are very useful, perhaps to cover a small container or a pinholder. They can even be attached with adhesive on to a branch or a piece of suitable driftwood.

Alternatively three or four fresh pink-gilled button mushrooms can be fun if added to a country scene created on a moss-filled dish; perhaps at the base of a 'tree' made from hawthorn or seedheads of cow parsley. Cocktail sticks taken up into the base of the stem will help secure them to the pinholder or into the moss.

Preserved flowers and seedheads

Preserved flowers, leaves and grasses seem particularly to go with country homes. There are various methods of preservation.

Seedheads and flowers look most attractive when

A pine box makes an effective setting for country-garden fruits, flowers and foliage arranged in hidden containers. The round fruits at the front are from the strawberry tree

drying while hanging upside down from a beam or suspended by ribbons from a hook in the ceiling. Indeed, so pretty an appearance do they present on long scarlet or bright blue ribbons that they can become an indoor decoration in their own right. I especially like bunches of soft green grape hyacinth and bluebell seedheads in late spring. Later these turn to a charming creamy colour which is useful in so many little designs.

As autumn comes it is the turn of many seedheads which, gathered on a dry and sunny day, can be preserved in a warm dry place to bring variety to our winter flower arrangements; love-in-a-mist (nigella),

poppyheads of every kind, clematis, angelica, bulrushes, Chinese lanterns, cow parsley, grasses, verbascum, alliums, and many more come to mind. Flower arrangers soon learn to recognize a good thing when they see it and will preserve many a handsome item which others might think only fit for the bonfire!

Among a host of recognizably lovely flowers to dry in the same way I suggest larkspur, achillea, echinops, delphinium, heather, helichrysum, statice, acanthus, eryngium, and love-lies-bleeding. Gypsophila (called babies' breath by the Victorians) has been out of favour with flower arrangers for many years. Because it is unusual nowadays, it makes a good addition to anyone's stock of preserved plant material and it dries easily. I love to have it in great informal bunches about the house, and like it particularly in country baskets of mixed dried flowers.

Throughout the drying seasons, search the garden and the country lanes regularly for suitable subjects. Leave them hanging airily bunched for a few days until they feel quite dry to the touch. Then they may be arranged at once or stored in some dry place until needed. Flowering grasses, both wild and from the garden, will also preserve nicely either by hanging aloft or more simply popping them into a deep container and enjoying them as they preserve themselves.

Drying in water Hydrangea flowerheads are actually bracts, and these will dry out if left in a warm place, standing in an inch or so of water. They must be completely mature or they will not preserve, so do not gather them except towards the end of the season, when the texture of the heads changes considerably. Bells of Ireland (moluccella) and verbascum are among other subjects you will find dry well in the same way (though the glycerine method is better). Sometimes, too, as summer ends, garden roses and their buds can be gently dried out by this method, standing them in a little water on top of a warm radiator or boiler.

Preserving in glycerine Many leaves and such things as sprays of fruiting or flowering dock can be easily preserved for winter decor if left to drink in a mixture made up of two parts boiling water to one part glycerine for a week or so. Leaves such as beech, rosemary and elaeagnus, and seedheads such as old man's beard, angelica and many others can be successfully treated in the glycerine mixture. A depth of 2 to 3 in of the mixture should be sufficient but this should be kept topped up as it is taken up into the plant.

Landscape designs

Small landscapes are a specially interesting side of flower arranging and are sometimes seen at shows. Such a design makes a very good form of flower decoration with a look of the country. It is certainly different and is adaptable to both sophisticated and informal surroundings. In our homes we arrange exactly as we like and to please no-one but ourselves. We do not have to worry about whether accessories (objects other than plant material) over-dominate the flowers, leaves and other natural plant forms, as we must do when designing for competitions. All the same, the finished effect will probably be better and more pleasing if we have a plan in mind as we gather together suitable flowers, figurines, bases and containers to suggest some sort of natural scene.

Work with what you have to hand, to suit your surroundings. The very traditionally-furnished home will probably have a naturalistic ornament of some kind around. It might be a representation of an animal, bird or human figure, which it could be amusing to link with flowers and grouping all together in such a way as to suggest a natural habitat or landscape on a base or in a flat dish container.

Informal landscapes are fairly easily suggested. Such things as miniature daffodils arranged on a pinholder as if growing at the foot of a nicely curving tree (a branch) and so on. You do not, of course, have to have an accessory, and a few pebbles or stones along with some tree-like driftwood or a lichen-covered branch to give height might be enough to spark off an idea which can be developed. The only aim is to catch a general mood. It could be a wind-swept moorland with a gale-bent tree or shrubs, a placid wood, a country lane or even a town garden.

To achieve a well-proportioned landscape arrangement we must be able to shrink in our imagination down to its size. A scaled-down 6-in high figurine requires a setting which is neither too small nor too large; with flowers, leaves and fruits chosen with thought as to scale. Obviously a large blowzy garden rose would look too big in a 12-in high landscape arrangement, while a few tiny roses (such as from one of the miniatures) might be exactly right.

In relation to a tiny garden landscape a normal-sized bunch of grapes might well be suggested by a spray of black privet berries, while a grouping of baby acorns and a few ordinary garden plant seedheads could suggest rather more exotic plant forms when presented in some 'tropical' setting. A stem of *Euphorbia wulfenii*, with a tuft of leaves at the top, might impersonate a palm tree, for example, and with a toy lion at its foot we have exotica!

Using a base A base is sometimes useful to link a landscape group attractively into one entity, making a picture for the eye to enjoy. To hold the stems use either a pinholder in a low dish or a well pinholder. Place this to one side of the base and at the back, so as

A pleasant landscape design for early spring can be made from catkins, ferns, some moss, two potted primroses and a few daffodils arranged among pieces of driftwood

to allow plenty of room for your scene in front of it. It really does not matter overmuch but if you measure the tallest stem, which you put in first, to about one-and-a-half times to twice the width of the base (or your flat container), the effect will generally be good.

Clearly, therefore, the base is of importance to the whole effect, so it should be chosen with care. A base can be made from a suitable piece of flat wood, a plain mat or a tray, or sometimes an upturned tray will be found useful. Interesting bases can often be found at flower arranging clubs' sales tables, or we can make our own by covering cake boards with fabric to suggest grass, sand or some other natural setting.

Landscapes can be of fresh or dried material, and the latter will go on being interesting for weeks. The fun of landscape designing opens up a whole new, fascinating world and fresh trains of thought, to the flower arranger. It makes us remarkably observant, too, so that when walking in the country or on the beach, or doing everyday chores we can be looking out all the time for things we can add to make our landscape designs more realistic and pleasing. Do not throw away a pineapple top, but dry it off and keep it to use like the spikes of a desert cactus, and try not to see a particular piece of driftwood as looking like a seahorse or a monster or some more abstract shape but rather as a castle, a bridge or a cliff face with caves and chasms.

The Habitat Style

For people married within the last few years, home will probably be influenced to a greater or lesser degree by the Habitat style of furnishing, with its clean, confident lines, simple, clear, strong paintbox colours usually featuring basic fabrics in stripes and plain colours rather than flowery in any way. All this will be found behind the glossy newly-painted front door opening on to a hall where, directly opposite the entrance, an arrangement inspired by the same style could well be displayed. Flower pieces to integrate here can be very imaginative and exhilarating.

Containers which 'go' with such settings might successfully be a grouping of jewel-coloured tube shapes or chunky square block shapes in plastic, pottery, or glass; while stainless steel, undecorated terracotta, and stained and coloured woods with inner liners are effective. Peasant pottery, or the work of modern British and oriental potters, is something one can also collect over the years.

Handsome and off-beat

Textures and colours, shapes and styles of flower arranging should steer away from the very feminine and pretty, and lean more towards the handsome, the off-beat and the original. Displayed on tables of chrome and glass, colourful or very plain wood, or plastic surfaces, the effect should be visually exciting, snappy, and brightly different.

Choose flowers, leaves and fruits of large clean-cut shapes and strong, distinct personality in impact colours to go with the room and its furnishings and with the choice of shapely, green, potted plants. Present cut plant material in concentrated masses of pure colour or as daring individuals; for example one big scarlet rhododendron flowerhead with its leaves in a striking black container, or pure orange rose heads close-grouped in bright yellow pottery or glossy plastic with very clean lines.

A standing piece of driftwood, perhaps painted in a matt or glossy primary colour, to match the base on which it stands, might be included in a grouping, in conjunction with one or more splendid modern containers holding a few dramatic flowers.

Consider fruits, such as oranges, piled up in a slick dome shape and stuck about with a few sturdy green leaves, such as laurel, which will last out of water for a time. Or, try strings of shiny red apples on knotted cords of different lengths, as an unusual hanging decoration for a party window. Create a still-life with a melon, apples and some grapes on a large plastic serving platter, displaying it near suitable free-style or abstract painting, or to make a striking centrepiece for a party table.

Watch out for modern 'fun' flower-holding items in pottery or some other material. These are young and certainly different and often made to look like fruits, hands clutching a bunch of flower stems, or affecting the look of white tissue paper in which bought flowers are often wrapped. Others are in the form of way-out animals or female heads which take a top-knot of flowers. There are also such items as jugs and bowls with irridescent stripes, offering surprise effects and masses of impact, which can inspire new looks and new ways with flower decoration. For quickie flower designs choose plant materials which are more bold in colour and shape and have the prospect of a long life, instead of the more delicate items which other rooms may carry.

Because your eye enjoys this sort of furnishing you can develop a taste for contrasting strong, pure colours and shapes in your flower arranging, whether you live in town or country. Both garden and shop flowers and fruits and, more importantly perhaps, leaves will all have their uses and will prove suitable subjects for you.

IMPORTED NOVELTIES

Many preserved leaves, stems, strange husks, cones and other parts of exotic plants are coming into Britain each year by the lorry load. Bleached to a natural creamy colour, or dyed to take on all those Arabian Nights fantasy colours, they make possible many off-beat autumn or winter arrangements. One importer tells me that each year sees a different colour combination popular with the buying public. One year we seem to choose all the natural brown and tawny shades, the next it will be yellows and oranges, and then we may go mad for a while on all the pinks through to mauve, fuchsia and lavender.

Imported grasses of every handsome shape, size and colour are other pleasant items to cheer our winter designs. Watch out for fluffy rabbit's tail grasses or, for positions demanding really very large designs, we may find ten-foot-tall pala grasses (so beloved by shop window decorators) of great use. All grasses add valuable pointed shapes for making outlines of arrangements.

Giant fir cones come to us all the way from India, and a dyed preserved bracken arrives in the shops from Italy. It is interesting that American oak leaves are imported first to Italy in their natural state and there they are preserved in a special way so as to keep their splendidly vivid autumn colours for a very long time. Every season unbelievable amounts of dried beech leaves from the huge Italian woodland plantations arrive, selling at a price which makes it hardly worthwhile to preserve our own even if we know where we can find fresh beech leaves. By the way, the somewhat odd smell of much freshly-bought preserved plant material comes from the sulphur and chemicals used in the preservation process, and this wears off after a little while.

Look out for smart modern containers; this one, shaped like a hand holding stems, sympathetically displays a bunch of daffodils and a few leaves picked from house plants

Spray-painting If the colours of any imported materials are not exactly right when you get them home, or if you want to add a touch of fresh new sparkle to last year's dried material, why not spray-paint some items? Do this out of doors or in an airy room, and try not to breathe in any fumes. You can gild or silver these preserved items too, or they may be individually painted with poster paint or car-body spray paint.

FOLIAGE IS IMPORTANT

Any of the bold leaf shapes from suitable large houseplants such as aspidistra, fatsia, monstera, mother-in-law's tongue (sansevieria), palms and cordyline will be a delight. Most well-grown house-

The soft colours in a modern home

The drama of space

Stems cut from flowers such as daffodils and irises can at times be trimmed down to different lengths and presented on a pinholder simply as interesting design material, their flowers being used elsewhere. Useful flowers like gladioli, presented to take full advantage of their splendid shapes, are available in both town and country. Any confident flowers, fruits, and seedheads provide solid emphasis, and a dramatic feeling to all this lighthearted working with and in space. Though, in fact, we may find that many arrangements look so splendid without flowers that we can sometimes consider not even including them at all. Chrysanthemums, lilies, large open roses, gerberas from the florist, oriental poppies, rhododendrons and any other big flowers will be useful when they are included.

Globe artichokes from the greengrocery will dry and last for ever and their leaves may be spray-painted for extra dash. Preserved imported artichoke seedheads, like big fluffy drumsticks, can be found in the florists' shops, in their natural creamy colour or dyed flamboyantly. From the wild, seedheads of Queen Anne's lace and mares' tails are just a few of the things we may find to please us.

If you become very interested in this rather abstract form of flower arranging you will find that to control the stems, so that they stay where you really want them, you will often have to use a strong pinholder, crumpled chicken wire or water-soaked flower foam. However, this form of decoration, because of the strong inbuilt character of the plant material, will stand well and last a long time even in centrally-heated rooms, and so will be worth the extra time involved in arranging.

All settings surely differ, of course, and close-packed or airy masses of garden flowers might look equally at home. 'Stemmy' flowers arranged casually in smart tinted Thirties' glass vases can be in absolute harmony in some surroundings; for example, on shelves or table tops of looking glass set against such things as pale linen chair covers, curtains or blinds.

That 'stagey' look

Novelties are imported from all over the world, and I recently found four tall red-stained wooden candlesticks which look handsome when accompanying scarlet pottery on the dinner table, linking up nicely with peasant wool braid edging the plain dark forest

plants in situations of good light with central heating will cheerfully spare the odd leaf or two, or full decorative use can be made, in flower designs, of occasional dead or dying leaves with their changing colours.

From the garden there might be superb New Zealand flax (phormium), strappy iris, *Arum italicum*, and a hundred and one other things. From the wild there will be broom (which can be easily coaxed into bold curves), well-shaped branches of shrubs and trees, ivy and rhododendron. Learn to see all plant forms first as design elements rather than as 'pretty-pretties' and in ultra-modern rooms feel no sense of hurt when bending and cutting leaves down so as to create new shapes and the possibility of very individualistic patterns.

Bend suitable plants such as reeds and iris leaves into curving or angular shapes, so that when placed in a design they capture space; for unlike the familiar traditional massed use of flowers they may often have areas of planned airy space within the design. These will not only appear in the outline of the arrangement but also within it, giving spaces through which we can look, as in modern sculpture.

green of the tablecloth. With glossy evergreens and white Christmas roses and holly berries, this looks particularly stunning at Christmas.

Hand-made toys can often be found at craft markets or toy shops which import Scandinavian wooden toys. These may be just the things to add dash to a flower display in a modern room so do look at them with fresh eyes before handing them over to the children! Close to my home there is a school for handicapped girls and they design and make quite beautiful wooden horses and carts of this kind. The colours are bright, strong, clear and cheerful and very English-looking. An inner dish can generally be fitted into the carts to hold water, and such items look excellent piled high with fruits or preserved and dried flowers.

Another rather stagey look can be created by placing candles of modern shapes among flowers to give height. The specialist candle shops have dozens of these surprising shapes. Some, indeed most, are far too beautiful to be lighted and so may be placed in an arrangement and enjoyed for a long time. There are candles shaped like Twenties' white porcelain ladies, fishes and fruits, even like those boxes of jelly sweets with fruity centres! There are birds and lovely tumbling clowns, mock jam tarts, and memorable knickerbocker glories in tall wax 'glasses'. Integrated in a variety of ways, they add something new and fantastic to flowers and foliages in a certain style of setting.

Party flowers

Half the fun of a party is visual and if on entering a room the table looks interesting or amusing the evening might very well be off to a good start. Lighted candles with flowers are always useful to set the mood and their soft sparkle need not necessarily be in the high-flown banqueting style with silver candelabra and 'precious' flower designs which have taken us too long to complete.

Try a series of fat and cheerful candles set to stand in brightly painted tin lids to catch the drips, or on colourful little plates to match the dinner service. Among and round them flowers such as daisy chrysanthemums can trail and swing along the table-top. Many flowers will last well for a few hours out of water and I often use flowerheads grouped on the plates of a side table alongside home-baked pies, cheeses, and so on.

Almost until the present day flowers were regu-

larly used to decorate the food itself, but an unusual decoration to intrigue the guests at a party can be made by using vegetables and fruits cut into flowery shapes and presented as the table centre – an edible one! These look particularly appealing when displayed in a glass bowl.

You have to think of it a few hours earlier, preferably the day before the party. Spring onions and celery may be persuaded to take on attractive new shapes if the ends are scored gently before being dropped into iced water and left overnight in the refrigerator. By party time their ends will have curled back prettily on themselves. Radishes, too, can be deeply scored to create a flower-like shape.

Cucumber slices can also be made to look flower-like, while scarlet and green peppers could be cut into the shapes of leaves. Again, refrigerate overnight in iced water. Tomatoes, too, may be cut into fancy shapes and added to the decoration, which can be served on a crisp base of finely-chopped cabbage or lettuce – it is a dish of fresh edible plant material attractive enough for a maharajah! Watercress, forced chicory, and many other salad vegetables and fruits

Handmade toys can make unusual containers. This smart little horse and cart came from a workshop for handicapped girls and is shown here heaped with artificial crabapples

are as pleasant to look upon as to eat, when attractively and unusually presented.

Cheering up a kitchen

Different rooms in a house may quite well have utterly different characters. However beautiful, or unprepossessing the aspect of your kitchen and whether sunny, with modern work-saving surfaces or old-fashioned and cosy, flowers play a vital part.

I am a keen soup maker and I enjoy having many of the ingredients – the pretty pulses like lentils and split peas, pearl barley and suchlike – grouped in baskets about the kitchen as a source of instant yet constantly changing colour. I have an arrangement of fresh green parsley usually to hand on the window ledge, displaying itself in a little jug or a flower-sprigged pottery basket. Shop cress, crisp and growing and ready for daily cutting, makes a pleasant decoration in the neat white plastic container in which it is sold but is prettier still planted in a low container. I also save, and use in my kitchen for posies of garden flowers, those bright plastic baskets in which the high-class food halls sometimes offer grapes. These show off particularly well scarlet geraniums and a few leaves, fresh cut herbs or holly at Christmas-time.

Flower arrangements in the ever-busy surroundings of a kitchen definitely look odd if over-arranged. So keep them really simple, just popping in a few quick garden gatherings or leftovers from other arrangements or wild leaves and fruits as they come to hand, and use homely containers. Aim to delight and cheer the chief cook and bottle-washer!

Tall slim containers are usually out of place in a kitchen, as they can so easily be knocked over and become tiresome. Anything with too wide a spread is equally undesirable, as it gets in the way. However, a tiny bunched posy can generally be tucked in somewhere. Choose such a spot as the back of the breakfast bar, a window ledge with its potted plants, or the top of a kitchen fitment.

If your kitchen outlook is, like mine, rather dull, resolve to do something about it. Lighten your heart with something good to look at, make your own bright little scene. Using a bit of board as a base, and a couple of well pinholders (from the florist) for holding water and stems, right the way through the year you can have your own seasonable scaled-down 'view'. Coax a few just-budding branches into precocious flower or leaf and add two or three of the first primroses or the last blooms left from the indoor bulbs at their feet. A knot of shop-bought anemones might follow after.

A House by the Sea

Wide, open, luminous skies, reflections of water and tide-washed sand give many a home at the seaside a quality of light which is visually exciting. This same exuberance can be echoed in the flower decorations of modern coastal homes, their double glazing letting in all that clear strong light to add impact to designs in primary 'Mediterranean' colours which might seem garish in many other surroundings.

Old cottages at the seaside, with tiny wind-defying windows, allow in little of this splendid light, of course, and here it is good to retreat into their cosiness, with small, intimate arrangements, as in other cottage interiors.

In particular, seaside houses look good when decorated with arrangements on themes linking up with their salty surroundings. Such things as little shell boxes holding prettily-coloured dried seaweeds and simple wild flowers picked on the dunes, look

effective here; while in larger-windowed houses designs featuring wind-honed driftwood and wave-smoothed stones may have the addition of clustered flowers such as scarlet geraniums massed in blocks of vivid colour. These look well against a plain modern textured wall.

Driftwood

The seaside is a place where all flower arrangers seek driftwood, but in fact possibly the best is to be found up the inland creeks, edging land-locked lakes, and in old coppiced woodlands. Those of us lucky enough to live at the seaside, however, may enjoy the moments after the great winter storms when on the tideline we can pick up bits of ancient shell-encrusted plank (to make into bases for flower designs), pieces of discarded net, fishing floats, old spars, and other odd and interesting items brought in by the waves. Sometimes we will be lucky and find driftwood of beautiful texture and fine colour. But wherever we find it, driftwood undoubtedly looks well in the seaside home.

Carefully examine the wood from every angle before deciding how to place it decoratively in your design. Any pointed pieces often look best pointing skywards, to give a slim top to the decoration and a lead-in for the eye. Some driftwood stands well, with no help, while other pieces may take a little ingenuity to get them to stand up in the desired manner. The wood might be very lovely just by itself, and can be mounted on a slim base or larger block of wood. A big pinholder could be all that is required to make some driftwood stand upright, or a saw used to cut a level end to a piece. Two or more pieces interlocked together can be sometimes arranged, while a screw taken up through a wooden base and into the drift-wood is another method of standing, the base being perhaps made large enough to accommodate a small container for flowers or other plant materials.

Wood can be spray-painted if you wish, using car body paint, to suit the colour scheme of a room, or one can stain it with shoe dye, or polish it. At Christmas it may be frosted for yet another effect, using a light application of glue sprinkled with packet 'frost'.

For semi-permanent winter decoration use dried plant materials in company with your standing piece of wood. Such a group can look most effective at night if spotlit.

A piece or pieces of tall slim driftwood look striking when displayed wedged in the neck of some tall, heavy, vase-shaped container of bold character. You may, if you wish, add a few strong, visually heavy flowers or sculptured leaves as accompaniment, for a 'quickie' decoration. Aim for a well-defined, confident, flowing movement. As a counter-weight if the container is in danger of becoming top heavy, fill it with pebbles or wet sand.

Should your container, slim in itself, have width at the top this can look pleasing and unusual if after positioning the driftwood you fill the empty spaces at the top to the brim with sand, crushed marble or even broken windscreen glass for an echo of seaside sparkle. Similarly, a plain-coloured shallow dish with a pinholder towards the back and to one side can be filled with coarse sand or small matched pebbles to show off the distinctive tailored interest of the wood, with clusters of slightly larger rocks, a few flowers,

A seaside arrangement of wild flowers picked behind sand dunes and placed in a dolphin vase. The pebbles and the colour of the table make a perfect setting

and perhaps a figurine in sympathy with the line and the theme. Both ideas can produce a very calming oriental seascape effect.

Shells, stones and coral

Arrangements of shells and sea-stones in a low dish of modern shape can make a perfect backing for a few very short-stemmed flowerheads and leaves, which may provide an ever-changing pattern of colour. These can be charming on a windowledge where we can look down on them, or make a simple decoration for the dining table or the breakfast bar. The necessary water so stains and dapples the stones that their colours and textures are intensified. In a low bowl, possibly of coloured glass, an attractive arrangement can be made with bits of coloured bottle glass – so often found on the shore – with an arrangement of matching or toning long-stemmed flowers. If the pebbles are placed well under water the effect is rather like a little placid rockpool sprouting mysterious flowers.

To the holidaymaker or those who live by the sea, seaside gift shops 'in season' may be a flower arranger's delight, a perfect place to spend a damp or dismal day in seeking out treasure in the way of inexpensive accessories such as pottery seagulls or seahorses, little crab baskets, handsome foreign shells, ships in bottles, and all the paraphernalia with which these shops stock up. Perhaps because they can look gimcrack, many of us will pass them by. Maybe many of their items will be cheap-looking or tawdry, but not everything. The flower arranger will see possibilities in many ordinary-looking things, for she develops a 'seeing eye' as part of the hobby.

Sea fan and coral may be useful as a means of making a semi-permanent setting for a few strong shapes of wild flower seed skeletons, some pieces of shapely foliage, fruits or flowers, and certainly allow a few things to go a long, long way. Filigree sea fan, or sea fern (which by the way, is not from the vegetable kingdom but of animal origin) is usually rather difficult to impale on the pinholder, through the openings in chicken wire, or into a piece of flower foam, for more often than not it still has a hard piece, like a foot, sticking out at the base. With some sharp scissors or a knife trim it down to a slimmer shape, then wire or tape it to a short piece of stick, which not only provides a little additional height but also makes it possible to position it more easily in the design; on to the pins of a pinholder, for example.

Sea fan can be soaked for a few minutes in water to make it more malleable, and it will then take on gentle curves if rolled softly around the handle of a wooden spoon. It can be spray-painted any colour, and can look a million dollars at Christmas if dabbed lightly here and there with glue and dusted with gold, silver, blue, or green glitter from a packet.

Make a seascape

Creating a seascape – a seaside 'landscape' – can be fun. Sandpaper can be used for the base or another idea for making a base which I have found very successful is to cut a piece of thick cardboard into an interesting wavy-edged shape. Cover this all over with a little glue and apply a sheet of clear food-wrapping film, ruckling it into wave shapes as you stick it down, so that the effect is of wave-patterned sand or shallow water when the tide has receded.

Spray-paint it lightly with a mixture of delicate greens and blues and you will have an ever-useful base which will look lovely with blue-green sea holly (eryngium), pale roses, delphiniums, or small dahlias in soft blues, cream or salmon, with shells and pebbles. Pink tamarisk, which often grows near the sea, is useful for giving height, as is eucalyptus, and grasses such as maram grass from the sand dunes.

For large or complex designs, chicken wire or flower foam might be used, but a large well pinholder will often suffice. Small pieces of old garden fencing can be positioned in such a way that they suggest the old character of ancient sailing ships or wooden breakwaters.

Exciting collage

A suitable small piece or pieces of driftwood can be incorporated excitingly into a hanging collage. Using a backing such as a piece of chipboard or hardboard smoothly covered with hessian, linen, or some other fabric harmonious with the theme, you then create your own design upon it. I have successfully used an old cork bath mat for this purpose and have also found that woven rush place mats are equally effective.

If you wish your collage to stand away from the wall a little, secure four cotton reels or large corks behind it to keep it just proud of the wall. This can be useful if the plaster wall is rough or uneven, as often occurs in old properties, but as with all collage this feeling of extra depth adds a little drama to the effect overall.

Arrange shells, driftwood, dried flowers, perhaps undulating string to suggest wave movements, maybe a bit of fish netting made from the small bags which hold tangerines and nuts. Carefully position and move them around until you feel satisfied with the design, which is best kept flat in front of you on a table as you work.

Make quite sure the overall effect looks well balanced and as interesting as you can make it before sticking the pieces finally into position. Enjoy yourself interplaying textures and colours and provide depth by recessing some items; sticking them nearer to the backing than other items. The collage may be framed, but often looks as well just as it is, or edged with thick rope.

Town and Period Houses

A typical little town house in a terrace or square close to the centre of a town or city perhaps has only a small, neat front garden and a tiny walled affair at the back, with a square of lawn or paving and a bit of well tended border. Here tubs or a window box may be the only source of odd snippets of foliage for an arrangement with a geranium or two, if we are pressed, for a special occasion. A sheltered wall, however, could provide year-round sprays of ivy, roses in summer and sprigs of golden jasmine all winter. Such situations can be quite easily coaxed into providing a really wide variety of tremendously interesting things for seasonal cutting, with tubs well able to grow everything from bright spring bulbs to heathers, shrubs and summer annuals, and lots and lots of attractive evergreens with really pretty leaves, in a wide range of desirable colours.

Naturally, all new plants take some time to get sufficiently well established for us to cut much from them, or we may not wish to spoil the growing display. Women, however, are admirably adaptable and in such a situation can work well with what they have, backed up by the few flowers and sprays of foliage which can be bought from time to time. Here it is really possible to develop skills; to see all the wide possibilities of one-flower designs, for instance. Take a single shop-bought or garden rose with a short stem and back up its beauty with a few pressed autumn leaves (pressed with a hot iron under an old cloth to keep their full colour) for a really delightful flower-piece.

Or float flowerheads in a shallow dish of water with a few fresh leaves (possibly taken from a pot plant). Three flowers could be used in the setting of a well-shaped piece of branch wood, driftwood or tree bark, with the aid of a pinholder. Be on the lookout for, and treasure, all seedheads – those from the garden and wildlings too. You can spray-paint these for extra zip.

EXOTIC EXTRAS

Keep your eyes open in all the fascinating little delicatessens where they sell so many strange-looking fruits and vegetables nowadays; such things as fat and oh-so-beautiful French garlic, or exotic peppers with magnificent shiny orange, green or yellow skins,

and feel well blessed indeed. Our country cousins are less likely to have such sophisticated luxuries available to them for their arrangements!

Flower shops in towns and cities are usually far better stocked with a greater variety of plant material than elsewhere. There will be both fresh and silk flowers in more profusion, and stock will change more rapidly. There may well be wood 'flowers', fresh and preserved foliages and fir cones either bleached, or offered in the same warm colours as they grow. All of which can bring a country look to a house in town. There is certainly no need at all to go without the joy and the charm of flowers, nor is it necessary to break the bank to buy them; a single spray carnation when arranged in company with a few home-grown leaves will make a small design that will last for a fortnight.

Buying flowers

I believe anyone who lives in a town, far from green and growing things, specially needs to allow themselves the regular weekly treat of a few bought flowers. I would put them very high on my own shopping list, and we should all encourage our husbands, boyfriends, or children to 'think flowers' rather than buy us chocolates! I am not thinking of pounds to be spent but simply a cheerful spray of daisy chrysanthemums or such, even in the depth of winter, or a sweet posy or two of violets or February snowdrops.

An orchid, as an occasional luxury, may not be out of the question, for it will last for weeks and weeks and so is not all that expensive in the long run; it will certainly give a feeling of opulence to a room and to ourselves. Sprays and stems carrying a number of flower heads can all be cut so as to make a number of short stems if desired.

Spend your flower money wisely. Always choose fat budding or semi-open flowers, and this particularly applies to all the bulb flowers. Make sure any flowers with leaves on their stems, such as chrysanthemums, do in fact still carry the leaves. Market stalls and small flower shops where the turnover is not very fast will sometimes remove the leaves from ageing flowers. Always gently insist on selecting your own bunch or individual stems even if the florist actually takes them from the container. Leave behind any-

Flowers to match fruit, container to match accessories

Bunched French garlic on stiff stems, arranged as it was bought

thing which makes you feel it is even slightly suspect, such as drooping heads or a little browning on the petals, or in the case of chrysanthemums and dahlias any of the back petals beginning to drop.

As we get into the habit of buying flowers fairly regularly we will not only get to know the florists' shop assistants but also learn to recognize good buys when we see them. These may be the surprise treat of something out of the ordinary, such as a protea head or two which we can dry off in the container after enjoying them for a week or so as fresh flowers.

FLORISTS' FLOWERS

All those flowers we buy from the florist's shop should have been conditioned and be at crisp perfection at the time of purchase. And in any case, the more usual florists' flowers are specially chosen for their long-lasting qualities. All you need do on getting them home is cut off the bottom bit of each stem before arranging. If any flower flops over after it has been put into water – something anemones, roses, lilacs, and gerberas may sometimes do – simply re-cut their stalks and give them a shallow pep-up drink in some very hot water until, like magic, they pop up again.

In winter, when flowers are expensive and less plentiful, give them the longest possible life by not standing them on that dear little table next to the fire, on top of, or close to, a hot radiator, or in any other place where heat or a draught will strike them directly.

POSITIONING FLOWERS

Determine to make the very most of what you have by placing an arrangement right opposite the entrance to a room. A position such as a small table in the centre of a room can also be ideal and really catch the eye. Another idea is to gain added interest by linking an arrangement visually with the colour of a book jacket or magazine cover apparently casually placed close by, or linking up with a suitably coloured ornament or cushion cover.

Arrange fresh flowers in among the foliage of a flowerless pot plant, using small hidden containers to hold water, for an instant effect. Standing an arrangement against a complementary picture on the wall can be a very striking way indeed of drawing attention, for no more outlay than imagination in placement.

OPPOSITE Florists' shops in towns often carry unusual plant material. Here, dried embryo palm fronds and protea heads (which will dry off in the arrangement) accompany small antiques

Cut foliage

Even in the smallest town house which has no garden to speak of, it is usually somehow possible to grow a little foliage for cutting; use a tub or a window box out of doors; never be defeated! I would certainly grow hostas, for as cut fresh leaves they are marvellous and last for ages. Eventually they will dry out in the arrangement and turn a warm biscuit colour, in twisty shapes of the greatest usefulness. Though crisp and fragile, these last all winter long with care. Hostas have flowers, too, as does tough-as-old-boots bergenia (elephant's ear), which may colour well for you in winter when grown in a tub.

Ever-grey eucalyptus and evergreen skimmia (with the latter you have berries into the bargain), gold-dappled green *Elaeagnus pungens maculata* (sorry, I don't think this has a pet name), ivies, hellebores of every kind, rosemary, euonymus and blue rue are among a host of things possible for even a town house's tiny garden to produce.

Any strappy leaves such as iris (shop bought or from the garden), New Zealand flax (grown in the garden or in a big tub in a paved area), aspidistra (a few leaves from a pot plant) or yucca (grown in the garden or in a tub) may be arranged in a variety of interesting ways. To suit very up-to-date homes, use a pinholder in a bowl or small dish and impale one leaf firmly on to the pins then bend the tip right over to touch its own foot, pressing this on to the pinholder too; thus making a shape which encloses space in a very up-dated way. A design of great interest can be made using a number of leaves. This will last for months and might accompany a piece of driftwood, a few clustered flowers or some round-shaped leaves.

Don't throw away fallen or dying leaves from houseplants such as aspidistra, fatsia and grevillea. Instead, use them again and again in arrangements as they dry off to warm brown or creamy colours. They can be used with so many florists' and garden flowers.

Silk flowers

These are so realistic nowadays that often they have to be touched to prove they are artificial. As central-heating systems are switched on, possibly as early as October, and left on until spring, these flowers really do come into their own, for, of course, they will put up with the hot dry conditions which are an anathema to most flowers. I think they are lovely; small works of art in their own right. I enjoy using them about the house to back up the real flowers and plants, particularly on days when I am very busy.

Some silk flowers are real fantasy blooms, thought up by the people who produce them, in lovely opulent dream colours not seen in nature. But most are absolutely recognizable as our own well-loved garden or wild flowers; naturally, we take our choice. The 'new' colours may be chosen to link up with the colours in a room, and can be most decorative, especially if the décor is a little offbeat.

I have some pale apricot-pink oriental poppies which suit my dining room well, and I enjoy them in a tall alabaster Victorian container, arranged with toning carnations and their own silk leaves. The fact that their long slim stems bend easily is not the least of the advantages of silk flowers. They can be gently curved to assume absolutely any position and allow for the soft downward-flowing line over the rim of a container that is often so desirable. Endeavour to produce natural-looking curves rather than angular or erratically bumpy ones, which can never look like a growing stalk.

To curve them, hold each stem horizontally and stroke smoothly but firmly between finger and thumb in a downward movement until you are satisfied with the shape. Cutting the hard wires of the stems is another matter, and often defeats my flower scissors! Goodness knows why the makers provide them with such stout stalks, as in all flower arrangements it is usually necessary to cut stems down somewhat. Even informal flowery mixtures, casually displayed in low bowls, need some shaping to size. I find that wire-cutting Snips or garden secateurs and lots of bending the wire backwards and forwards on itself is required to sever the stems.

Silk flowers of springtime are exceptionally valuable, I find. For instance, I enjoy adding them to bowls of bulbs just waiting to come into flower. 'Planted' in real soil, moss or bulb fibre, silk flowers look lighthearted and pretty. I take them out as the real blooms begin to colour their buds, but return them to the bowl when these have gone over. With this method a bowl of bulbs can go on looking attractive and colourful for some months rather than weeks.

Bunched crocus and polyanthus are specially lovely, the mock hyacinths are superb, and though the snowdrops I have are rather too much on the large side to be really natural-looking, they too are a delight. Among the leaves of over-wintering house

A charming arrangement of real and silk strawberries and flowers in a doll's basket. Keep the silk flowers fresh by washing them regularly

plants without blooms, silk flowers have a real role to play.

And, simply clustered in a small container, the lily-of-the-valley are totally convincing. I particularly enjoy them opulently massed with their own light green mock leaves against the white woodwork of my bathroom window, where they innocently disport themselves with a pale soft backdrop of grey winter skies.

I use spring flowers made of silk most of the winter and on into early spring, as we await their real sisters coming into bloom. As with summer flowers, they only look right when used in their season. For summer, geraniums are very good indeed, as are lilies (orange, yellow and gold), cornflowers, peonies, nasturtiums, snapdragons – and there is even a most acceptable wild rose. For spring, sprays of forsythia and flowering dogwood are attractive and last year I bought silk tulips which I thought truly fine, and some very believable sprays of pussy willow.

When I come back home from a holiday it is nice, I always think, to be greeted with flowers about the house no matter what the time of year. Silk ones present a welcoming look in any room and they can be an excellent idea for leaving – along with a well-stocked freezer – if the woman of the house has to be away from home for a day or two!

Silk flowers turn up for sale all over the place. Flower-club sales tables are a good source of supply, as are the big stores, but florists' shops and nurseries invariably seem to hold the best stocks.

Many of these imported silk flowers are superb in every tiny detail, even down to the different shadings and textures on the stem of a rose. Some that I have at home have even been supplied with realistic thorns and sideshoots. Though I would never let them take over from real flowers completely, I must admit that I like, too, the sprays of geranium, rhododendron and hydrangea. These can be used to good effect in a little indoor window box, where they shine through the panes and give a jolly look from outside.

There are branches of silk ivy to use in a Christmas arrangement or to make up into an ivy ball tree. Silk flowered alpine strawberries, with tiny scarlet fruits, look endearing when 'planted' in pots all along a kitchen windowledge in a gardenless town house or flat at any time.

I personally dislike to see silk house plants but if you really cannot grow house plants well, and if a sunless corner indoors demands the colour of a croton, dieffenbachia, dracaena or ivy, then the cash outlay on a silk plant could be the answer.

Foliage is often extremely difficult to get in towns, of course, and silk leaves and sprays can be helpfully realistic, either teamed up with real fresh or preserved flowers or with silk blossoms. Don't leave your mock flower, fruit or foliage arrangement standing around forever gathering dust and failing to charm any more because it has become so familiar. Rearrange it, change it and store it away from time to time.

All the silk flowers and leaves will wash, by the way. Simply swish them around in water with detergent in it, rinse and, although it looks odd, hang them out to dry on a good blowy day! In very damp conditions, silk flowers can get mildew and this is almost impossible to remove.

Wood 'flowers'

Also most popular at the moment, and easy to find in the shops and on flower club sales tables, are imported 'flowers' made from wood shavings. Many of these are made from left-over shavings in the furniture-making industry in Florence, and very attractive they are too, often stained in the most amazing colours. It should be possible to find something to 'lift' even the most dull or difficult of colour schemes.

Though not cheap to buy, they do last for years. However, the colour may fade a little if an arrangement is left in strong sunlight. These flowers are all hand-made and coloured with natural dyes and look well with antique wood. Flower making has now become a surprise cottage industry in many parts of Italy, with mothers and daughters sitting round their kitchen tables and taking for their real-life patterns the many fresh mountain flowers of Italy.

Wood flower stems are usually rather straight and stiff but they can be coaxed to take on curves suitable for specific designs. These 'flowers' can be arranged with fresh or preserved leaves, of course. Using fresh foliage necessitates water for the stems, so, preserve the bottoms of your wooden 'flower' stalks and prevent them from rotting by varnishing the lower parts with paint or nail varnish.

I much enjoy using these lovely make-believe flowers cascading informally among fresh fruits; simply sticking the somewhat shortened stems into spaces around them, possibly adding a few preserved leaves. At the moment I have a low design on my dining table, using these flowers in a variety of tones and tints of warm rich apricot and peach. They are arranged with trails of grapes, and clusters of fresh apricots, and nectarines. With dark brown beech leaves to match the 'eyes' of the flowers and set on a soft toning cloth, the effect is really rather grand!

Table decorations

For a dinner party when days are overfull, you may very well find that silk or wood flower and foliage arrangements are most useful, for they can be done in good time – even the weekend before – and look most acceptable and pleasant when seen under the soft light of lamps or candles.

Possibly you should choose different flowers, whether fresh or artificial, for a lunch party as the different lighting should be taken into account. Blues and dark reds, for example, sometimes do not light as well as yellow, white and pale pink. Silk flowers light up very well.

With today's informal eating, however, it is the warm unspoken note of welcome all flowers provide which is their main delight. Even though we may not have very many flowers around the house normally, when friends come for a meal most of us like to make that extra effort. If you are serving the meal at the dining table it is worth taking a long look at the table itself, trying to see it afresh as a plain, clean shape in the room upon which, like an artist, you can 'paint' your design, using the place settings, tablecloth, and so on with a flower container to create a really superb effect.

Take into account whether the table is round or oval, square or oblong. Is its surface plain or highly polished? Does it show off beautiful markings in the wood? Or is it old and badly marked and so has to be covered with a cloth? Is it surrounded by dining chairs with plain wood or rush seats, or are there

White and yellow roses arranged with easy grace make a splendid table centrepiece for a summer party

cushion squabs made to tone or match with the curtains? When you first enter the room how do you first see the table – long and running away from you or across your line of vision? What lies at the back of it – plain or patterned window curtains which at night will be drawn; a view of garden or fields, an un-cluttered wall, or a wall with pictures or decorative plates, or a display of books? How do you like to lay the table – with or without a table cloth; picture table mats, or mats of rush? Do you serve the food from the table itself, or do guests help themselves from a side table or from a heated trolley, so leaving a little more space to play with on the dining table?

If you keep these things in mind, you can always achieve a table which will link with your own unique setting and so reflect your own lifestyle. If you have chosen a room which is comfortable and friendly, possibly a little cluttered already, the table decorator with its background of the table's own wood or a plain cloth, can be effective but quietly soothing. Spotlit it can be stunning, the darkness round about adding drama to the effects of the flowers.

A low, natural rush basket (a round shape for a round table), or a number of tiny baskets with handles and hidden containers for water by each place setting, can look remarkably effective. The baskets might be filled with tiny mixed garden flowers or all one kind of bloom, such as bunched-in-the-hand scarlet roses frilled with their own leaves. Seasonable fruits like

Another, but quite different, arrangement using roses with mixed foliage all held low on a concealed pinholder in a shallow glass dish

shop-bought or garden cherries and strawberries, redcurrants, or even pretty small vegetables, winter oranges, grapes, or lemons – which your guests could take home – interspersed with plain green leaves, might pick up the colour or the design on patterned plates and vegetable dishes or the colour of the table napkins and cloth.

A china rabbit sitting on a deep plate with little spring flowers massed around him can be fun, especially if children are present. Plain china or pottery, pewter, brass or copper (the metals looking very pleasant when reflecting night lighting) always fit in well in a rural setting. Flowers arranged decoratively on to a base with a hidden container make pleasant decorations. But for the very important occasion do bring out the sparkle of silver if you have it and arrange the flowers – though still informally –

around candlesticks, a silver cake dish, or whatever you happen to have.

An idea from the past Anyone who has ever fancied that flower arrangement is something only of our own age would perhaps be surprised at this description of an Edwardian 'yacht luncheon' from a book of the period:

'A miniature toy yacht filled with dark red clove carnations stood in the centre of the table on a low waving bank of greenery and moss to give the effect of foaming billows. Little vases in the shape of dolphins held the same flowers. The dinner service was pale green, the glass very pale green too.'

Women have always enjoyed dreaming up unusual schemes for parties. The fact that this particular affair was on the deck of a houseboat, under a brilliant awning, with ropes of flowers hung from the rigging, matters not at all. A similar centrepiece, suitable for a special party could easily be worked out and children would love it.

Period rooms

Period rooms with small antiques and a light feeling of calm and gracious living are lovely to decorate with flowers. However, as with any other sort of home, the arrangements do not need to be very ornate or elaborate and the plant material used need not be very expensive.

These days, antique containers are often far too valuable to risk being broken while in use, but such things as flower-painted china urns and classical tazzas can often be incorporated into the decoration by arranging the flowers so that they encompass it, using hidden containers. Fruits and, of course, leaves in company with flowers seem especially harmonious here, and long-lasting very decorative still-life groups can be arranged very easily.

Silk, leather, and velvet-covered bases are particularly effective. You could incorporate an antique clock, a picture or a figurine into the design. Marble-topped furniture is an ideal setting and is less liable to water damage. Care must clearly be taken with fine wood, and one can copy an idea often seen in stately homes of using a piece of clear glass under each container.

Vegetable tureens and deep flowery bowls make idyllically deep water containers for the mixed border flowers of any season, and fit in well with the feeling of these period rooms. Though our own home may not be of exactly stately proportions, it can well carry such decorations. Merely cut them down to size by down-grading the size of the container and the number of flowers.

Not so often seen is the all-one-kind-of-flower arrangement, but this can look stunning when flowers are plentiful and is an excellent way of displaying, say, one's whole collection of preserved hydrangea heads. When flowers are featured on a china container, their colours and possibly a repeating of them in the real flowers can be attractive.

An unusual and very distinctive decoration for a library or shelves groaning with grand-looking books is to decorate an occasional spine with a bookmark made of ribbon decorated with flowers. Use bright silk or preserved flowers and leaves, their individual stems pressed into a small square of dried flower foam stuck firmly to the ribbon. Imported wood 'flowers' or small cones can look magnificent. The effect is specially fine at Christmas, with wide red flock bookmarks used along with the festive decorations.

A bookmark of silk and preserved flower heads, their stems pressed into flower foam stuck to a broad ribbon

IN THE SITTING ROOM

Any sitting room, to please me and I hope to please you too, must have its flowers. The flower arranging experts used to advise no more than one arrangement in a room. I could never see the sense in that. I am just greedy, I suppose, and like a number of arrangements around my sitting room; nothing too big or over-dramatic, just interesting or very pretty.

One arrangement may be quite simply a trail of grapes running across the top of a shallow urn, with three magnificent garden roses or yellow azalea heads. I find plastic grapes very acceptable. The double pink Constance Spry roses look tremendous with purple grapes. By the way, dried flowers are particularly suitable for use with valuable containers in that they are very light, don't need water, and if no mechanics, such as chicken wire, are used there is nothing to cause scratches or damage. A third arrangement might feature a mixture of jewel-coloured leaves, clustered, like gems, in a box.

Wine and coffee tables, any little antique table by the side of an armchair or sofa, are obvious places to stand a few flowers. The mantelshelf, the focal point of many rooms, is another prime position. Try running an arrangement grandly, all along the top of

Tiny artificial grapes show off two lily flowers all arranged in an antique tazza

it, using one or more hidden containers, or try a collection of small posy holders placed between the usual ornaments, arranged like Victorian posies with neat frills of leaves.

A small bunch of fresh flowers can make life seem special, too, when friends call for a gossip over tea. It does not have to be over-showy or difficult to make; just a few stems can be put together in a moment even for an unexpected visitor to make a talking point and a feeling of extra warmth. Certainly low mounds of fresh flowers, such as massed rose or geranium heads, marguerites, or daisy chrysanthemums – anything of a round shape – with a few pointed leaves make quickie eye-catchers. Again if they match the china in some way they are perhaps nicer still.

Reflected glory I often stand flowers in front of a looking glass to make a few look remarkably like a lot! Of course, then it is necessary to make sure that the back of the arrangement looks as good as the front. Arrange some leaves and a few blooms at the back to look at themselves in the mirror, so that the reflection is of flowers and not just a back view of a lot of stalks.

Placing the arrangement onto a bit of mirror glass is always charming, and very Edwardian, fitting in well with small antiques as well as with the more

modern furnishings. I have often thought I would like to have special light-reflecting mirror glass tops made for low bookshelves and occasional tables, for just this purpose. A mirror in a gilded or modern wood or metal frame could be used as a base for an arrangement in the centre of a dinner table. Mirror tiles are available from the shops, and these too can be used, either singly for small designs or with a number placed together to form a base for a bigger arrangement.

When using mirror glass in this way, arrange for some flowers or little trails of leaves or fruits to peep down at their own reflections. Snowdrops are particularly endearing when arranged in this way – try it and you will see why.

IN OLD WINDOWS
I much enjoy flowers in old windows. However, very sunny windows are obviously not really suitable on those rare very hot days, and even winter sunlight can generate a lot of heat through glass.

The antique dining table is a most suitable place for flowers. It seems a shame only to have flowers here on those high days and holidays when someone special is coming to eat with us. If there is just no time for more, use preserved or mock flowers and fruits. Alternatively foliage plants can be decked out with additional fruit or flowers, silk or real, or very uncomplicated designs can be made with a few flowers and leaves floated on water or grouped on pinholders in a shallow dish.

For a party, neat knots of flowers in low containers (even something as low-life as painted margarine tubs if you have nothing else handy) may be attractively grouped together or run the length of a long table. Most attractive and easy on the eye for a party are looped ribbons and flowers in colours to match the table mats or the tablecloth and napkins, with trailing fruits between them.

BEDROOMS AND BATHROOMS
Perhaps you do not think of flowers in association with your bedroom, but I do with mine! I like flowers by my bed on a small table covered with a pale green silk cloth. A poor sleeper, I enjoy simply-bunched scented flowers, such as summer jasmine or sweet

A stately autumnal arrangement of berries with a variety of foliage frames a window. This can be made well in advance for a party

Even in a town house with no garden it is usually possible to find a few individual flowerheads and some foliage taken from a pot or windowbox

peas clustered with a few leaves in a low container. On summer nights the odd spray of night-scented stock or mignonette I do commend to you, and I always arrange to have posies on the dressing table when visitors come to stay.

In a very feminine bedroom a friend of mine has arranged a delightful decoration of artificial and dried flowers as a frieze round the top of the walls. Caught up with ribbons, the flowers are wired on to fine rope in romantic garlands and swag drops, to match the delicate colours of her bedroom curtains and dressing table drapes.

Another idea is to arrange flowers in association with something you collect. A collection of pottery animal ornaments, for instance, might be decked out with flowery neckbands or halters, by sticking preserved flowers to fine ribbons. A base is effective when displaying them as a group.

Personally, I like to see a flower or two in the bathroom. And in my own home scarlet fruits and flowers seem just the thing to enliven the bathroom window ledge, for the room has a blue and white theme. Preferably the flowers will be fresh; in practice, and more realistically, they are usually mock!

But when guests are expected I usually find time to pop a specimen or two of anything a little out of the ordinary or very pretty into a little container for the downstairs cloakroom. I think it gives pleasure and adds interest. The sort of things I have in mind are very tiny flowers, such as childhood's 'hundreds and thousands' (Virginia stock) which I find are always commented upon, as they are not often seen nowadays, or flowers from a Christmas cactus, or a sprig from an African violet house plant.

Breakfast in bed It is always enjoyable to treat an overnight visitor to the luxury of breakfast in bed. Why not take a little bit of extra trouble and make the day begin doubly delightfully by decorating the breakfast tray with an under-six-inch high flower arrangement in a small container of some kind, perhaps in colours closely matching the crockery? A few sprigs of moorland heather kept from a day in the country, a stem or two of lightly-scented freesia, some daisies from the lawn or a knot of shop-bought snowdrops would be lovely. Even in the tiniest flat there must be somewhere to hide the posy overnight so that it comes out as a complete surprise.

CHILDREN'S BEDROOMS

Young girls' rooms these days are often sweet and very endearing, having a fresh just-blown-up-from-the-country look about them. Flowers here can be most appealing, adding the delicate finishing touch. Perhaps chosen to match the lacey bedspread or the daisies or rose sprigs on the curtains, flowers can be arranged in soft and romantic ways.

Mums can do a lot to encourage even an untidy girl to take an interest in her room and indirectly to become enthusiastic about flowers and flower arranging. Many girls, although bogged down with homework, will see what they can do to make their room a happier and more relaxing place. They might even like to spend pocket money occasionally or receive a surprise present of a little beribboned bunch of tiny silk or preserved flowers to sit on the bedside table or on the floor by the window.

A young girl I know collects dolls' hats and these make an enchanting collection which is displayed by her bed on the pegs of a pale-blue painted hatstand made for her by her father. She has framed the hatstand with trails of pale flowers and decorates the little hats with knots of ribbons and little artificial flowers. Even her old teddy bear, I noticed, sits on her bed holding everlasting flowers in his paws. The imaginative person will realize that things for holding flowers don't always have to be the conventional ones!

A tiny bunch of blooms picked fresh from the garden, perhaps chosen to match the first pots of make-up she has ranged on her dressing table, or a basket of dried creamy-white gypsophila (arrange it fresh, out of water, and it will dry itself) looks equally delightful and picks up the light airiness of curtain nets or bedspreads. Set the gypsophila with coloured butterflies (cut out of magazines or other pictures) to win an instant feeling of liveliness and romance.

There are many most attractive dried flowers available, and they come in all the clear fresh pinks and yellows and blues so suitable in this kind of room. There is statice (don't go for bunches containing lots of dark purples for this room), pink acroclinium and

Spoil guests when they stay overnight; take them breakfast in bed with a tiny arrangement of seasonal flowers – even more charming if the colours match the crockery

delicately-coloured grasses in all the sweetpea colours to arrange in airy ways.

These ideas will equally well apply to any romantic feminine room setting, whether upstairs or down. Very young children (and some girls) will possibly be more appreciative of bolder and more vivid schemes, using real or mock plant material in blocks of primary colours, rich scarlets and clashing reds and pinks, butcher blue, all the singing yellows and sunny oranges, arranged in cheap pottery or plastic of bright colours.

Get them to help you arrange giant-sized silk sunflowers, or home-made ones produced from coloured card. Arrange the flowers around a favourite toy and you indirectly teach a child really to look at things – I began flower arranging when I was four. Youngsters, once hooked on the idea of flower arranging, can become very imaginative, and anything at all which will hold flowers, such as a toy wooden train or fire engine can be used.

Bring in budding catkins in the spring so that the children can watch them opening, and slice off carrot or turnip tops which, put in a little water inside a colourful plastic saucer, can be watched as the days go by, to see the emerging new green leaves.

Flats and Bedsits

Though we may live in a tiny rented bed-sitting room or a sky-high flat we need never feel deprived of beauty, for we can make flowers very much a part of our lives. On a wet Saturday or Sunday afternoon life can sometimes seem dull and drab. But it need not be if we have flowers to amuse us. If we have no flowers we can design with fruit and vegetables, even things like lentils, slipping out to the shops to choose a few items for their exciting shapes and colours, discovering as we mass them the possibilities of interplaying their textures and shapes, and just have fun relaxing with them – and eating them later on!

In a small compact home housework is, happily, usually quickly done, and so we are lucky to have more time to make flower arranging into a really special hobby. Living in a small space possibly means that lots of large and splendid containers cannot be accommodated, or plant material stored, or big designs attempted. Turn the problems into advantages. One idea is to concentrate on, and make your own speciality, the petite and miniature designs, dried plant collages for hanging on the wall, and pressed flower pictures – the ideas are endless.

Get together an intriguing collection of very small containers in metal, pottery, glass, or wood, and you may even like to make a few of your own designing.

OPPOSITE Flowers preserved from summer days, arranged in a basket. These butterflies are hand painted on card but could easily have been cut out of a magazine

Select everything carefully and thoughtfully. Don't buy or hold on to uninteresting shapes or poor quality things you will never use. If you have enough room you can make a feature of your pretty collection, which certainly does not have to be large to make an impact. Grouped together in an alcove with shelves, on a room divider, or in a china cabinet, arranged with care such a collection can become a really unusual and enviable eye-catcher, and ever-useful into the bargain. Small-scale figurines might make a secondary collection.

Adapt everyday objects and learn to look at all things with an eye to their possibilities as flower holders. This is exactly what people did in the past. Some of the earliest paintings of flower arrangements show flowers in jugs and tumblers.

You may like to spend time in creating and designing quite complex flower arrangements, working towards scaled-down perfection. You could think about entering flower arrangement shows, where even the gardenless flat dweller can become famed for miniature and petite designs.

Miniature arrangements

Miniatures for competition work are tiny delights which would fit into the palm of your hand, measuring not more than four inches in any direction. Think of them standing in an empty cube of that size. Of course, at home they can be made slightly larger than that, but it is fun to try your hand at the true show miniature.

Miniatures can be displayed alone, or perhaps even better in a group, at eye level on a shelf or even a suitable window ledge. Often the container chosen is far too large. An eggcup or wineglass may look very small in relation to a clematis flower, but in relation to a truly miniature bloom, such as a hawthorn flower, it then appears too dominant. Little shells, a lipstick case, a bottle top, a button, a jar lid, a pill box, a bit of driftwood, a pebble with a small indentation in it, such things can be adapted or used as they are as containers.

Suitable bases might be a tiny mirror glass, a thin flat pebble, a small oval of coloured card, a scrap of velvet-covered card, a bit of lichened tree bark. For a winter scene in miniature, sea salt or granulated sugar can suggest snow inside a tiny flat container when using dried flowers.

Hold fresh stems in place in a little damp Oasis foam on a carpet tack stuck into the bottom of the container with Plasticine or glue. For dried miniature arrangements, use one of the dry foams such as Drihold in exactly the same way. Do not have too big a piece of the foam or it may be difficult to hide it with your tiny pieces of plant material. A few twists of fuse wire may be useful, but do experiment for yourself; an informal placing of flowers can be charming.

Some people find tweezers useful for inserting stems in miniature arrangements, but I have always been more at ease arranging in the normal way with my fingers. Manicure scissors can be ideal for pruning tiny branches. A cuticle stick is invaluable for pressing minute things into place or making holes in the foam to take soft-stemmed flowers. An eye-dropper is often used for watering, and a fine mist spray will keep the fresh things alive and well for a long time if suitable long-lived plant material has been chosen in the first place.

Clearly, a miniature of preserved flowers and leaves will last a long time – until you are sick of it or it accidentally gets knocked over! Fresh or dried materials which are suitable for sketching in the outline shape of a miniature include such things as vine tendrils, a few tips of conifer, sea lavender, or golden rod, grasses, curvy twigs or tips of ferns, and for main interest individual flowers of plants such as escallonia, stonecrop, anaphalis (pearly everlasting), *Alchemilla mollis* (lady's mantle), and many teeny-weeny rock plants or individual flowers removed from larger sprays.

Tiny rosettes of succulents are excellent, and when looked at as suitable material for a miniature many minute seedheads are just as enchanting. Blue-grey, gold, copper, and tan heathers or sprays from miniature roses and the smaller ivies, as well as grass blades, can be used for tiny foliage.

Miniature accessories As you begin experimenting with miniature flower arranging you may well be inspired, as with other forms of the art, to extend your interest by going on to collect special accessories to scale. A shop close to my home specializes in dolls' houses and their furnishings. Many toy shops hold similar miniature items, though these will possibly be mass-produced. They make an excellent extension to flower arranging as a hobby. Displayed together

A miniature arrangement needs miniature accessories

with miniature arrangements, you can create a most intriguing form of decoration in tune with a small home – an endearing little room within the room.

I recently bought a miniature Victorian doll measuring under 5 in, a number of miniature containers, a pint-sized model of a Victorian plant stand, a tiny white table, a silver candlestick not as big as a match, and made myself a circular table to hold the candlestick, using the stopper from a tablet tube and, for the table top, a slim circular box which once held cream rouge. They are all displayed together like a small scene; I love it, and it creates tremendous interest when friends come to call. In such ways we can bring extra attention to our small-detailed flower arrangements which might otherwise never gain such an interested public! Other accessories might be a birthday cake candle, a little animal or bird figure, miniscule seashells, cake decorations and various farmyard or zoo toys of the right size. Many of these will even make possible tiny landscapes with great appeal and individuality.

Petite arrangements

A petite arrangement, at any rate for those who enter competitions, is something which measures under nine inches but more than four inches. In other words, it is the next size up from the true miniature. Arrangements round about this size are really very useful, fitting so well into many of today's rooms. A petite arrangement is the sort of sweet little decoration which looks delightful on a coffee table or a small table by the side of a favourite chair.

It is a very suitable size indeed for the informal bunch of leaves and flowers gathered from the very small garden or some spring or winter violets bought from a flower shop. Most of us have lots of little containers around which will hold such a small display easily and prettily. I am always on the lookout for containers of this so-usable size; they are, I find, usually inexpensive.

For instance, I recently bought a pair of charming Twenties' vases shaped like tulip heads. These cost under two pounds from a market junk stall, and a modern gourd-shaped bowl found on another day was about the same price. Wine glasses, with both plain and coloured bowls and stems, a copper milk measure, a rose-sprigged china cup and saucer, a small green-stained wooden paper clip box which will hold a water container, and a 'Present from Hastings' mug are all part of my collection.

I also collect pottery birds, with holes in their bases, and I find these turn up quite often on junk stalls. The fact that many seem to have lost the tips of their beaks doesn't really seem to matter! They were all the rage between the wars, for standing in the centre of shallow pottery bowls. They display a few flowers in an interesting way, for the bases will usually hold water.

A petite arrangement in a vase shaped like a tulip head bought from a market junk stall

The doll measures under four inches and is accompanied by an arrangement made of real and silk blooms. An attractive way to display flowers when space is limited

From a Cotswolds craft shop selling turned wooden items I recently bought a delightful little 'grass pot' made for displaying just a few stems of grasses or a dried seedhead or two in a homely way. I chose one made of sycamore, beautifully turned so as to show the fascinating patterning of the wood. All of them were different, individual, and I wished afterwards that I had bought more in other sizes. I thought how they would have made a pleasant grouping of slightly different heights, with the delicate tints of the various woods mingling casually with small dried plant materials arranged in them.

One thing, of course, leads to another and in seeking suitable things to please the eye when displayed in my grass pot I noticed how, in a late summer garden tub, Livingstone daisies had made strikingly-shaped seedheads like tiny carved wooden sunflowers of a perfect size for these containers. At the foot of the tiny group, which I placed on the dining room mantelpiece, I ran a trail made of a few creamy-coloured beans and thought how a few lentils would have suited a wood which had a more apricot-coloured glow. Acorns and beech mast would go with other woods.

Mounds of fruit I am always charmed by the effect of low richly-heaped mounds of small fruits or ever-lasting flowers, bunched berries, fresh flowerheads on short stems, nuts and cones displayed in close clusters. At the moment I have a delightful small flowerpiece in my sitting room, made of lightly-massed heads of dried pink roses, informally grouped on top of a low bowl holding rose-scented pot-pourri.

These diminutive, appealing designs require no special mechanics; they simply support themselves – so long as you don't attempt to go too high! They show off any small dried or preserved things to great advantage in many a suitable container, which can be anything from textured modern pottery to a china

A varied mound of real and mock fruits and flowers, shells and foliage displayed in a vase of alabaster and surmounted by a bird

bowl, an antique tazza to a saucer, or a wooden box.

Delicately-coloured dried flowers and leaves in all the creamy pinks, softest baby blues, delicate apricots, pale yellows, and almond greens can look specially enchanting when arranged this way in a mother-of-pearl shell. Wrap clear kitchen film right over the top and round the container, and you have a very acceptable small Christmas or birthday gift – the wrap can be removed on presentation if you wish.

Flowerball trees

The most delightful standard rose or other flowery 'trees' can be made, for standing in the centre of your dining table, in a window, or on a side table for a special 'do', using a piece of dowel covered with ribbon, pushed into a block of Styrofoam fitted securely inside a decorative container. On top of the dowel, spike a round ball of Styrofoam held in place with a crosspiece made from a bit of dowel or a stick, bound on with sticky tape.

Now press short-stemmed silk or dried flowers and leaves all over it in a fairly regular pattern, so that it resembles one of those formal clipped trees in a tub which you see in old-fashioned pictures of doll's

houses. Flowers can be cut with short stems and pressed close all over the Styrofoam or arranged, still close-packed, but in a more casual and 'fluffy' manner, to make a larger tree.

At Christmas, brightly-coloured plastic fruits, mock birds, and real leaves make a truly festive decoration. Indeed, this could even be turned into your inexpensive Christmas tree by hanging doll's-house size items, and tiny parcels for your guests, on ribbons all over it. Fresh flowers and leaves can be used, of course, in exactly the same way, except that then you will require a water-soaked ball of Oasis foam (in place of the Styrofoam) to hold the living stems.

'Wall flowers'

When home is small, anything which can be hung on a wall will be an advantage. It is possible to create something pleasing to suit the room exactly and its owner very inexpensively indeed. It can be whatever our fancy makes of it. Some of us might dream up an idea for a beautiful seed collage, others an old-world dried or pressed flower picture, and most of us would enjoy a fresh or dried flower posy in a wall holder. The flowers used can be sweet and traditional, with masses of character or in a different kind of room can seem strong, up-to-date and vital; much depends upon the container.

Certainly the size can be made to fit exactly the space available and the design might be hung by itself on an uncluttered wall, or grouped imaginatively with other things to create an impact. This can be bold or gentle, just depending on exactly how we choose to present it.

Containers to hang on a wall, both modern and antique, are a pleasure to seek out and, once again, collecting these can make an interesting hobby. Particularly in a small room it is good to be able to have a selection of containers which can be changed now and then.

Try not to think of a wall vase as being something like a picture which, in the average household, once placed has to stay in situ for ever and ever, so that nobody notices it any more. Use your wall as an artist would use an empty canvas, as a means of displaying things which give you pleasure.

With a number of wall containers to hand, they can be used singly or in groups to show off a single full-petalled rose, a gathering of mixed garden flowers, or a few attractive woodland leaf rosettes. Massed with a

Magnolia flowers, iberis, prunus and viburnum in a pretty cherub wall vase. Such an arrangement can be linked to the colour of the room curtains

cascade of such things as ivy or fruits such as grapes, or clustered with any short-stemmed plant material you happen to have, they can do a lot for a room which may need a little extra visual interest.

I have a good variety of hanging containers collected with pleasure over the years, and which I bring out from time to time – all do not need to be on display at once. Some are even amusing, such as a pair of modern black and gold lacquered owlets which I hang together, one slightly higher and to one side of its fellow. They do not, in fact, hold water but with a small wedge of modelling clay or dried flower foam set tight inside tiny apertures at the top of each head they look very striking when decoratively presenting things like jewel-coloured dried helichrysum flowers. They also make an offbeat decoration with scarlet berries, rosehips, or haws (sprayed with clear varnish or painted with nail lacquer, these last very well). The addition of pale cream and emerald-coloured leaves (possibly dried and spray-painted) and small cones is visually exciting.

Sometimes for a party I hang them above the drinks table, where they look well, each displaying a low headdress of green leaves on which I cluster shiny gold and scarlet foil-wrapped luxury chocolates. A stainless steel or coloured plastic knife drainer (with a hidden container inside for water) can look just as effective, making possible some very novel wall hangings in a modern setting. Heaped with little oranges or crab apples (real or artificial) set off with gilded leaves, no-one could possibly pass them by!

Interesting hanging shapes in pottery, such as mock paper bags held up by strings, ballet shoes, and similar novelties might well suit a town flatlet with a young light-hearted family, possibly echoing the special interest of one of them. Otherwise, antique wall containers in the shape of cornucopias, woven baskets, cherubs and such are decorative in the extreme in more traditional surroundings.

Very up-to-the-minute painted metal containers of generously wide triangular shape can be found to fit in with most interiors. All wall arrangements look best, on the whole, at eye level and they are then easier to tend. When topping up water levels do remember that water will drip devastatingly down the wall if your over-generous hand pours the water above the hole for the hook. Indeed, this is a point worth watching when choosing such a container as the hole is sometimes a long way below the rim. If your container starts to syphon water over the rim, look for the offending leaf or stem, for you will usually find that one is touching the rim and acting as a syphon.

Seed pictures

During the past few years many people have become fascinated by the homely art of making pictures and collages from seeds, and have been amazed to discover the wide variety of beauty easily obtainable from the shelves of the supermarket or the petfood and garden shops. In the grocery chainstore we can find a whole range of visual excitements for our purpose from rough-textured black peppercorns to bright orange lentils, split green peas, grey or white pudding rice and dark-rosy-red beans.

From the pet store come pretty tan-coloured linseeds, sunflower seeds (with their beautiful brown-black striping) and golden maize. Garden seeds include many which can be saved from the borders or vegetable plot like the jet-black seeds of grape hyacinths, the dark brown and oddly-shaped seeds of honesty, and purple kidney beans. Then there are the dessert fruit seeds of oranges, grapes and melons saved after enjoying the fruit. Once we start on *this* hobby, life is never quite the same again!

As well as a mix of interesting seeds you will need something to stick them on, such as a piece of stiff cardboard, hardboard, or plywood. This may be covered with silk, felt, rough linen or coloured card, or it can be used as it is. A frame to fit the backing will be desirable in some cases. Adhesive such as Uhu or Copydex, tweezers, a flat stick for spreading the glue, and possibly some polyurethane varnish to give a protective coating to the completed design, are other requirements.

Start by sorting the seeds into small boxes or jars. Roughly sketch onto the backing the design you have in mind. I have found very useful the special paints which can be removed from fabrics with a damp cloth if you make a mistake with the drawing. Begin with some very simple outline shape like a sunflower or daisy head, a tree, or a leaf form. You might eventually go in for clever abstracts or human and animal figures or landscapes, and so on, even portrait heads! Those who do not draw can use an iron-on transfer.

Attach the seeds by spreading a thin film of glue over the design, a little at a time. Work from the top downwards. Press each seed into place with a teaspoon handle or a nail file. Do not allow any glue to come over the top of the seeds. A seed dispenser bought from a garden shop can be really useful for placing small seeds accurately. Bigger items could be positioned individually.

Allow to dry thoroughly before brushing over the completed design with polyurethane varnish. Then frame or mount the work to suit your room. It could be fun to make a series of linking pictures, perhaps depicting the seasons or subjects which are personal to you, like up-dated Victorian samplers. You could pick out your name, the date, and perhaps a little motto, spelt out in seeds or preserved flower petals. Absolutely anyone can develop a flair for this if they are willing to have a go at being inventive and ingenious.

Window Boxes, Balconies and Patios

The successful growing of plants in containers on
balcony, patio and roof garden reflects the owner's ingenuity
in painting a picture with plants. Local conditions,
such as the aspect, amount of light, available
soil, exposure to wind must all be considered but even the
smallest space offers a foothold for a pot of flowers.

Window boxes and containers

The majority of people, I believe, first think about their patio, balcony, roof garden and window-box plants in the spring, although to my mind the gardening year really starts with the autumn planting season. There is a very good reason for this, in that many of the plants we grow get away to a much quicker start in the following spring, after autumn planting.

Spring-flowering bulbs such as crocuses, daffodils and hyacinths may of course be purchased in pots just as they are coming into flower and placed in a window box, but it is much more interesting and far less costly to plant these bulbs out in October or November, and have the pleasure of seeing them develop and come to maturity.

AUTUMN PLANTING

When bulbs and plants are planted together in the autumn, making one job of it, little further attention will be necessary, except for occasional watering during dry weather. Watering should be done only in mild weather during the winter and sparingly, just sufficient to keep the soil moist. As growth increases in early spring, then more water will be required unless sufficient is provided by nature.

When planting, the bulb should be placed so that the amount of soil above it is twice the depth of the bulb itself. The soil should be pressed gently but firmly round the bulb.

Stem-rooting lilies, such as *Lilium regale*, require a deep tub, because the bulbs must be planted with about 6 to 8 in of soil above the nose of the bulb. When planting lily bulbs it is wise to sprinkle a little sharp sand beneath them to ensure good drainage. If the tub is of generous proportions the bulbs may be left undisturbed for several years and will give an annual display of unsurpassed elegance.

SPRING PLANTING

In the spring our garden centres, nurseries, and local markets are usually well stocked with plants in boxes or pots, many already in bud, which have been grown in cold frames during the winter and are hardy enough to plant out for a spring display. Some will have been grown in the open all winter and these will not be quite so far forward as those protected in cold frames.

This will make a difference of a week or so to the flowering date, and should be borne in mind when making your selection. Personally, I prefer to bed out plants that are not too far advanced, as one can then have the pleasure of seeing them develop.

If you want an immediate show of colour, some plants can be moved in the bud stage but will require more careful watering and perhaps shading should the weather turn hot just after they have been put out. At least if the plants you buy are already showing colour there can be no doubt that you are buying just what you want for your colour scheme, whereas if you buy plants in tight bud and they turn out to be the wrong colour, it will be too late to do anything about it when they are in flower.

When choosing plants for containers, sturdy young plants will always give the best results. If they are pot grown, so much the better, but they will naturally cost more than plants that have been grown in boxes.

When buying plants from boxes, see that the young plants have not been over-crowded and allowed to become 'leggy' or starved, with the lower leaves turning yellow. Such plants are unlikely to recover satisfactorily, so choose bushy, healthy little specimens which will transplant much more readily. Even pot-grown plants which have been crowded on a greenhouse bench or in a frame for too long can become lanky and prove unsatisfactory.

Watering Some hours before planting, or preferably the previous evening, the plants should be thoroughly watered in their pots or boxes so that when they are planted out they will not immediately flag. Place the plant fairly low in the hole, then firmly but gently press the soil around it. Make sure that the soil is firmly round the roots and water the plants at once to settle the soil into place.

Should the weather be hot it will help the plants to get established if they are lightly sprayed over with water in the evenings, particularly those in window boxes in sunny places. I have seen young plants completely ruined by being neglected for 48 hours immediately after planting when the weather has been hot and dry.

For similar reasons I do not recommend sowing seeds directly into window boxes. Conditions are usually too rigorous for small seedlings, and, as seed growing is a slow process, the boxes are bare for a considerable time. Though the germination of seeds can be of great interest to children, even if their interest lasts long enough they will probably be disappointed in the results. Far better to let them grow some mustard and cress which will germinate very quickly in a light place in a warm room, and they will have the added enjoyment of eating the crop (see page 152).

TOOLS

The only tools that are really necessary for container gardening are a light-weight fork for use if there are beds, a trowel and a hand fork for use in window boxes and other containers. An ordinary coal shovel will be quite handy for filling window boxes and containers with soil, and an old household fork will suffice to loosen the surface soil should it become caked after the plants have been growing in containers for some time.

A pair of secateurs or garden scissors will be useful for trimming plants from time to time and a small syringe or sprayer is an excellent investment to keep the foliage free from dust and grime, which is only too plentiful in towns, and to keep pests and diseases under control. Plants 'breathe' through their leaves and when these are coated with dust they will never look happy. A small watering-can with a slender spout is a boon for window boxes and hanging baskets. For larger areas a 2-gallon galvanised can, or

a 1½-gallon can if that is too heavy, will save too much walking backwards and forwards to a tap.

FERTILIZERS

There are numerous proprietary brands of well-balanced fertilizers which give excellent results when used in accordance with the manufacturers' instructions during the growing season, which normally begins when the warm spring days arrive. Some fertilizers are very economical and only require one teaspoonful to two gallons of water, so do read the instructions on the packet carefully.

Obviously it is a waste to use most fertilizers in winter when the plants are making no growth and, in fact, it might prove harmful. Bonemeal is a slow-acting plant food which can be used with full confidence and added when the compost is being prepared for filling containers; bone flour, acting a little more speedily, is useful for topdressing when plants are established. A topdressing of moist peat or leaf soil, applied to the beds or containers in early summer, will help to conserve moisture.

I believe that more plants are ruined through overfeeding and irregular watering than from any other cause. It is easy to tell when this is happening for they look lethargic and flop, just like a fat, pet dog.

SOIL MIXTURES

I am surprised how often people will go to considerable trouble and spare no expense in choosing

A mixed planting of bulbs and violas in containers brings a breath of spring to a small backyard

just the containers they like and then fill the tubs, boxes or pots with any old soil they can lay their hands on. There is a saying: 'Gold on the cage won't feed the bird', and this is equally true of plants, which will never thrive in rubbishy soil, however elegant an 18th-century lead trough or Provence pot may be.

Soil used to be a problem for flat dwellers and town gardeners but now that soil-less composts are obtainable in polythene bags of varying sizes, ready for use, life is much simpler. John Innes Potting Compost is often recommended, and provided it has been properly prepared, it is excellent. From experience I know only too well, however, that it is often mixed by far-from-skilled labour, so if you are buying John Innes Potting Compost, be sure to get it from a reliable source.

Soil-less composts, on the other hand, are prepared by manu-facturers in vast quantities under careful control and can be relied upon for their uniformity. I am not suggesting that they are cheap, but they are clean to handle, there is no waste, and all the necessary plant foods are there in a well-balanced mixture. This means that no further use of fertilizers will be necessary for many months. As the soil-less composts are often based on peat it is important that they should not be allowed to dry out, because in a container once they do become dry it may prove difficult to get the whole bulk thoroughly moist again and the plants will suffer in the meantime.

For those of you with roof gardens or lots of tubs on a balcony, special lightweight compost is available, but again, great care must be taken to ensure it doesn't dry out.

If good soil and the facilities for preparing a suitable mixture are available, an ideal compost is 3 parts of good loam, 2 parts of well-rotted leafmould or moist granulated peat, and 1 part of coarse silver sand. A liberal handful of bonemeal, which is a slow-acting fertilizer, may be added to each bushel of the compost. What is a bushel? It is sometimes described as being approximately one barrow load, but barrows vary considerably in capacity and the correct volume of a bushel is contained in a box measuring 22 in × 10 in × 10 in, that is, 1·28 cu ft.

PREPARING WINDOW BOXES

The size of window boxes must, of course, be governed by the amount of space available on the window ledges where they are to stand, but balcony boxes can often be considerably larger, large enough, in fact, to allow clematis, climbing roses or, say, the yellow winter-flowering *Jasminum nudiflorum* to be grown.

It is advisable to treat the inside of a new box with a wood preservative. Choose one that is non-injurious to plants, and on no account use creosote. The outside of the box can be painted to match the paintwork of the house. Plain oak or teak boxes are very attractive, but the cost is a matter that may need consideration. Containers made of cement may also be used, but the lime from the cement may give trouble for a time to those plants that cannot tolerate alkaline conditions. Containers of this kind also tend to be very heavy.

Extremely handsome glass fibre troughs including replicas of 18th or 19th-century decorated lead plant containers are also available. They are by no means cheap but

they are very light in weight and impervious to the weather. Much more easy on the pocket are the modern lightweight polystyrene containers which are now easily obtainable. These lightweight troughs and containers are particularly suitable for using on balconies and roof gardens where weight must be limited as much as possible.

To assist drainage, a window box should have strips on the base and not stand flat on a windowsill, balcony or roof top. Such strips should raise the box by ½ in or so and if the windowsill slopes slightly downwards, wedge-shaped struts should be nailed to the bottom of the outside of the box to ensure that it will stand level. By placing these struts at the extreme ends of the box, it will then be possible to have a shallow metal tray underneath to collect any surplus water that may drain away after watering. This can be a wise precaution for flat dwellers – otherwise water may drip down on to neighbours' windows or balconies, which could easily cause squabbles.

It is essential that the box is

A window box, when fully loaded, is heavy and must be well secured in position, preferably by being screwed to the window frame

There must always be a layer of drainage material in the bottom of the box

securely fixed in position, especially where the window is exposed to strong winds, and this can be achieved by means of metal brackets screwed to the box and the window frame. Where the sill is too narrow for the box to rest with safety, supporting brackets can be fixed to the wall below the level of the window so that the flowers, but not the box, are visible from the room. The keen plant lover will find many ways and numerous types of containers in which to grow his particular favourites.

Drainage Another most important matter for plants in tubs, window boxes or other containers is drainage. To prevent the soil from becoming sour, all such containers should have drainage holes in the bottom, and be raised slightly off the ground so that excess moisture can drain away. These holes, which should not be more than $\frac{3}{4}$ in. in diameter, must be covered with broken pieces of flower pot, commonly called 'crocks'. Small stones will also

answer the purpose, the object being to keep the drainage holes clear of soil which would in time clog them. The 'crocks' should be placed over each hole with the concave side downwards. Over these a thin layer of pebbles, coarse leafmould or coarse moist peat should be spread to a depth of about 1 in. Pieces of old turf,

The problem of a narrow window ledge can be overcome by attaching the box to brackets fixed to the wall

placed grass-side downwards, may be used instead if they are more easily obtainable, and this will provide nourishment for the plants when the roots reach the bottom. If really good loam is used and the ingredients are carefully mixed, with the addition of a sprinkling of a well-balanced general fertilizer, the resulting compost should be satisfactory for about three years.

The container should be filled to within about one inch of the top with soil or compost mix which should be pressed firmly, but gently, to ensure that the corners and space along the sides are filled in. Be careful not to over-fill, or watering will be difficult and messy.

Later on, if necessary, a light topdressing of moist peat or leafmould can be added around the plants in early summer. This will help to conserve moisture, particularly where window boxes are exposed to sun and wind, and are liable to dry out quickly in hot weather. The smaller the container the quicker it is likely to dry out, so always use as large a box or tub as space will permit.

Creating year-round interest

The smaller the garden the more difficult it is to plan for colour and interest throughout the year and even more so when it is a question of just a window box or two. However, with a little thought it can usually be achieved so do not let this problem disturb you.

I have mentioned earlier, but have no hesitation in repeating, that if you wish to succeed completely in what you set out to do then do first consider the aspect and the soil so that you get the right plants in the right place. If your balcony, patio or roof garden is quiet with the mood of centuries of sun – which is unlikely in most parts of the British Isles – then choose sun-loving plants, but if you are on a wind-swept position choose hardy plants that will withstand such conditions. When in doubt consult a nurseryman who knows your local conditions. It is an awful waste of time and money to try and coax plants to grow under unsuitable conditions.

BULBS FOR COLOUR
Spring-flowering bulbs are a joy to behold after the dreary months of winter, and particularly for those who live in flats, for they bring thoughts of brighter days to come.

There is considerable scope for individual taste when planting a window box or tub with bulbs, but the following suggestions may be found helpful by the less experienced. Daffodils such as the magnificent deep golden yellow Golden Harvest or Dutch Master, Trousseau, a bicolor with blue-green foliage or Semper Avanti with creamy white perianth and a orange cup, are most effective when massed or interplanted with a dwarf evergreen shrub or some winter-flowering heathers, among which they will grow and flower. If you prefer a white trumpet then Mount Hood is a massive flower with white perianth and elegant trumpet that opens as a soft yellow and becomes ivory-white.

For those who prefer the small-flowered bulbs, or where window box space is limited, there is an enchanting choice. Such favourites as chionodoxa (glory of the snow), scilla, crocus, snowdrop, muscari (grape hyacinth) especially *M. azureum* 'Blue Pearl' and *M. botryoides* 'Album' which is scented, and the exquisite early-flowering *Iris reticulata*, with its fragrant, glowing purple-blue flowers, or the clear yellow *Iris danfordiae*, a real miniature gem, will make a delightful picture. They will not all flower at once, but will give a succession of colour and interest in the early months of the year, when it is most acceptable.

The shorter-growing double tulips are also most colourful and attractive in window boxes or tubs. They revel in a sunny position, start to flower during the second half of April and last longer than single-flowered varieties. They seldom exceed 1 ft in height and are usually slightly less. The colour range is fascinating and includes the rosy-pink Peach Blossom, Orange Nassau, a deep Indian red; Rheingold, pastel yellow becoming deeper as the flower opens, the red Vuurbaak with an orange sheen and the pure white Snow Queen.

Of the lilies that do well in tubs or large pots the exquisitely fragrant *Lilium regale* is one of the easiest to grow, and can be most effective when half a dozen or so bulbs are planted in a deep tub to stand on a balcony, patio or sheltered roof garden. The large, trumpet-shaped flowers are in all their glory in July; cream, flushed with rose-purple outside and white within, with a delicate suffusion of gold in the throat. The majestic golden-rayed lily of Japan, *Lilium auratum* and the numerous splendid hybrids, make an outstanding display in August and September. The late-flowering *Lilium speciosum* does well with me in a large container and in September the large, reflexed white flowers, heavily spotted with crimson, 10 to 12 to a stem, are borne erect up to 5 ft in height. It is best left undisturbed for several years and will grow in sun or partial shade.

MINIATURE ROSES
Roses that grow between about 6–18 in. in height have a fascination for some people but they have never really 'got' me, possibly because I have not, to be quite truthful, had much success with them. With one or two exceptions they have not been long lived. I must admit, however, that the little blooms are admirable for miniature flower arrangements, and those who raise these little fellows certainly pick some fetching names, such as Darling Flame, Dresden Doll,

OPPOSITE This well designed roof garden provides year-round interest with conifers, evergreens and flowering plants

134

Mon Tresor, New Penny and Royal Salute.

An old polyantha rose which is popular is The Fairy. With soft pink clusters of flowers it is very suitable for balcony boxes but is too tall for window boxes as it will reach a height of 2 ft. There is now an excellent range of hybrids from this variety, some of which – Fairy Changeling and Fairy Crystal – are reasonably compact.

I have no misgivings, however, in recommending the good old *Rosa roulettii*, which grows about 6 in high and produces its tiny pink flowers over a long period. After all, it has been cultivated in gardens since 1815, if not before, so it has proved its hardiness.

When planting miniature roses choose a reasonably sheltered spot – not on top of the white cliffs of Dover – and use a well-drained, soil mix.

PINKS

Although flowers are very much a matter of personal choice, some of my own favourites are the dianthus and pinks family, and this is for several good reasons. The silvery-grey, spiky foliage is attractive throughout the year, some have a glorious clove fragrance, and the flowers have a serene beauty all of their own.

The modern forms of dianthus are ideal for a sunny window or balcony box, because they like an open, airy position, and do not object to dry conditions. There are many varieties from which to choose, but I mention the following as being among the best for our purpose. For rich fragrance, *Dianthus* 'Rainbow Loveliness' and the Fragrant Village Pinks are unsurpassed, and on a warm summer evening the air is full of their scent. Growing about 12–18 in. in height, they flower over a long period, provided the dead flower heads are removed.

For the front of a box, *Dianthus* 'Delight', growing about 6–9 in. in height, is an excellent plant in a good range of colours which produces its single flowers from early summer until the frosts. Also for a front position, *D. allwoodii*

By the use of a hanging basket, window boxes and pots a small town balcony can be transformed into an oasis of colour and interest

alpinus will be found most suitable. Dwarf and sweet scented, it forms a compact cushion of silvery foliage, which is charming even in the winter months. The colours range from crimson, through lilac and pink to white.

The Allwoodii perpetual-flowering pinks are admirable for our purpose, particularly Laced Monarch which is scented and with a pink ground laced with chestnut. There are many other fine varieties including Cilla, white with a red eye; Sandra sugar pink and fragrant; Robert, also scented, rose magenta with light maroon centre and Susanah, white with a lilac eye and very fragrant.

The best way to obtain pinks (other than raising your own seedlings) is to purchase them from a reliable nurseryman. They will provide a delightful display in a wide range of colours. Where a particular colour is wanted, then plants of named varieties will have to be purchased. Spring planting is advisable in town gardens and window boxes.

FUCHSIAS

Fuchsias are some of the most rewarding summer-flowering plants to grow in tubs for they continue for months and thrive in sun or partial shade but, like hydrangeas, when grown in full sun they require adequate moisture at the roots. They are admirable for growing in containers and some varieties of cascading habit are seen at their best when grown in hanging baskets.

Some fuchsias are too tender to be left in the open all the year but among the hardy varieties an old favourite of mine is the bright scarlet Corallina with a dark purple corolla, and another reliable variety is Madame

Summer-flowering bedding plants

Many varieties in the following list can be bought in the early spring as small plants for bedding out, and, with careful choosing, will give a good display throughout the summer.

NAME	COLOUR/REMARKS	HEIGHT	FLOWERING TIME
Ageratum Blue Danube	Blue	6 in	July–September
Antirrhinum Floral Carpet Mixed	Various colours	8 in	July–September
Begonia semperflorens	Red, orange, pink and white	8–12 in	July–October
Calendula (Marigold)	Yellow, orange	8–12 in	May–October
Calceolaria (dwarf varieties)	Yellow, brown	12 in	June–October
Celosia (Cockscomb)	Red, pink, yellow	18 in	July–September
Centaurea Polka Dot Mixed (Cornflower)	Blue, pink, white	12 in	June–August
Chrysanthemum (annual varieties)	Various colours	1–3 ft	July–September
Convolvulus Minor	Blue, pink, white	12 in	July–September
Dahlia Coltness Hybrids	Various bright colours	18 in	July–October
Fuchsia	Pink, red, purple, white	1–2 ft	June–September
Heliotrope (Cherry Pie)	Mauve, purple. Sweetly scented	1–2 ft	June–September
Lobelia String of Pearls Mixed Dark and Light Crystal Palace	Blue, white, pink, red, purple	4–6 in or trailing	June–October
Nasturtium Tom Thumb Mixed Gleam Hybrids Whirlybird Mixed	Golden, yellow, scarlet, maroon	6–12 in	July–October
Pansy	Various bright colours	6 in	April–September
Pelargonium (Geranium)	Scarlet, pink	12–18 in	July–November
Penstemon	Various bright colours	1–2 ft	June–November
Petunia (numerous varieties, all excellent for window boxes)	Various bright colours Single and double flowered varieties	6–18 in	June–August
Phlox drummondii Mixed Twinkle Dwarf Star	Crimson, pink, purple, blue, white	6 in	July–October
Salvia Hot Shot Compact Purple	Vivid scarlet, purple	1 ft	July–September
Stocks, ten-week varieties	Various colours	15–18 in	July–August
Tagetes (African Marigold)	Yellow, red	6–10 in	July–October
Ursinia	Bright orange	9–12 in	June–July
Verbena	Pink, blue, white. Both bushy and trailing	12 in	July–October
Viola Blue Heaven Bambini Choice Mixed	Blue and mixed bright colours	6 in	May–July

This planting uses a range of containers on a base of artificial grass

Cornelissen, with scarlet and white flowers. Other good varieties include Tom Thumb, crimson and mauvy purple, Alice Hoffman, rose and white; Pearl White, white flushed pink, and Mrs Popple, scarlet and dark violet. For planting in a hanging basket or for trailing over the side of a container I suggest the rich red Marinka; the free-flowering Claret Cup with pale pink tubes and sepals and rich red corolla, the low, spreading Tinker Bell with pinkish-white flowers, and Eva Boerg, ivory-rose and violet-purple. If you cannot get these varieties locally there are plenty of others that will make an equally good summer show if planted out in May.

CHRYSANTHEMUMS
Modern chrysanthemums are diverse in form and colour and if grown in pots they can be transferred to window boxes or containers to follow summer-flowering plants as these fade. Or they can, of course, be left in the ground for several years until division becomes necessary.

Particularly suitable for small gardens are the pompons, bearing a profusion of double, button-like flowers in a variety of delightful colours. No disbudding is necessary and they flower from August to October, according to the variety. In height they vary from about 1–2½ ft. The Lilliput varieties are even more compact, making bushy plants about 12 in. in height covered with tiny double flowers.

New varieties continue to appear each year and the best of them will be well worth growing.

EVERGREENS FOR WINTER COLOUR
Evergreens and hardy heathers will provide some interest throughout the year. Some suitable evergreens include Japanese laurel (aucuba); *Berberis buxifolia* 'Nana', a bushy shrub with dark green foliage and amber yellow flowers in April and May; common box; *Cotoneaster adpressus*, which is not evergreen but retains its leaves well into the winter and bears cheerful red berries; *Euonymus fortunei* 'Silver Queen', one of the best variegated forms with handsome white and silver leaves up to 2½ in. in length,

also *Euonymus japonicus* 'Aureo-pictus', a golden variegated form; and, where space permits, laurustinus (*Viburnum tinus*), the variety Eve Price being the most decorative, bearing pink-budded flowers turning to white from January to April.

Where something dwarf or prostrate is required, plant the evergreen *Cotoneaster congestus* which makes a compact shrub of umbrella-like growth bearing round red berries; *Erica carnea* and its varieties for winter flowering in shades of pink, carmine and white, and those varieties with golden foliage are also most attractive. Other suitable plants are the prostrate double broom (*Genista tinctoria* 'Plena') covered with yellow flowers in June; the dwarf, erect little ivy, *Hedera conglomerata*, the variegated varieties of *Hedera helix* such as Glacier, Gold Heart, and Little Diamond, and the miniature roses, *Rosa roulettii*, about 6 in high with dainty pink flowers and R. *pumila*, with soft pink flowers from June to September.

Conifers with golden foliage are pleasing throughout the year and one of the most effective is *Thuja occidentalis* 'Rheingold'. This has an ultimate height of about 5 ft, but is slow-growing and makes a dense, broad pyramid of bright gold in summer, and in the autumn the finely-fronded foliage turns bronze-gold.

An attractive little pine that associates well with hardy heathers is called *Pinus mugo*, or the European mountain pine. It does well in almost any soil, including chalk, and eventually makes a rounded, gnarled tree. There is a dwarfer form known as *pumilio* which makes a spreading bush that occasionally reaches a height of 6 ft. P. *mugo* 'Gnom' forms dark green mounds and P. *mugo*

'Mops' is very slow growing.

These dwarf trees are full of character and planted in an open sunny position they will soon lend an air of permanency to the scene. This is one of the attributes of the conifers, but it may take several years to achieve a similar effect of a well established planting with the taller-growing varieties.

Shrubs in tubs

These may be used with effect throughout the year at the entrance to a house, on a roof garden or wide balcony so long as the position is not too draughty. Evergreens in particular resent being stood in some bleak corner where the wind whistles round them. Too often one sees shrivelled, neglected specimens adorning the entrance of a block of flats where it seems to be nobody's responsibility to water the unfortunate plants, let alone spray them over with water to freshen them up from time to time in dry weather. Obviously the soil in a tub will dry out pretty quickly if it is in a sunny position and is standing on paving that

gets really hot in summer, therefore regular watering is essential during periods of drought, and a good syringing overhead will help to remove the layer of dust which may accumulate on the foliage, particularly in town gardens.

Suitable shrubs for tubs include pyramid and standard bay trees, and box in various forms.

For a formal setting, on either side of a door for instance, a pair of pyramid bay or box trees can be quite effective and are less likely to blow over than the standard types with a large ball of foliage at the top of a bare stem.

Among the dwarf cupressus (now called chamaecyparis) are narrowly pyramidal, bright green and golden forms.

Shrubs and bamboos planted in containers and wooden decking create a pleasant outside living area in a small space

Yews are not fully satisfactory in large towns due to the fact that the foliage is liable to become clogged with grime which is extremely difficult to remove; in the country it is a different matter and they are most desirable, particularly the golden varieties. With care these evergreens will last several years in tubs and can always be planted out when they become too large.

Among the shrubs which I have grown in a teak tub, 18 × 18 in, is a maple (acer), which is as sound as ever after 30 years, and the weeping evergreen *Cotoneaster*

It is useful to include some evergreen shrubs and herbs in any group of plants as these provide year-round interest

'Hybridus Pendulus'. After about 25 years the maple (*Acer palmatum* 'Osakazuki') became top heavy and seemed liable to be blown over by the summer gales. We therefore planted it out in the garden where it has since made exuberant new growths. This variety has delightful fresh green leaves in spring and summer, which turn a brilliant scarlet in late October.

We then planted the tub with the weeping cotoneaster, which has a 4-ft stem and is quite effective with its long branches hanging down to the ground. The clusters of flowers are creamy-white, the leaves glossy green and in the autumn the berries are brilliant red.

Care of container-grown shrubs

Where permanent shrubs are grown in tubs or other containers

it is important to fork the surface soil over lightly, say every three months or so, otherwise it will become compacted. This is easily done with a hand fork in the same manner as one does with a garden fork round the shrubs in a border. If the soil has become impoverished, remove the top inch or two and replace with fresh compost: early spring is a good time to do this.

Only too often formal shrubs such as bay and box trees are neglected, merely existing for a time before giving up the unequal struggle. Regular watering is essential, and in addition, during hot weather, they should be given a good overhead syringing with water once or twice a week. This should be done in the evening when the hot sun is no longer on the leaves and they cannot therefore be scorched. In addition to freshening the plants and improving their appearance, the removal of grime from the leaves will make respiration easier, since plants 'breathe' through their leaves. The syringing should be done with

some force, for a gently spray will not remove the dust, but it should not be harsh enough to break off the leaves.

Both evergreen box and bay shrubs are reasonably hardy and with care will last quite a long time in tubs, but no shrub will survive if it is placed in a position where there is a perpetual draught. In really severe frosty weather the tub should be protected with old sacking or straw and, of course, the plant should not be watered.

Remember that such shrubs as the rhododendron, azalea, kalmia and some of the hardy heathers must have a lime-free soil, so be sure that your topdressing is lime free.

Plants for screening

Trellis and screens Bare walls can be so much more attractive if easily-erected cedar wood trellis is used, or plastic mesh made of high density polythene in various colours, which does not rust or corrode. I am not suggesting that this is cheap, but such mesh is long lasting, which is an important consideration. I have found it most useful and decorative for training sweet peas, and it is easy to roll up and store for the winter. Or when permanently attached to a wall it makes the tying of roses, clematis, jasmine and other climbers an easy job.

Trellis is most useful for forming a quick screen, even only a few feet in height, as is often to be seen in Continental open-air restaurants, or as a screen beside tables at pavement level. Known as *treillage decoratif*, its value is widely appreciated. It is also pleasing on the walls of a porch,

In a restricted area it is essential to make use of all the available space. Wooden trellis or plastic mesh attached to walls or balcony railings will allow a wide range of climbing plants to be grown

OPPOSITE Bare walls and screens look much more attractive if covered with climbing plants and evergreens

Climbing roses take up very
little ground space

light and will be welcome both for
sitting in and as a protection for
your plants.

Climbing plants for containers

The yellow, winter-flowering
Jasminum nudiflorum, useful for any
aspect including a north-facing
wall, can be grown in a balcony
box which may be large enough to
accommodate a climbing rose or
clematis, or even a passion flower,
Passiflora caerulea, where there is a
warm, south-facing wall on which
it can be trained. *P. caerulea* is a
decorative twining plant with
exotic mauve flowers and in mild
districts it will remain green
throughout the year.

Quick-growing annual climbers
are both decorative and useful for
covering walls or trellis to provide
a screen so long as the site is
reasonably sheltered. By this I
mean that I am not recommending
the following plants to grow on a
trellis on some exposed, windy
roof garden, but a sheltered roof
garden or balcony is a different
matter.

The half-hardy cup-and-saucer
flower, *Cobaea scandens*, a native of
Central and South America, makes
rapid growth when planted out in
the open in late May and its large
greenish-violet flowers are a
delight from July to October.
Where there is a frost-free lean-to
greenhouse or garden room it
makes an excellent perennial
climber and will grow to 20 ft or
more.

Morning glory, or *Ipomoea
tricolor*, with its freely-produced
sky blue trumpets, starts to flower
in late June and continues for
months. Being a member of the
convolvulus family it likes to
twine itself up some form of
support and may grow to 6 ft or
more. The convolvulus-like
flowers are produced for many
weeks during the summer and

or in the entrance hall of a light,
modern house where such plants
as the kangaroo vine (*Cissus
antartica*), the wax flower (*Hoya
carnosa*) and the small, narrow-
pointed green-leaf ivy (*Hedera
helix* 'Pittsburgh') can be grown
quite happily.

Where a windbreak or screen is
required on a roof garden or
elsewhere there is the rigid
transparent vinyl sheeting, which
may also be used for covering
garden frames, car ports and the
like. This is most useful to form a
sheltered corner without excluding

autumn, with new ones opening each morning. Heavenly Blue is a glorious shade, and Scarlet O'Hara is a soft red-wine. A near relative to the morning glory is the Mexican *Quamoclit lobata*, with funnel-shaped flowers that open rosy-crimson, becoming orange and later yellow.

Sweet peas in a wide range of colours will provide a fragrant screen by July when the young plants are bedded out in April or early May. The dwarf Patio, Bijou and Knee-hi varieties are the most suitable for growing in containers.

Particularly effective against a white wall in a sunny position is the purple-leaved vine, *Vitis vinifera* 'Purpurea' or the Teinturier grape, when it is neatly trained to a trellis.

The less rampant climbing roses can be grown quite successfully in largish containers or are delightful when planted against a reasonably sunny wall. Suitable varieties include the fragrant, daffodil-yellow Golden Showers which grows to about 8 ft or so on a wall, or the exquisite Pink Perpêtue which climbs to about 15 ft.

A rose that has proved a great success with me is climbing *Rosa chinensis minima* 'Pompon de Paris' to give its full title, which appeared in Paris in 1831. On a west-facing wall it grows to about 7 ft and in May and June it bears a profusion of dainty little double pink flowers and fern-like little leaves which prove to be ever-green in severe winters. The original R. *chinensis minima*, which is said to be extinct, did not exceed 1 ft in height.

Planted at one corner of the same wall in a large container is *Clematis alpina*. Its slender stems ramble up through Pompon de Paris to a height of 4 ft or so and

bear nodding heads of soft lavender-blue flowers at the same time as the rose is at its best. This is one of those plant associations which has worked out happily for they are both in flower at the same period. So far as the clematis is concerned, this likes to have its roots in a cool, shaded place and its top growth in a reasonably open sunny position. Cool conditions can be achieved for the roots by placing a slab of stone over the soil by the stem of the plant.

From Chile comes the fast-growing, deciduous climber known as *Eccremocarpus scaber* (meaning with pendent fruit, the seed pods being pendulous, and *scaber*, rough to the touch) which is easily raised from seed and is perennial in mild gardens, where self-sown seedlings will often appear. It bears clusters of orange-scarlet, yellow-tipped tubular flowers throughout the summer and autumn and perennial specimens may reach to 20 ft or so. Those grown as half-hardy annuals and planted out in May attain about half that height.

Plants for shade

Hostas, which we used to call plaintain lilies or funkias, with their broad, cool-looking leaves are effective throughout the spring and summer. Their mauve-lilac flowers are not spectacular but are quite pleasing, growing on slender stems from 1½–3 ft in height mainly in July and August. Those with variegated leaves are the most striking and are usually much in demand for decorative arrangements.

Hostas, although often grown beside a pool in dappled shade, may also be grown in a container so long as the soil does not dry out in summer.

Once planted, hostas should be left undisturbed for several years and when division becomes necessary it should be done in the spring just when new growth is evident. In a patio garden they lend a refreshing sense of coolness, as do hardy ferns with their grace-ful, slender fronds. Both are most useful for filling a shady corner in moist, peaty soil, and both are perfectly hardy.

Also for shade is a prostrate, variegated member of the nettle family which the botanists have dubbed with the unfortunate name *Lamium galeobdolon variegatum*. This has yellow flowers in May which are much loved by bees and the leaves are a fresh green with prominent silver markings. A word of warning: it is a vigorous grower which can swamp its neighbours, so do not plant it with any particular treasure, but it has its uses in a tub or window box in either sun or partial shade; and it has the advantage of providing attractive foliage from early spring until the late autumn. There is also a golden-leaved variety.

Ivies and vincas (periwinkles) come in beautifully variegated varieties and do well in cool shady conditions.

Fragrant plants

I always remember a sizzling hot day in southern Portugal when the sun and hot sandy soil released waves of mingled scent of pine, gum cistus and wild lavender. The dusty roads were lined with graceful eucalyptus trees, adding a further tang to the quivering air.

Fragrant and aromatic plants are one of the great delights on a balcony, patio or roof garden where space is limited and there are many suitable plants from which to make a selection. I have for years collected such plants for I find the scent of flowers and the spicy aromas of lavender, rosemary, pelargoniums and some of the herbs such as the various mints, thymes and marjoram, much more refreshing than over-fed, scentless dahlias and the like. The night-scented stock, *Matthiola bicornis*, does not have spectacular flowers but when grown among other plants it gives a wonderful scent in the evening.

Even in the winter months there is the sky blue *Iris unguicularis* – better known as *Iris stylosa* – which has a pleasing fragrance, particularly when cut and brought into a warm room. This plant likes a poor soil and a sunny position where it will get well baked during the summer.

Viburnum fragrans and *V. bodnantense* produce sweet-scented, rose-tinted flowers from November to early spring and are charming for a sheltered corner. *Lonicera purpusii* is another winter-flowering shrub, with cream, sweet-scented flowers. *Cytisus battandieri*, with silver foliage and yellow, pineapple-scented flowers, and *Trachelospermum jasminoides*, a less well known evergreen climber with white scented flowers in July, are suitable for a south or west-facing wall. These shrubs will require large containers.

In mid-May one can plant out the Peruvian heliotrope, or cherry pie (especially the dark purple variety Marine with dark foliage) which for generations has been cultivated for its most delicious almond-like scent, and another old-fashioned plant, the pelargonium, is again being appreciated. There are a large number of these with a variety of scents – citrus, nutmeg, peppermint, almond and aromas indescribable,

but delicious. These plants must, of course, be overwintered in a frost-free greenhouse.

A real favourite of mine, which requires similar treatment except in really sheltered gardens, is the lemon-scented verbena, *Lippia citriodora*, a dainty perennial shrub from Chile. The leaves have a peculiarly penetrating refreshing sweetness when pinched between the finger and thumb. A single leaf placed in a book will retain its aroma for a long period. I grow this plant in a small tub (12 × 12 in) where it has been for years. It is cut back fairly hard each March and stands outside in a sunny corner from mid-May until the autumn.

Many of the lily family, too, are delightfully fragrant, and those I have described earlier on page 134 are particularly suitable for a patio or balcony.

No garden, however tiny, is complete without the dainty mignonette, or *Herbe d'Amour*, known in prosaic botanical terms as *Reseda odorata*. As it resents being transplanted the seed should be sown in April where it is to flower and the seed germinates better if the soil is made firm before sowing. This little gem is much loved by bees and has found a place in the armorial bearings of an old family in Saxony. The story is that the Count of Walstheim loved the fair and sprightly Amelia of Nordbourg, who was a spoiled child and a coquette. She had a humble friend named Charlotte.

One evening at a party all the ladies were called upon to choose a flower each, and the gentlemen were to make verses on the selection. Amelia chose a sumptuous rose and Charlotte the modest mignonette. During the evening Amelia coquetted so desperately with a dashing colonel that the

Count could not suppress his vexation. Of the rose he wrote: 'She lives but for a day, and pleases but for a moment'. And he then presented the following lines on the mignonette to the gentle Charlotte: 'Your qualities surpass your charm'.

Having transferred his affection to Charlotte, they were in due course married, and a sprig of sweet mignonette was added to the family arms, together with the motto.

Well, those are some of my favourite fragrant plants which I have come to appreciate over the years. I hope that my readers may enjoy these and others which are their own particular favourites.

As the poet Thomas Gray has written: 'Full many a flower is born to blush unseen, and waste its sweetness on the desert air', but a keen gardener will know where his treasures are and will look forward to the day when their sweetness is brought forth.

Herbs in containers

A number of different varieties of herbs will grow quite happily on a sunny balcony where they are not only attractive in appearance, but their fragrant or aromatic leaves are in many cases delightful, and for culinary purposes they are always in demand. An omelet made with freshly-gathered herbs can be delicious, and it is not beyond the realms of possibility for the flat dweller to grow a few varieties, even if they are only grown in pots.

Herbs are best planted in the spring just when they are starting into new growth, that is, in late March or April. Given reasonably fertile, well-drained soil, they will thrive with the minimum of attention. Naturally, they will not last as long as plants growing in a sheltered kitchen garden, but if new plants are introduced from time to time, there is no reason why a small collection of herbs should not give infinite pleasure to the eye, nose and palate for many a long day.

Where they are grown as individual plants in pots, they must not be allowed to dry out. This can occur in a matter of hours if they are in an exposed position on a window-ledge on a hot sunny day, but by plunging the pots in moist peat, that is, surrounding the pots with peat up to the rim, moisture will be conserved in the soil around the roots of the plants, and will reduce the amount of watering required. At the same time it will greatly improve the condition of the plants, since it is bad practice

Sweetly-scented plants like lilies grow well in pots and provide an attractive display outside the window

to allow a plant to become excessively dry and then saturate it with water.

Chives (*Allium schoenoprasum*) Plant 6 in apart in March. A delicious mild onion flavour is imparted to a salad or omelet by the addition of chopped chive 'grass'.

Garlic (*Allium sativum*) Plant the bulbs (cloves) in March about 6 in apart and 2 in deep; lift and store in July and August. Used for flavouring meats and salads, the cloves should be used with discretion: a little goes a long way, particularly in this country where garlic is not over popular. In the old days it was said to cure jaundice and to be used as a relief for asthma, but one suspects its effect might be matched by the story of the Scot, desperately ill in hospital, who cried out for the sound of the bagpipes. Played all night up and down the ward they

saved his life – but all the other patients died.

Mint (*Mentha spicata*) Plant the roots horizontally, 2 in deep, in moist, peaty soil and grow in a partially shaded position. Water freely in dry weather. Much used for sauce with lamb, new potatoes and green peas. There are numerous different kinds of mint, not all of culinary value. According to mythology, Mentha, a daughter of Cocytus, was changed into this plant by Proserpine who was jealous of her.

Parsley (*Petroselinum crispum*) A hardy biennial which should be sown thinly where it is to mature. Germination is slow in early spring when the soil is cold, so do not become impatient: it may be hastened by pouring boiling water on the soil before sowing. Seed may also be sown in July and August to provide a crop for early spring and summer. There

are many old superstitions about when to sow parsley seed; Wiltshire folk always used to sow on Good Friday, 'else the devil gets into it'.

Sage (*Salvia officinalis*) A low-growing perennial shrub making rather too large a plant for a window-box but quite suitable for a tub in a sunny position, or a sizable pot filled with a light, well-drained soil. Young plants should be planted in March or April, and the leading shoots should be pinched out to keep the plants bushy. Those of us who can remember the flavour of home-killed pork will not have forgotten the sage and onions which were gathered to accompany the roast meat.

Sweet Marjoram (*Origanum majorana*) The garden species is a smaller plant than the wild marjoram. It should be treated as an annual in this country, the seed being sown thinly in the open in April or May. Where greenhouse facilities are available, sow in pans containing light sandy soil in February or March and transplant the seedlings to a sunny position in the open in May. The fresh sprigs are highly esteemed.

Thyme (*Thymus vulgaris*). Plant about 4 in apart in well-drained soil in a sunny position in March or April. Pot-grown plants from nurserymen may be planted at almost any time. Thyme has a warm aromatic flavour and is most useful for seasoning.

Lemon Thyme (*T. citriodorus*) Suitable for similar conditions. It is a delightful little plant with a most refreshing fragrance, the lemon flavour being pleasing with fish or poultry.

There are numerous other varieties of thymes suitable for the rock garden and for growing between paving stones, where they are most attractive, but they are not of any culinary interest.

Hanging baskets

Another good way of breaking up the depressing expanse of a blank wall is to suspend a hanging basket or two. It is possible to get green plastic-coated wire-mesh baskets which many people think more attractive than the old plain galvanized-wire baskets. It should be remembered that they are very heavy when full of moist

OPPOSITE Trailing pelargoniums and *Helichrysum petiolatum* look well together in a hanging basket

soil and plants, and so must be securely suspended.

Before planting a hanging basket, it should be lined with damp moss laid thickly enough to retain the soil in the basket, or strengthened by a lining of strong plastic sheeting pierced with holes to allow for drainage. Pot-grown plants which are just coming into flower are knocked out of their pots and, if the plant is well rooted, the roots loosened gently at the bottom of the ball of soil. This will encourage them to spread into the new soil in the basket. A medium-sized basket – one measuring about 14 in across the top – will take three plants that have been grown in 5-in pots, and probably three or more small plants from 3½-in pots. Such plants will usually have been grown in a greenhouse and it is unwise to put them in a hanging basket in the open until towards the end of May when the danger of frost is past.

Hanging baskets, for obvious reasons, dry out very quickly in hot weather and they may need watering twice a day at such times.

Planting up a hanging basket Stand the basket in a large pot to give it stability and line it with moss

The lining can be strengthened with a sheet of plastic and the basket is then filled with light-weight compost

A cross section to show the arrangement of the plants; trailing kinds should grow over the sides

Plants suitable for hanging baskets

Most of these varieties can be bought in the spring as small
plants for bedding out:

NAME	COLOUR/REMARKS	HEIGHT	FLOWERING TIME
Abronia (sand verbena)	Lemon-yellow, pink, white. Trailing plants with fragrant flowers resembling verbena	6–18 in	July onwards
Asparagus sprengeri	Green. Trailing fern-like foliage	1–3 ft (length)	
Begonia, tuberous and fibrous rooted	Various colours	12 in	June–September
Calceolaria	Yellow, brown, red	12 in	July–September
Campanula isophylla	Lilac-blue	3–6 in	July onwards
Coleus	Most colours. Attractive coloured and variegated foliage plants	18 in	
Fuchsia	Pink, red, purple, white	12–18 in	June–September
Pelargonium (Geranium)	Scarlet, pink, white. The ivy-leaved varieties are most effective when growing over the side of the basket and the upright zonal varieties for the top of the basket	12–18 in	May–October
Heliotrope (cherry pie)	Mauve, purple	12–18 in	June–September
Lobelia	Blue, white, pink, red, purple. There are both compact and spreading varieties	4–6 in or trailing	June–October
Nasturtium	Orange, yellow, red. Single and double flowered varieties. Extremely free flowering and decorative	6–9 in or trailing	July–October
Petunia	Blue, purple, pink, red, white, yellow. Single and double flowered varieties	6 in or spreading	June onwards
Phlox drummondii	Crimson, pink, purple, blue, red, white	6 in	July–October
Tradescantia zebrina	Dark green leaves, striped white above, purplish beneath	Trailing	May onwards
Verbena	Blue, scarlet, pink, mauve, white	Trailing	July onwards

It is important, therefore, to place them at a reasonable height and in an accessible position.

Sink gardens

Old stone sinks make charming homes for small-growing alpine plants, such as edelweiss, and such plants are naturally happy in exposed places. These sinks are not easily found nowadays, but over the years I have been lucky enough to collect five. One lovely old, deep stone trough was given to me by a Cotswold quarry owner. I filled this trough with specially prepared lime-free soil, planted it with the autumn-flowering *Gentiana sino-ornata* and learned a curious lesson. The trough happened to stand below a bird table and the lime content in the bird droppings killed all the gentians along one side immediately below the table, while the others flowered happily.

Should you have no luck in finding an old stone sink, then I suggest making use of a glazed

Many plants are suitable for both window boxes and hanging baskets. Here petunias are combined with creeping Jenny

domestic sink, which can sometimes still be picked up in a builder's yard where they now have little use for them. Such a sink can be made quite attractive by painting it over with a bonding adhesive, first having cleaned off any grease or dirt. The adhesive should be allowed to dry partially and then a cement mix, a little at a time, is pressed firmly on to the surface and left in a rough state. The mix should consist of one part cement, three parts of sand and one part of peat, with water added and mixed to a thick paste. If the new cement can also be painted over with cow manure, it will encourage the growth of moss

on the surface to give an old-world effect. The drainage hole in the sink should, of course, be left open and the sink stood on bricks to ensure good drainage. Allow the cement to dry for a few days

before filling with compost and plants.

A sink garden provides year-round interest and is a charming addition to a small area where it can be easily viewed

Plants for the sink garden An old stone sink planted with suitable rock plants, dwarf conifers and small bulbs can make a charming feature in a patio or on a roof garden. It will be at its best in the spring but it can be made interesting all the year by including a few small houseleeks such as the cobweb houseleek, *Sempervivum arachnoideum*, and the Noah's Ark juniper, *Juniperus communis* 'Compressa' which makes a compact little column, measured in inches.

My own five sinks are filled with a variety of small plants and dwarf conifers, including the Noah's Ark juniper which, after many years, is only about 8 in high. Another plant that I have found to do well is the diminutive rhizomatous *Iris cristata*, a little gem with tufts of 3-in high sword-like leaves. It produces soft blue flowers with a golden crest on short stems from May onwards.

Edelweiss from the Alps can also be grown in a sink but should be protected in winter with a cloche or sheet of glass from excessive wet which ruins its grey, felty foliage. In its mountain home it is protected by thick, crisp snow for many months and it does not like our winter mixture of fog, wet, frost and sunshine.

Entirely different are the house-leeks, or sempervivums, from the Latin *semper*, always, and *vivo*, alive, which is very true of these trouble-free little plants that form interesting clumps of rosette-like plantlets in shades of green, steel-grey, violet and ruby, or cobwebbed so they are like ping-pong balls in cotton wool. They thrive in full sun and in gritty, but not impoverished, soil and once established they should be left undisturbed for evermore. They may often be seen growing on the top of a stone wall, or even on a tiled roof where, in fact, I have had a clump growing for many years with practically no soil at all.

The nomenclature is involved, to put it mildly, and one nursery-man I know lists nearly 100 varieties, which should be enough to satisfy most people. A stone sink planted with several different varieties is interesting at all times, and during the summer months flower heads arise bearing spikes of pink, yellow or reddish Catherine-wheel flowers. They should also be quite happy in a shallow window box on a sunny balcony or roof garden.

Aquatic plants

Where it is not feasible to have a pool, yet it is desired to have small-growing water lilies or other aquatic plants, these can always be planted in a half-barrel, deep stone sink, or old water-trough, of about 12–18 in. in depth half filled with heavyish soil and about 9 in of water.

Choose one of the smaller-growing water lilies, such as *Nymphaea odorata minor* with dainty, fragrant, pure white flowers and fresh green leaves; *N.* 'Paul Hariot', apricot-yellow, becoming orange-pink and deepening as the blooms mature; or *N. pygmaea alba* and *N. p. rubra*, a charming rose-pink. *N.* 'Paul Hariot' should be planted in water 12–18 in deep and the other species in water 6–12 in deep.

Also decorative in a trough water garden are the Japanese *Iris kaempferi* with flowers of velvety texture in shades of violet, blue, crimson and yellow; the free-flowering marsh marigold or kingcup (*Caltha palustris*), a native plant that bears golden-yellow heads of flower from March to July, contrasting well with the dark green leaves; cotton grass (*Eriophorum angustifolium*) with silky down, and the outstanding zebra rush, burdened with the name *Scirpus tabernaemontani zebrinus*. A native of Japan, it has erect stems 3–5 ft in height, marked with alternate bands of green and white. It looks delight-fully cool on a hot, sunny day.

A roof-top water garden

Vegetable and Fruit Growing in Containers

Growing food plants is always a satisfying pastime
which even those people without a garden can share. As long
as there is a windowsill or balcony available, a wide
selection of salad vegetables and also some
fruits can be grown. Tasty varieties should be selected
to add an extra zest to summer repasts.

Windowsill

In the absence of a garden, or even to make use of as many facilities as possible, a windowsill can provide an added dimension to the growing of food plants indoors.

Mustard and cress

Perhaps not surprisingly, mustard and cress tend to be thought of as the only food plants that can be grown indoors. Indeed mustard and cress are very easy to grow and are probably two of the best things to start with in order to gain a little confidence and to have a little fun.

Apart from the seed all you will need is a water-absorbent material, such as peat, blotting paper, paper tissue or cotton wool, and a plate or saucer.

Place the material of your choice, paper tissue is as good as any, on the plate or saucer and moisten with tap water. Sow the seed, not too thickly, on the damp tissue and check daily to ensure that the tissue remains moist. During warm weather check the tissue twice daily as it can dry out very rapidly.

At average room temperature white mustard will germinate and be ready to eat within four to six days. The seedlings should be eaten when approximately 1 in in height when they will be at their best. If you leave them too long they tend to become rather bitter.

Cress, on the other hand, will germinate within two to five days but will not be ready to eat for about two to three weeks after sowing the seed.

Whatever time of the year, mustard and cress provide an easy-to-grow salad crop that can either be used as a tasty and nutritious part of a salad, sandwich filler or as a garnish to the main course.

Seed sprouts

Unfortunately seed sprouts have assumed something of a 'health freak' image and this is a great pity, for not only are they one of the easiest and most varied of vegetable crops to grow, but they are also even more fun than mustard and cress.

Seed sprouts are available in a very wide range of varieties including Salad Alfalfa, Alphatoco Bean Sprouts, Fenugreek, Chinese or Mung Bean Sprouts and even mustard and cress. Whichever you choose, the following method of cultivation is probably the easiest and most foolproof.

All you will need is a jam jar or kilner jar, a piece of cheesecloth or muslin and a rubber band. Simply place one or two dessertspoonfuls of seed (no more or your vegetables may take over the house!) in the jar and cover the jar with the cheesecloth or muslin securely fixed over the rim with the rubber band.

Then fill the jar two-thirds to three-quarters full with tepid water and shake for about fifteen to twenty seconds holding your hand over the muslin to prevent the water coming out. The water should then be drained away by tipping the jar, which will allow the water to escape through the muslin whilst retaining the seeds.

This operation should be repeated twice daily for between three to seven days when the seed sprouts will be ready to eat.

As a point of added interest, the seed sprouts can be grown in the light or in a dark cupboard, it is really up to you. If you like green sprouts then grow them in the light. If, however, you prefer them pale yellow in colour then simply grow them in a cupboard.

Finally, try not to allow the seed sprouts to get cold as average room temperature encourages rapid development.

As mentioned previously, mustard and cress can also be grown by this method and these need no further description, but what about the others mentioned?

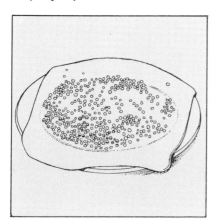

Mustard and cress is sown simply by sprinkling the seed on damp tissue

Water frequently and cut the crop when it is about an inch high

Seed sprouts Place the seeds in a jar and cover with muslin

Add tepid water, shake the jar and drain

Repeat twice daily until the sprouts are ready for eating

Salad Alfalfa has a sweet, almost pea-like flavour and is a useful addition to salads, sandwiches or as a garnish. Chinese Bean Sprouts or Mung Beans are ideal for many culinary uses, and are probably the best known seed sprouts available. Alphatoco Bean Sprouts have a sweeter flavour and crisper texture than Mung Beans and can be fried or steamed or used in salads.

Another seed sprout worth trying is Fenugreek, which when freshly sprouted is similar in flavour to curry, but if left for longer develops a more subtle, less strong taste and provides a useful

vegetable for use in salads, soups or as a garnish.

Lettuce

Somewhat surprisingly, lettuce can be grown indoors on a windowsill and although they may tend to become rather leggy, they can provide a useful meal with relatively little care. However, not every variety of lettuce is really suitable for this method of growing and one such as Ramcos or another variety that will grow over winter under protection should be selected.

To grow the lettuce simply sow

the seed in a shallow pot or seed tray nearly filled with seed compost, covering the seed with approximately $\frac{1}{8}$ in of compost. Gently water the compost and germinate the seeds in a well lit position at about 13–16°C (55–60°F). Avoid temperatures above 24°C (75°F) or the seed will not germinate.

After a few days the seedlings will appear and after a further two or three weeks when the seedlings are large enough to handle they should be gently pricked out and potted up. To do this, first water the seedlings, then holding them by the leaves – never

Sow lettuce seed by sprinkling it thinly over the compost in a pot

Once the seedlings are large enough they can be pricked out

Remove each one gently and insert it in a separate pot

the stem – gently tease them from the compost using a small stick. Each seedling is then potted into a $5\frac{1}{2}$-in dwarf or half pot using a potting compost. Simply fill the pot with compost, make a hole deep enough for the seedling's roots and gently place the seedling in the hole, lightly pushing the compost around it with the stick.

Water carefully and place the pot on a windowsill. Do not allow the compost to dry out during the following weeks and after about two months or so the lettuce will be ready to eat.

Tomatoes

Tomatoes do not always end up as tall gangly plants. There are a number of dwarf-growing varieties that can be grown in a pot indoors on a windowsill where they will fruit prolifically despite their diminutive stature, which is only about 24 in. Varieties such as Minibel or Pixie are very easy to grow and can be sown at any time of the year.

Sow the seed in a seed tray or half pot using a suitable seed compost and cover the seed with

A home-grown lettuce from the kitchen windowsill

about $\frac{1}{8}$ in of compost. Water lightly.

Keep the pot or tray containing the seeds at about 18–20°C (65–68°F) in a well lit position and germination should take between seven and fourteen days.

After about three weeks the seedlings should have started to produce their characteristic true

leaves and can then be pricked out. Gently water the compost and tease out the seedlings holding them by their leaves.

Each seedling should be potted in a $3\frac{1}{2}$-in pot using a potting compost and then placed back on the windowsill until they have grown to about 6 in tall. Keep the compost reasonably moist, but try to avoid over-watering.

When they have grown to about 6 in tall, pot each plant into an 8-in pot, again using a potting

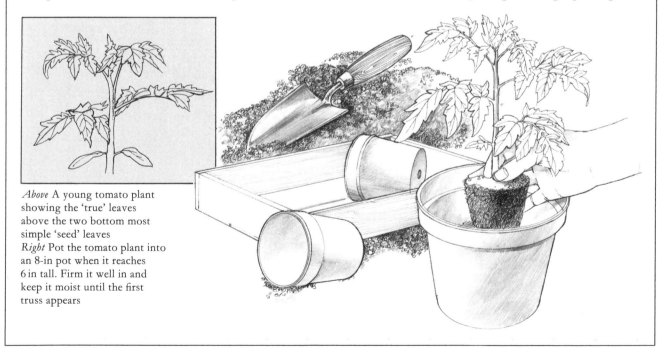

Above A young tomato plant showing the 'true' leaves above the two bottom most simple 'seed' leaves
Right Pot the tomato plant into an 8-in pot when it reaches 6 in tall. Firm it well in and keep it moist until the first truss appears

You may have to assist nature by pollinating the flowers

Peppers

Peppers can be grown on a windowsill as easily as tomatoes. Germinate the seed at about 20°C (68°F) and prick out the seedling, first into a 3½-in pot and then into an 8-in pot using a potting compost each time.

When the plant is about 6 in tall feed once a week with a tomato fertilizer. The peppers will be borne fairly readily and can be picked green or when red and fully ripe.

Aubergines

compost. Continue the previous treatment until the first truss appears. When this happens you can then start to feed the plants using a tomato fertilizer at the rate recommended on the label by the manufacturer.

Unlike the more conventional types of tomato there is no need to remove side shoots or pinch these little bush varieties. Indeed, if you do pinch them they do not like it and do not grow as well. During the winter when there are not many insects around, you can increase fruit set by tickling the flowers with a small paint brush.

Although the fruit of these dwarf varieties are rather small they are really delicious and well worth growing.

Aubergines can again be treated in much the same way as tomatoes and peppers, although aubergines and peppers are more suitable for growing during the summer months only. Germinate the seed at about 20°C (68°F) then pot into a 3½-in pot and finally into an

8-in pot using a potting compost.

When the fruit becomes apparent, feed with a tomato fertilizer once a week and provide the plant with a cane or stick for support. The fruit are ready to be picked when they are about 4 in long.

Melons

Obviously the larger melons are not really practical to grow indoors but Ogen is an ideal small variety that will grow particularly well in a south-facing window. Hardly surprisingly the Ogen melon, which originates from Israel, requires lots of sunshine (so it is only successful as a summer crop) and, as it grows, an increasing amount of water.

To start them off, sow one seed to a pot in a 3½-in peat or plastic pot nearly filled with a seed compost. Do not cover the seed but simply place it on its edge on the compost. The use of a peat pot helps to avoid root disturbance when the plant starts to grow actively. The seed should be germinated at about 21 °C (70 °F), any lower and the seed will not

Cucumber seeds are sown on their sides, one to a pot

germinate and may even rot.

When the plant has produced four or five leaves, pot it up into its final pot. If you have used a plastic pot take great care to avoid damaging the roots as you remove the plant from its pot. With a peat pot you have the advantage of not only avoiding root damage, but also not having to remove the pot, as you simply pot up the plant complete with its pot.

Pot the plant into a 10-in pot using a potting compost. Take care not to over-water following repotting and increase the supply of water as the plant grows.

When the plant is about 12 in tall, feed once a week with a tomato fertilizer, watering in between if the plant requires it.

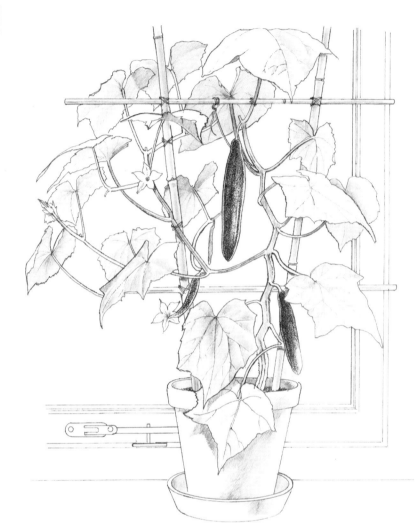

This pot-grown cucumber plant is being supported by a framework of bamboo canes

With luck and, of course, a reasonable amount of care your plant may yield up to ten melons.

Cucumbers

A suitable variety for windowsill care is Fembaby, a less vigorous all-female kind that produces bitter-free fruits. However, it can become rather leggy and does need careful training or it can get out of control.

As with the melon, sow the seed one to each 3½-in pot, preferably using a peat pot, laying the seed on its edge on the top of the compost; again a seed compost is ideal. Do not cover the seed otherwise it may rot.

Germinate the seed at about 27°C (80°F) but reduce the temperature a little as the plant produces its true leaves. When four true leaves have been produced, pot the plant into a 10-in pot using a potting compost and place the plant in a south-facing window.

A temperature of about 18°C (65°F) will be adequate from now on. Apart from watering and feeding every week, once the plant has reached 18 in high it does have a rather exacting requirement for support and training.

Support the plant with bamboo canes or sticks and when well established remove the leaves from 20 in of stem and from that point pinch out the lateral growths. This will help to encourage the production of flowers and subsequent fruits.

When the plant has grown as tall as you wish it to grow, pinch out the top. Train down two of the side shoots from the top as they grow, as this will help to make a well covered plant.

Fembaby requires a surprising amount of water and may need as much as 2–3 pints during warm spells, but the plant will reward your efforts with fruits that reach 6–8 in in length.

Pineapple

If you are lucky enough to obtain a pineapple with a complete top rosette of leaves you may be able to grow your own pineapple fruit.

Cut off the top about $\frac{1}{2}$ in below the base of the rosette. If the leaves are healthy and lush allow the base to dry off for a day or so before potting. However, if the leaves look dry then dip the base in rooting powder and pot up immediately. Use a $5\frac{1}{2}$-in dwarf pot and a compost made from three parts of seed compost to one part sand. Water infrequently and the rosette should produce roots and grow.

When the plant is about a year old place two or three ripe apples beside the pot and cover the plant and apples with a polythene bag for about a week.

After removing the plant from its 'tent' it should fruit within about six months, if it doesn't try again. The pineapple reacts to the ethylene gas given off by the apples and will initiate a fruit which, apart from being much smaller, is also rather more sour than those naturally grown.

Peanuts

Not everything you grow will provide you with a meal, but peanuts apart from eventually producing a light snack give a tremendous amount of fun.

Sow fresh peanuts – not roasted or salted – preferably still in their shells in a $3\frac{1}{2}$-in peat pot containing seed compost, allowing about two peanuts to a pot. Moisten the compost and germinate at about 27°C (80°F).

Once the peanuts have germinated keep the plants well watered until established and white roots start to appear through the bottom of the pot. Pot the plants into a 10-in pot in a potting compost.

Apart from watering frequently,

Why not try growing your own pineapple plant? *Left* root the top in a $5\frac{1}{2}$-in half pot containing a sandy compost. *Above* encouraging it to fruit by covering it with a large polythene bag containing two or three apples

A peanut (or groundnut) plant showing the nuts forming under the surface.

the oddest part of the cultivation occurs when the plants start to bloom. Green shoots appear from the yellow blooms and these then disappear into the compost where they then start to form new peanuts beneath the surface. The yield of nuts will not be high!

Citrus

Orange and lemon plants are relatively easy to grow from seed, but they may be disappointing because they do not produce the heavy crop of fruit that most people expect.

The orange or lemon pip can be germinated in a $3\frac{1}{2}$-in pot of seed compost, one seed to each pot. Keep the seed at about 20°C (68°F) and when germinated grow the seedlings on in full light – a south-facing window is best.

As the plant grows, pot it up into a 5-in and later a 7-in pot using a potting compost. Feed during the growing season, which is from April to September, once every two weeks with a tomato fertilizer applied at half concentration.

Just like a fruit tree in the garden, a lemon or orange plant should be trimmed or pruned to encourage compact growth. Unfortunately citrus plants rarely bear fruit but when they do they are worth waiting for – but be warned, the fruit are usually too bitter to eat.

Growing bags

Growing bags offer tremendous scope to grow a very wide range of crops. Although they are usually only thought of for growing tomatoes, in fact they will grow virtually anything, and for those without a garden they will provide that facility.

Courgettes and marrows

Courgettes and marrows are treated similarly, in fact baby marrows are really courgettes. Germinate the seed, placed on its edge, one to each pot in a $3\frac{1}{2}$-in peat pot filled with seed compost at a temperature of about 21°C (70°F).

When about 6 in tall, plant the marrows or courgettes, complete with their peat pots, two to each bag, taking care not to plant them out until mid-May when the danger of frost is over.

Make sure that you do not allow the growing bag to dry out, particularly during warm dry spells. When the first fruits have been picked start to feed with a suitable tomato fertilizer at the recommended rate once or twice a week, allowing about 4 pints to each feed.

Keep picking the fruits as they develop. This will allow you to enjoy them at their best and will also encourage the plants to produce more. Useful varieties of marrows are F_1 Zucchini and F_1 Golden Zucchini; the latter looks most attractive, too.

Cucumbers

For outdoor cultivation the ridge cucumber Burpee is one of the best varieties to grow.

Sow the cucumber seed on its

Two ridge cucumber plants in a growing bag

edge in a peat pot filled with seed compost and germinate at about 21°C (70°F). Once germinated grow the plants to about 6 in tall and then plant, complete with peat pots, two to each growing bag.

Do ensure though that the plants are hardened off for a week or so outside in a sheltered position before planting up. The end of May is a suitable time to plant up your cucumbers outside, when weather conditions should be improving.

Do not allow the compost to dry out, particularly during dry periods, but conversely do not over-water the bags. When the first cucumbers have been picked start feeding with a tomato fertilizer once a week for two or three weeks and then twice weekly.

Unfortunately, ridge cucumbers are not as elegant and well formed as glasshouse-grown cucumbers which do, of course, require a high temperature and humidity level. However, they are certainly

worth a try as a growing bag crop outside.

Lettuce

Although on first consideration you might think that it is not really profitable to grow lettuce in a growing bag, they really are worth the effort. Lettuce require little care and attention and can be grown repeatedly as the growing bag is cropped again and again.

First choose the variety or varieties that you prefer. Webb's Wonderful is still one of the most popular as are the cos varieties with their more distinctive nutty flavour. Salad Bowl is a useful variety which provides a successional supply of leaves that can be pulled as required.

Germinate the seed in a seed tray or half pot nearly filled with seed compost. Sow the seed thinly and cover with approximately $\frac{1}{8}$ in of compost and keep at about 13–16°C (55–60°F) indoors in a well lit position. Alternatively, germinate outside but this may take longer.

Once germinated, leave the seedlings in the pot or tray outside for about two weeks until they are large enough to handle. Then moisten the compost and prick them out, holding them by their leaves, directly into the growing bag at about twelve to each bag, in two rows of six. Then, simply keep the compost in the bag reasonably moist and within a few weeks you will have a superb crop of lettuce.

A succession of lettuce, courgettes and aubergines growing on the corner of a balcony

You can, of course, stagger the availability of the lettuce by sowing and planting in batches with a gap of one or two weeks, planting two, three or four plants to each bag each time. This will then keep you supplied with lettuce for weeks!

Between each crop of lettuce, remove the root stumps that have been left behind otherwise they tend to rot and can infect future crops with grey mould fungus or botrytis, which is a common disease of lettuce.

So easy to grow are lettuce, that they can be grown in a growing bag after it has been used for growing tomatoes or other crops.

Peppers

Although peppers grow better in a greenhouse, where protection from the elements helps to ensure a good crop from commercial varieties, you can still grow peppers outside in a growing bag. Varieties such as F_1 Early Prolific and F_1 Canape grow very successfully outdoors and require no special care and attention.

Sow the seed thinly in a seed tray or dwarf pot nearly filled with seed compost. Then cover with about $\frac{1}{8}$ in compost and germinate at about 20°C (68°F).

When large enough to handle prick out into $3\frac{1}{2}$-in peat or plastic pots in potting compost. Leave the seedlings in a sunny, warm position indoors until about 6 in tall before planting out. Plants growing in plastic pots must be removed from their pots before planting in the growing bag whereas those in peat pots can be planted directly in the bag, three to a bag. Peppers are not frost hardy and should not be planted until mid-May outside.

Keep the compost moist and when the first fruits have set start

Runner beans are a satisfying crop to produce in a growing bag

to feed with a tomato fertilizer once a week.

The fruits will then develop and can be picked green or red. As the fruits develop increase feeding to twice a week. If you pick the fruit when they are green you will encourage the plants to produce more peppers. Alternatively, you can leave them until they are red, but this takes longer and reduces the amount of peppers produced.

Runner beans

Runner beans are another crop that can be grown in a growing bag provided they are given

sufficient protection from the wind. Thread strings through the bag to provide support for the plants and train to a fence or even up a sunny wall.

Runner beans can be sown or planted when the danger of frosts is past but must not be grown in an exposed position. Sow the beans directly in the bag in two rows, and about 12 in apart along the length of the bag.

Feed once a week when the plants are about 2 ft high using a tomato fertilizer and increase to twice a week when you start picking. During warm dry spells you will find it necessary to water in between feeds to keep up with the plants' requirements. Good varieties worth trying are Enorma and Red Knight.

Strawberries

Strawberries must surely be one of the most enjoyable fruits to grow during the unpredictable days of summer.

They do, however, tend to grow somewhat rampantly when planted in the garden and produce myriads of runners that spread and entwine all over the place. This is one of the reasons why they are an ideal crop for a growing bag. And this may be used in either a conventional or unconventional way.

First of all strawberries can be grown in a growing bag that is laid flat in the normal way. Plant ten plants to each bag in two rows of five along the length of the bag. Apart from watering there is no need to do anything else but they must be fed after fruiting with a tomato fertilizer to encourage

This unusual method of planting strawberries in a growing bag is very space saving

strong healthy growth for future cropping.

Earlier crops of strawberries can be produced by planting up the bag in September and leaving it outside until January. It can then be placed in a greenhouse or conservatory, where it will fruit earlier. An increased 'set' of fruit can be obtained by transferring the pollen from flower to flower with a small paint brush. This does the job of pollination in the absence of insects in the early part of the year.

Although the conventional way of using the growing bag is effective you may get rather bored seeing the bags always laid flat. So why not use them in a different way?

Take the growing bag and instead of laying it down stand it on one of its ends, so that it looks like a narrow sack. Cut 4-in slits opposite each other and plant the strawberries in the slits. The strawberry plants will trail down the sides of the bag and will then crop prolifically.

Alternatively, if you can obtain the smaller growing bags that are sometimes available you can even hang the bag up in the air either on a wall or a fence. A smaller growing bag will accommodate between six and eight strawberry plants.

To add a further touch of variety, Alpine strawberries are worth a try – don't plant up a complete bag but simply substitute two or three of the usual plants with the Alpine sort. The berries are smaller and sweeter but are produced through most of the summer.

Tomatoes

Tomatoes must still be the most popular plants grown in growing bags. Inside a greenhouse, outside in the garden, or simply laid outside the back door, there are a number of varieties that will provide a veritable long-lasting feast of tomatoes from midsummer through to the autumn, when the first frost will quickly dispatch the plants blackening the foliage and fruits.

Instead of simply buying any variety of tomato – plant or seed – try to spend a little time in selecting the right one for the use you have for it. This is important because so many people are disappointed each year when their tomatoes do not grow vigorously or crop well when grown outside and are dissuaded from growing them again.

The Amateur is still an old favourite outdoor variety of tomato which crops reasonably well with average-sized good-flavoured fruits. However, why not try some of the newer varieties with the increased vigour that is provided by plants that are F_1 hybrids? F_1 hybrids have been specially bred to increase the crop

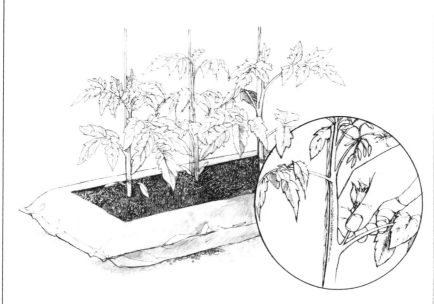

Inset Removing a side shoot from a tomato plant

potential and have certain other beneficial characteristics like improved flavour and shape.

F$_I$ Sweet 100 is a superb variety that produces delicious small fruits in abundance. This variety will need support and should have its side shoots removed.

Outdoor Girl again needs support and its side shoots removed but provides medium-sized fruits of good flavour.

Sigmabush and Pixie are bush varieties that do not require support or their side shoots removed. In fact all you have to do is leave them alone, apart from watering, feeding and, of course, picking.

Whichever variety you choose, sow the seed in the middle of March in a dwarf pot or seed tray in seed compost. Lightly cover with compost and germinate at 18–20°C (65–68°F). When the seed has germinated and the seed leaves have fully expanded and the characteristic tomato leaves are starting to emerge, gently prick out the seedlings one to each 3½-in peat pot using a potting compost.

Grow the plants on a sunny windowsill until they are about 6 in tall. In mid-May when, hopefully, the frosts have finished harden off the plants in a sheltered position for about a week then plant in the growing bag, three plants to a bag.

The bush varieties will obviously not need support, whereas the conventional tomatoes will require a frame. This can take the form of a proprietary ready-made frame or a home-made affair consisting of canes inserted in the compost or even strings running from the bag up a fence or wall.

A mixed planting of salad crops is decorative and useful

As the tomato plants grow, give water only until the second truss has set, then start feeding with a tomato fertilizer once a week, watering in between feeds as required. After this all you have to do is to wait for the fruit to grow and ripen and then pick it.

Other salad crops

Growing bags do not have to be used for growing a single crop at a time. Indeed, they can and should be used as a mini garden.

Apart from the crops already mentioned there are others that can be grown together. For example, spring onions, radishes, and baby carrots are all very easy to grow by sowing directly in a growing bag.

It is even possible to grow a mini crop of spring onions, radishes, baby carrots, lettuce and even a tomato plant in one bag – the possibilities and combinations are almost endless!

Even after a growing bag has been used for growing a major crop like tomatoes or cucumbers it may be used again for growing a crop of lettuce or mixed salad crops. Provided you rotate the types of crop to reduce the risk of disease and feed to make up for nutrients already used, you can actually keep a growing bag in use for two or three years.

Patio pots, tubs and planters

If you consider that growing bags are not particularly attractive, but wish nonetheless to make the maximum use of floor space, patio pots, tubs and planters can provide you with a more aesthetic solution.

However, prior to planting spend a little time and thought to ensure that the container you are using is suitable. Plastic or fibreglass containers are water-proof and weather-resistant and can be planted up immediately. Wooden containers should however be proofed first with a suitable timber preservative but preferably not creosote which is harmful to plants.

Although plastic or wooden containers are relatively inexpensive, they are usually rather light and more easily blown over. For this reason concrete or earthenware pots provide a sturdier alternative, particularly for taller growing subjects.

Bay trees

Although bay trees hardly supply a food crop as such, they do provide a most important item for culinary use i.c. the bay leaf. Freshly picked or dried, the leaves of the bay laurel can be used in soups, casseroles, stews, or a myriad of other dishes.

The cultivation of bay trees is quite simple and the beauty of the plant is that not only is a year-round crop of leaves always available from it but the appearance of the bay is always appealing.

The bay laurel should be planted in a potting compost to which has been added about 10

per cent fine sand. This will aid drainage and help to prevent waterlogging.

During the spring and summer feed the bay once every two weeks with a half-strength solution of tomato fertilizer. In the autumn and winter protect the plant from extremes of weather particularly frosts and strong winds. Bays are not very hardy and should be grown in a sheltered position or even brought indoors and grown in a cool light situation during the winter months.

The plant can be grown in a variety of shapes and these can be achieved by simple pruning, clipping or trimming of side shoots. The basic bushy compact habit of the plant can be maintained by pruning lightly any straggly growth.

If, however, you wish to grow the bay as a standard i.e. a long stem supporting a bushy mop at the top, the treatment is a little different. Start with a young plant and trim off any side shoots,

A wide selection of very attractive tubs and containers is available

Standard bay trees need good support and protection from strong winds

allowing the plant to grow straight up. Support the stem with a cane to prevent it bowing or snapping and until such time as it has reached the height that you wish. Then let the main stem

163

grow a little more and pinch out the top growth. The bay will then start to bush out at the top and within a year or two the stem will become more sturdy and the support can be removed.

Apart from the fact that the leaves of the bay may be picked fresh all year round and used, they may also be picked and dried and then stored in a glass jar.

Fig trees

Many people probably own a number of members of the fig family without really being aware of it. The varieties commonly grown are purely decorative; they do not bear edible figs and are better known as rubber plants, weeping figs, creeping figs and fiddle-leaved figs.

The true edible fig can be grown in a large tub or planter that is placed in a sheltered sunny

A fig plant requires a strong planter and is too heavy for a balcony

position. As the fig is likely to grow quite large use a sturdy container that provides stability. Figs require good drainage and are prone to root disorders aggravated by waterlogging. To improve drainage, place pieces of broken clay pot in the bottom of the container and use a free draining compost. A suitable compost can be a mix of 4 parts of potting compost to 1 part of sharp sand.

Figs require little nourishment and a feed of a tomato fertilizer used at half strength and applied once every two weeks during the growing season from May to September will supply the plant with adequate nutrients. The plant may become too dense in its centre and if this happens any offending branches that are cramping the plant's shape should be removed. The overall shape of the plant can also be improved throughout the season by simply trimming back any wayward growth in order to maintain a well-shaped tree.

When the fruit ripen and are picked, do ensure that they are eaten immediately. Unfortunately they don't keep very long and are best eaten fresh. Alternatively they can be dried and then stored before being consumed.

Peppers

Peppers can be grown very easily outside in small to medium-sized pots or tubs.

Germinate the seed in a half pot or seed tray in a seed compost at about 20°C (68°F). When large enough to handle prick out the seedlings one to each 3½-in pot of potting compost. Water the plants when required and grow them on in a warm well lit position. When they are about 6 in tall, pot up in the final container and place outdoors, but this must not be done before late May when the frosts are over.

Place the plant or plants in a sunny, well sheltered position to give them the best chance of growing successfully, and setting fruit that will mature. Start to feed, using a tomato fertilizer, once a week when the first fruit starts to set, then increase to twice a week after a few weeks.

If you pick the peppers when they are green and do not give them the chance to ripen and turn red, you will encourage the plant to produce more fruit. As peppers are a little more tricky to grow outside it is, in fact, better to pick them when they are green. Waiting for them to turn red may make all the difference between producing the odd one or two or a reasonable crop.

Tomatoes

Once again tomatoes fill the niche of providing a useful productive crop. The choice of the tomato variety can be made to suit the container. Dwarf bush varieties that grow only about 2 ft will suit window boxes, or planters where the restriction of space confines one to the smaller varieties. Alternatively, the conventional tomato varieties that require support can be grown in larger planters where space is not a problem.

Suitable dwarf bush varieties are Minibel and Pixie. These are bush varieties that should not have their side shoots removed but should be allowed to grow un-restricted. Even so their diminu-tive height of only about 2 ft is not often exceeded.

Conventional varieties that require support in the form of a cane or stick provide also a choice of fruits. F_1 Sweet 100 provides small but tasty fruits whereas Outdoor Girl will provide medium sized fruits. With these conventional varieties remove the side shoots or the plants will grow out of control and the likely crop potential will be dramatically reduced.

Whichever variety you choose, sow the seed in a dwarf pot or seed tray in seed compost, lightly covering the seed with $\frac{1}{8}$ in of compost. Germinate at about 18–20°C (65–68°F) and when the seed leaves have fully expanded

A dwarf bush tomato is a good choice for pot cultivation

and the characteristic tomato leaves start to appear, prick out one seedling to each $3\frac{1}{2}$-in pot in potting compost. Grow on until 6 in tall and in late May plant up in the container.

Feed with a tomato fertilizer when the first truss appears, once a week to begin with, increasing to twice a week after about a month.

Strawberries

Although strawberries will not provide much height, indeed they will tend to trail over the pot, they provide a useful crop for that odd situation on a balcony or in a window box where you do not want a plant that grows too tall.

Allow about three plants to each square foot of surface area of the pot or container and use a potting compost as the growing medium.

For a slightly taller variety use an alpine variety such as Alexandria. This can be grown on its own or together with more usual varieties like Cambridge Favourite.

Give water only to the straw-berries until after they have finished fruiting. Then feed with a tomato fertilizer as well to promote future cropping.

Mixed tubs

With larger tubs, troughs or planters there is absolutely no reason why a number of crops should not be grown together. Indeed to make the maximum use of space, long troughs are ideal for growing tomatoes, strawberries, peppers and even lettuce, radishes and carrots.

Even window boxes can serve as a mini vegetable garden, where dwarf tomatoes, peppers, straw-berries, lettuce, radishes and carrots can be grown with the minimum of care.

A mini garden of strawberries, tomato, lettuce and carrots

Hanging baskets

With growing bags, patio pots and dustbins occupying all available area on the ground you can still increase the crop potential by making use of space up in the air.

Growing bags can be tied at one end and hung from a sturdy bracket or similar support but they are rather heavy and do not look particularly attractive. Hanging baskets, on the other hand, look reasonable and can be hung almost anywhere.

Hanging baskets are available in a fairly wide range of forms. The most popular used today are the plastic baskets which should last three to five years. All they require is to be filled with an appropriate compost, planted and hung up.

Conversely, the original hanging baskets were made of wire mesh and these require a slightly different treatment. Obviously if you filled such a container with compost it would immediately fall out again and so some sort of material must be placed between the wire framework and the compost.

Traditionally sphagnum moss was placed on the inside of the wire basket and although rather difficult to obtain it still provides the best solution. Sphagnum moss looks attractive and may actually grow, providing a living lining. Sphagnum moss may sometimes be purchased from a florist who uses the material in floral decorative work.

Alternatively, a wire basket can be lined with polythene which does not look so attractive but works reasonably well.

Although wire baskets may require a little more time and attention to set up, they will last a great deal longer than plastic baskets.

Whichever you choose, use a potting compost as the growing medium and feed fairly regularly, for the container will not only dry out more quickly than pots or tubs, but will also require more feeding because of the lower volume of compost in the basket.

Courgettes

Courgettes can be grown quite effectively as a hanging basket crop.

Place the seed on its edge in a 3½-in peat pot filled with seed compost and germinate at about 21°C (70°F). When the plant is growing reasonably well and is about 6 in tall plant the courgette or marrow plant into the basket. Remember, though, that marrows and courgettes are not frost hardy and the young plants should not be put outside until the danger of frosts is over.

Once planted into the basket water in and check daily to ensure that the basket does not dry out.

Feeding should be commenced as soon as the first fruits start to form, using tomato fertilizer applied once a week for the first few weeks and increasing to twice a week to keep up with the plant's increasing appetite.

Marrows grown as courgettes should be picked as soon as they are large enough. If left any longer you could find the basket eventually coming adrift from its mooring. It is really preferable to grow true courgette varieties as they are more even in shape and are not likely to produce over-weight fruits.

Nasturtiums

As they say, now for something completely different! Unfortunately not everything you grow to eat looks particularly attractive – often quite the contrary.

Nasturtiums are, therefore, an ideal crop to grow, for they provide not only a useful food crop that can be used in a number of ways, but also an all-summer-long display of colour. For that reason alone nasturtiums can be

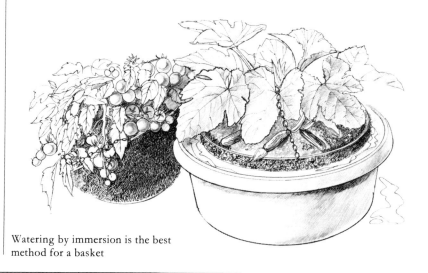

Watering by immersion is the best method for a basket

grown by the front door, where they will not look out of place.

As far as growing them is concerned, it really could not be easier. Sow the seed directly into the compost of the hanging basket in April or May, gently covering the seed with compost and watering in.

As the plants grow they can be used in a number of ways. The flowers, leaves and seeds can be used in salads providing a pepper-like vegetable that will liven up anything they are added to. The young seeds can also be pickled and used later.

Nasturtiums are quite modest in their nutritional requirements and you will probably not need to feed them all through the season. It really is up to you though, if you want plenty of flowers don't feed the plants much at all, alternatively if you want plenty of leaves, feed the plants about once a month with a tomato fertilizer.

Tomatoes

Even tomatoes are a good crop for growing in a hanging basket but you must choose the variety with care and not use conventional tomatoes. Instead use the dwarf bush varieties like Minibel or Pixie which only grow about 2 ft high and will also trail effectively over the edge of the basket.

Sow the seed in a seed tray or dwarf pot in a seed compost, lightly covering the seed to a depth of about $\frac{1}{8}$ in and germinate at about 18–20°C (65–68°F).

When the seedlings are large enough to handle i.e. they have fully expanded their seed leaves and have started to produce the true leaves, gently prick them out into $3\frac{1}{2}$-in pots filled with potting compost. Place them in a warm sunny position and water until the plants are about 6 in high.

They should then be hardened off outside for about a week or so from the middle to the end of May when the frosts are over. Plant up the basket with one, or two plants if the basket can take two, and feed as soon as the first truss appears. Use a tomato fertilizer at the standard rate once a week to begin with for the first month and then increase to twice a week.

Strawberries

Strawberries are also a useful crop to grow in a hanging basket. Depending upon the size of the basket, plant between three and five plants. The conventional strawberry plants like Cambridge Favourite trail and produce a reasonable crop from a restricted area.

Alpine varieties such as Alexandria can be used in the centre of the basket where, although they do not trail, they fill in the space between the conventional trailing varieties.

Unfortunately, you will be unlikely to harvest a large crop from strawberries grown in a basket, but nonetheless they are well worth the effort. Once planted simply water the strawberries until they have flowered and fruited. After that, feed once every two weeks for a couple of months with a tomato fertilizer to build up the plants for subsequent crops.

If you have a greenhouse, conservatory or even a porch, you can harvest an earlier crop by leaving the plants outside until January and then bringing them inside where they will fruit earlier.

Dustbin

One of the last items that you would think would serve as a container in which to grow plants must be a dustbin. Surprisingly though, a dustbin is ideal for growing a heavy and very useful crop of potatoes.

Potatoes must surely be one of the crops that demands the most hard work. First they must be 'chitted' (allowed to produce shoots), and then planted. A trench is dug and the potatoes are covered over with soil. As the potatoes grow, the soil is mounded up around the stems to encourage the plants to produce more tubers. Once grown, then comes the task of digging up the potatoes. The soil has to be carefully forked over and the potatoes removed. All of this requires a great deal of hard and often back-breaking work.

Not surprisingly, therefore, potatoes are usually one of the first crops to be dropped from the vegetable patch and are not usually considered as a crop that can be grown by any easier method. But growing potatoes in a dustbin requires very little care and attention.

First of all select a suitable dustbin, a plastic one is ideal. Galvanized dustbins tend to corrode and also can get damaged when the potatoes are harvested.

In the normal way 'chit' the potatoes in a cool shed or suitable situation. When the tubers have produced a number of shoots they are ready to be planted – this should be in early April. You can use soil to fill the dustbin but this does tend to make it very heavy and can make the eventual harvesting difficult. It is therefore a very good idea to mix up a

The potato is kept in the light until strong shoots grow from the eyes. This process is known as chitting

compost based on soil and peat. A mix of one or two parts of top soil to one part of peat will be suitable.

The soil or compost should then be placed in the dustbin to a depth of about 6 in. Take two potatoes and rub off the surplus shoots to leave either two or three sprouts. Place the potatoes on the compost in the dustbin and cover carefully with a 6-in layer of soil or compost.

Do not be tempted to grow

Below Planting the potatoes in a dustbin. *Right* The plants are earthed up as they grow

your potatoes in a sheltered or shady position for they must have full light or they will tend to produce weak growth.

Water the potatoes, but take care not to over-water as this will cause them to rot. Drainage can be improved by drilling two or three holes of about $\frac{1}{2}$-in diameter, but not everyone will want to drill holes in their dustbin!

As the potatoes grow, continue to top up the dustbin with more soil or compost, placing this around the growth, but taking care never to bury it.

Continue to do this until the dustbin is full of soil or compost, or until the potatoes start to flower. When they have finished flowering and the haulms (or top growth) start to die back, the potatoes will be ready to harvest. Probably the easiest way to do this is to simply tip over the dustbin and pick out the potatoes – you will be amazed at the crop produced by this method.

Incidentally, as a final point, take care where you leave the dustbin – your refuse collector might decide to harvest your potatoes sooner than you had planned!

Bonsai Growing Made Easy

Bonsai have a magic all of their own; ever changing,
ever growing they can be passed down from generation to
generation. The finest specimens are living works
of art of great value. So tenuous is their lifeline
that a few days of neglect can wipe out a hundred
years of constant attention.

Introduction

Many people believe that bonsai are a special species of dwarf tree that grows for a while into a strange and attractive shape then, having attained that shape, mysteriously stops growing. This, however, is far from the truth. Bonsai are not even dwarf trees but ordinary species which might just as easily be growing to 50 or 100 ft in a field but for the fact that they are being trained in pots. Their beautiful shapes are, in most cases, created by their owner who uses his gardening skill and imagination to train the small trees to a suitable style.

Over the last twenty years bonsai have become increasingly well known in Britain, being cultivated by many people who derive a great deal of pleasure from their hobby.

Trees have been grown in pots by gardeners of many nations for many centuries but to China and Japan must go the credit for the development of potted trees into works of art. The Chinese have cultivated bonsai for about one thousand years and have developed over that period a number of distinct styles of training, mostly geographically defined. The size of the country and its great wealth of indigenous plants could have led to even greater diversity but in recent times the majority of Chinese bonsai have been trained by the pruning and tying down of branches.

The Japanese almost certainly learned of bonsai from the Chinese, but early records show that the styling of Japanese trees has for centuries followed a different course to those of the Chinese and, especially in the last one hundred and fifty years or so, has been elevated to great heights. In both countries, bonsai had religious connotations. In China, they were, for the Taoist, symbolic of the power contained in natural phenomena, mountains, rock or trees which, when fortuitously found in nature, held that power in a greatly concentrated form. In Japan, however, bonsai were regarded as objects for contemplation by the Zen priests and, as such, valued for their great beauty and almost imperceptible progress towards perfection as a result of their training.

Bonsai were first displayed in Britain in the early years of this century and although at the time they were admired for their age and artistry, they did not become generally popular for many years. A few enthusiasts began developing trees as bonsai but interest remained at this level until the 1950's when Japanese-trained bonsai were imported into Britain in small numbers, to be purchased by curious members of the public. By the late 1960's this trickle had increased somewhat and bonsai, some good, many poor, appeared in the more adventurous florists' shops as well as in a very few specialist nurseries. However, it is only in the last four or five years that there has been a substantial increase in the number of amateurs growing their own bonsai in the same way that they might grow their fuchsias, house plants or tomatoes.

Despite this welcome increase in the number of enthusiasts growing bonsai, there are still a large number of people who, feeling that it would be all too difficult for them, have not tried this very pleasant pastime. However, to grow trees in pots is not difficult, the horticultural skills needed are quite basic and straightforward and the training of those trees, once growing, is also a straightforward and logical task, resulting in a little tree of great charm.

To help those people who would like to grow bonsai, easy-to-follow guidelines are laid out in the following pages.

Indoors or outdoors

The vast majority of bonsai in Britain today, either imported from Japan or cultivated by the growing band of enthusiasts, are of hardy trees, such as pines (pinus), beech (fagus) and crab apple (malus). These trees and many more besides are grown because they have particular features such as attractive foliage, blossom or coloured bark and they may appear very different in shape and character. However, they all have one factor in common, and that is as full size trees growing in open ground, they are hardy in our British climate. As bonsai, these trees do not lose their hardiness and the only concessions that need be made to them are as a result of cultivating them in pots. A hardy plant of any sort in a pot must be watered when it does not rain, for its roots cannot reach into the depths of the earth in search of moisture. It will also require some feeding as it will soon use the limited supply in the soil contained in the pot. Similarly, during the winter, when temperatures fall below freezing, the plant in a pot may require a little pro-

Pyracanthas are especially suited to bonsai training as both flowers and fruit are in good proportion to the tree

tection because, unlike its counterpart in open ground, its rootball may freeze solid.

Novices, faced with this fact, often feel that it seems a waste to have very attractive trees outside, sometimes turn to house plants to satisfy their desire for plants in the home. This is not, however, necessary as there are two alternatives available for those who wish to have bonsai indoors.

The first is applicable to the hardy trees first mentioned. In Japan bonsai are brought indoors for display and then taken out again, another being brought in after one or, at the most, two days. This is a simple routine and trees displayed in this way have a fresh, clean look.

For those who, either because they live in a flat or simply because they prefer it, wish to grow their

An English grown beech which is now about 15 years old

often seen in homes though rarely as trained bonsai, or even palms. As some readers may be aware, many of these plants can grow embarrassingly large when given a little attention in a house, what better then to train them as bonsai, ensuring by that means that they will fit into the lounge or kitchen for many years.

A golden rule in the cultivation of bonsai is, therefore, grow trees which in nature would live in an environment similar to that which you can offer. If this simple rule is followed, there is every likelihood that the tree, trained as a bonsai, will live a long and healthy life.

Equipment

In the same way as, for example, one would require tools such as a spade or a hoe to aid the cultivation of vegetables in open ground, there are certain items required for the cultivation of bonsai.

The most important of these is not a tool but a pot, this being essential to the growing and displaying of bonsai. For young trees or seedlings, flower pots, preferably the rather shallow types known as half pots, are adequate provided they have drainage holes. Either the clay pots, or the more modern and lightweight plastic or polythene pots may be used. Clay are perhaps to be preferred if there is a choice, as they are porous and ensure good drainage, which is all important to a bonsai.

Once the little tree has developed somewhat, it should be repotted into a shallow specially-made bonsai container. These are made of pottery which is both porous and frostproof, with excellent drainage. They are in quiet or neutral colours, unglazed or glazed,

bonsai indoors, there is a different range of trees suited to this type of cultivation. These are the trees originating from warmer climates than our own, that will thrive in centrally-heated rooms given simple care. Such trees range from the members of the citrus family, oranges, lemons, grapefruit, which are in fact often grown as potted plants indoors, to the coffee tree with its shiny leaves, and members of the ficus family, again

A selection of the tools required for training bonsai

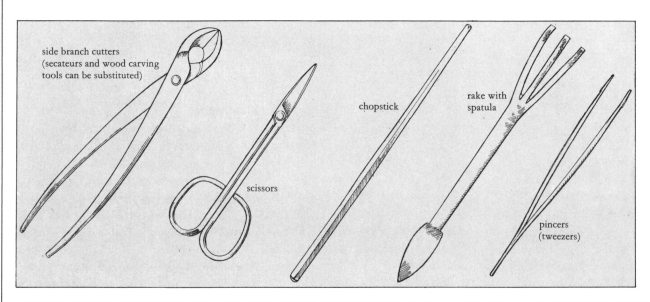

side branch cutters
(secateurs and wood carving
tools can be substituted)

scissors

chopstick

rake with
spatula

pincers
(tweezers)

and stand on small feet. Some are round, others rectangular or oval. Bonsai look very good in these containers and a selection of shapes and sizes may be obtained. Growers of indoor bonsai will not need to obtain frostproof containers, otherwise the requirements are the same.

Apart from potting compost, which is dealt with in more detail in the potting section, other needs are simple. A pair of scissors and small secateurs for pruning twigs or branches and a supply of wire, either copper or plastic-coated garden wire, in different thicknesses for bending branches to desired shapes are

helpful. A chopstick is an extremely useful potting aid, helping to ease soil between the fine fibrous root system of a bonsai with the minimum of damage. A small trowel and a pair of tweezers which are ideal for removing odd dead leaves from twiggy branches or removing intruding weed seedlings are two additional useful extras.

Many other tools, some specific to bonsai cultivation and training and others in more general use may be added. Their acquisition, though not essential, can make some tasks quicker and simpler and the most useful Japanese tools are illustrated on page 172.

Starting a collection

There are a number of different ways of obtaining the first trees for a bonsai collection. Of these the cheapest and perhaps the most satisfying in the long run is to grow from seed.

FROM SEED

Many trees are easily grown by this method and seeds of hardy varieties such as beech (*Fagus sylvatica*), oak (quercus), pine (pinus) and field maple (*Acer campestre*) can be collected when ripe. Other varieties of hardy tree seeds such as the Japanese maples (*Acer palmatum* and *Acer buergeranum*), the greybark elm (*Zelkova serrata*) and the larch (*Larix leptolepis*) may be purchased from specialist suppliers.

Seeds of such hardy trees would, in natural circumstances, spend winter on the soil, covered with fallen leaves, before germinating in the warmer days of spring. The period of winter cold is necessary for germination of most hardy tree seeds and, for those who wish to do this in a simple manner, there is the simple facility of the domestic refrigerator. If seeds are mixed with damp sand or peat in an egg cup and placed in the refrigerator for a period of a month or so, this will provide the necessary winter cold. The seeds must remain moist during this period, otherwise little attention is required other than that of checking occasionally to make sure the seeds have not started germinating. Under these circumstances the seeds must be removed and planted.

When the period of refrigeration is over, the seeds should be spread on a seed tray, prepared in the normal manner with a fine well-drained sandy compost. They may be covered with a very thin layer of the same

compost, no more than the diameter of the seed in thickness. After watering carefully, the tray of seeds should be placed outside or in a cool greenhouse and will not require covering, other than netting against the attention of cats or mice.

Seeds may, of course, be planted when collected, then left outside through the winter. The only problem occurs because the temperatures of an English winter can be alternately warm and cold, rather than being continuously cold.

Once seedlings have appeared and have grown two or more true leaves (except in the case of pines which should remain in the seed tray for a year before transplanting) the seedlings may be transplanted into pots. An ideal sized pot for the novice to use at this stage is a well drained 3-in half pot. Transplanting should be done with care and newly-potted seedlings should be carefully watered then placed in a sheltered spot until established and growing. They should then be moved to a sunny position and fed lightly but regularly with a general purpose fertilizer to encourage plenty of healthy growth.

For the cultivation of indoor bonsai, the process of growing from seed is similar, though seeds of warm climate trees do not, of course, require a period of cold. Most seeds of indoor trees appreciate being planted in a fine, well-drained lime-free compost in a pot or seed tray and this should then be placed in a position where there is plenty of light and a bottom temperature of about 21°C (70°F). The more tropical plants, such as date palms and mahogany trees, will require warmer starting temperatures up to 27°C (80°F) but, once growing, will happily thrive in average centrally-

This crataegus, collected as a young tree, has now been trained for six years in the windswept style

heated-house temperatures. The best source of seed for indoor bonsai is the seeds contained in fruit. These are, of course, fresh and more likely to be viable than very dry, long-stored seeds.

Growing seedlings under such warm and necessarily moist conditions can produce a condition known as damping off, when seedlings fall over and die. This can be avoided by watering the seed tray or pot at the time of planting with Cheshunt compound, a worthwhile preventive measure.

Once growing well with two or more true leaves, the indoor trees can, like their hardier brothers outside, be transplanted carefully into 3-in half pots and placed in a sunny window. After about four weeks, a programme of regular feeding with a well-diluted fertilizer will ensure plenty of growth ready for training.

FROM CUTTINGS

Another simple method of obtaining bonsai starter material is by rooting cuttings. Certain trees, such as beech, oak, birch and pines, are not suited to this method but there are plenty of trees and shrubs that make good bonsai and are readily produced from soft or hard cuttings.

Softwood cuttings, usually about 4 in long, are taken from shoots of the current year's growth, usually in early summer, and are firm, whilst in no way woody. They can be removed from the parent plant by cutting

below a leaf node (where leaf stem and shoot stem meet) or pulled from the branch with a heel (small strip) of older wood attached. One or two of the lowest leaves are removed and the heel, if any, trimmed. The cuttings are then ready to insert into a seed tray or pot filled with a suitable rooting mixture. A usual mixture is one part of moss peat mixed with one part of grit or sharp sand by volume. A hole is made for each cutting (a chopstick is useful for this job) and the cutting inserted and gently firmed in position. When all the cuttings have been planted the container should be watered, then placed in a light position where there is bottom heat of about 16–18·5 °C (60–65 °F). The soft shoots will wilt quickly if the air around them is not humid. For those without a propagator a polythene bag over the pot or seed tray may be used to retain moisture in the air around the cuttings. Regular spraying with water helps keep the cuttings cool and maintains the high level of moisture in the air around them. The cuttings will root in three to six weeks depending on species, after which they should be potted on ready for bonsai training; a suitable potting mixture being equal parts of loam, leafmould and sharp sand. Suitable hardy plants for propagation by this method include cotoneaster, pyracantha, chaenomeles and cydonia, *Betula nana* (the dwarf birch), crataegus and some varieties of acers. The easiest of the tender varieties which can be reproduced in this

Two popular types of cuttings are softwood (a) and heel (b)

174

This 19-tree group of *Zelkova serrata* (ages ranging from 10 to 30 years) was planted four years ago. The tray is 44 in long

way is perhaps the pomegranate, *Punica granatum*.

Semi-hardwood cuttings are similar to softwood cuttings except that they are of riper wood and should always be taken with a heel. They are also usually longer, about 6 in; as roots are slower to grow the cutting needs the greater amount of 'food' stored in the extra leaves of a longer cutting. These cuttings will root at a slightly lower temperature, 13–16 °C (55–60 °F), but still have the same need for moist air around them.

Hardwood cuttings are the easiest of all cuttings to take. They are shoots of completely ripe wood taken in the autumn and rooted in open ground or in the shelter of a cold frame. Such cuttings may be up to 1 ft long for deciduous trees but shorter if taken from coniferous species.

Cuttings in open ground are placed against one side of a V-shaped trench, made in a sheltered area of reasonably good soil, the bottom 1 in of which has been filled with sharp sand or grit. Soil is then pushed back into the trench and firmed down. These cuttings should be left for eighteen months before potting up. For bonsai cultivation the hardy varieties most suited to this form of propagation are junipers and poplar.

SELF-SOWN SEEDLINGS

Young trees of hardy varieties at least can often be found and transplanted for training. This is a quick way of obtaining material and even the average garden may yield a number of interesting seedling trees. The sort of seedlings found include laburnum, cotoneaster, pyracantha, ivy, cherry, almond and hawthorn. In wooded areas, many young forest trees may be found though the collector must remember that if the land is not his, he must have permission from the landowner to dig up any small trees he finds.

Such seedlings or young trees should be carefully lifted, retaining as much root as possible, and potted up in a suitable sized container. Once established, bonsai training can commence. It is usually recommended that wild trees be dug up in spring, just before actual bud growth starts and this is a good policy to follow. However, much success can be achieved when digging in summer provided that the trees, once potted, are treated for about a month in the same way as softwood cuttings.

Bonsai training

Once young trees obtained by any of the afore-mentioned methods are established and growing in 3- or 4-in pots, the process of bonsai training can begin. Pruning, especially of deciduous trees, is an essential part of bonsai training, normally carried out during the growing season. The novice, often being afraid of the consequences of cutting twigs and branches, frequently neglects this important part of bonsai development and maintenance. As a result, his trees look sparse and straggly instead of neat and shapely with a multitude of twiggy growth.

Deciduous trees can be grouped in categories according to their natural growth habit, some having two main periods of growth during a season whilst others grow throughout the summer months. There is a third category which, though their growth habit may be of the first or second type, are additionally characterised by their very dominant tip growth and which can to advantage have additional training in the form of bud removal during the winter.

CONTINUOUS SUMMER GROWTH
Notable amongst the first group, those which grow throughout the summer, are elms, maples, hawthorns,

cotoneaster and hornbeams amongst the hardy trees and shrubs and pomegranate and citrus amongst the tender plants. One could also include larch, swamp cypress and Japanese cedar (*Cryptomeria japonica*) amongst the conifers, the first two of which are, of course, deciduous.

All these trees (except cryptomeria which is ever-green) come into leaf in spring and, having produced foliage, continue their growth by producing shoots mainly from tips of existing branches, but also from buds in the leaf axils. These shoots should be pruned back to one bud (or pair of buds) when they appear, thus encouraging bushy dense growth giving the impression of maturity. Shaping can also be achieved during the growing season by pruning a badly-shaped branch back to a dormant bud pointing in the direction of required growth. A new shoot will grow from the bud and further training is developed by regular pinching back of new shoots as they elongate. By a combination of these two processes, an attractively-shaped tree will be created and maintained.

TWO GROWTH PERIODS
The second category of trees, those which have two main periods of growth during the summer months, are represented by several trees suitable for bonsai training, notably beech and oak. Some may consider these two trees unsuited for cultivation as bonsai because of their somewhat large leaves. However, over a period of time these reduce in size and look very attractive on a bonsai of, say 1½–2 ft in height.

Growth in spring consists of a shoot growing from each bud, on which there are several leaves. As soon as the leaves can be seen, such shoots should be pinched back, leaving one leaf on each. This will not only keep the tree compact, but will induce dormant buds on older wood to become active. During the second period during mid-summer, some of these previously dormant buds will produce a small shoot, as well as the shoots which grow as expected near the tips of branches. These should be treated as for spring growth.

DOMINANT TIP GROWTH
When considering trees which have very dominant tip buds in winter, one's mind goes to the horse chestnut with its characteristic 'sticky buds'. Other trees which

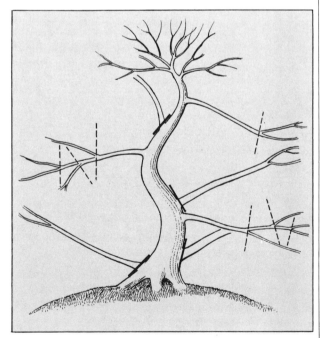

Pruning is carried out to remove unwanted branches (thick lines) and to promote a division of growth (dotted lines)

have very dominant tip buds in winter include ash, sycamore and oak. Though summer pruning is routinely carried out on these trees, removal of the tip buds in November or December encourages the development of smaller lateral buds during the winter. In spring, growth from such buds is shorter, finer and generally more suitable for bonsai than the rather coarse long shoots which would otherwise develop with great vigour from tip buds.

Evergreens are pruned according to type. *Quercus ilex* (the holm oak) a broadleaf evergreen, for example, is pruned in the same way as deciduous oaks but junipers, whose foliage has been considerably adapted to become leaf scales, are pinched out by hand every few days during the two main periods of growth to obtain and maintain the compact shapely layers of foliage so suited to this species.

Pines are different again. They normally have one period of growth annually in spring when a 'candle' develops from each bud. When this has elongated the needles begin to appear from the candle, extend and harden. To encourage the pine to produce more, and shorter candles, the extended candle is removed by hand or with scissors before the needles have begun to extend. This causes the tree to produce three to five new buds around the cut base of the candle, these becoming much smaller candles later on in summer, each with needles which are also usually shorter, if only because they are growing at a time of year when

the weather is drier and the sun stronger. Branch pruning of vigorous pines, such as Scots pine and Japanese black pine, can be carried out in July. This promotes growth from dormant buds. Otherwise major work should be carried out in winter, though not during frosty or snowy spells.

Wiring

Bonsai trees may also be shaped, or modified by wiring. This is a process whereby a piece of wire (usually copper, but nowadays frequently plastic-coated garden wire for thin grades or electricity circuit wire for thicker grades) is wound around the branch or trunk which is then gently bent into the required position. The wire holds the new position until, after a period of time, the trunk or branch will remain in its new shape unaided. The wire is then removed.

Trunks of sizeable deciduous trees are rarely wired, though coniferous tree trunks may be wired and bent, even when the tree is many years old. For this process, a thick piece of wire must be selected at least twice as long as the trunk to be wired and strong enough to hold it when bent. One end of the wire is anchored at the base of the tree by pushing it firmly into the soil between the roots. The wire is then wound round the trunk until the apex is reached, any spare wire being trimmed off. The wire must not be so tight that it bruises the bark, nor so loose that there are gaps

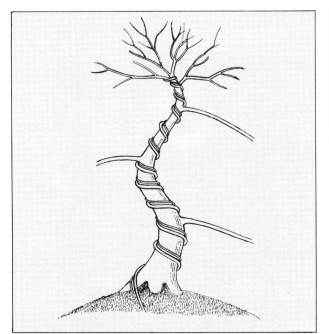

Wiring trunks Two wires, one thick and one thin, are wound side-by-side up the trunk and evenly spaced

Wiring small branches Thin wire is used for wiring the side branches and is anchored first to the main branch

between the wire and bark as it will be ineffective. The trunk should then be bent into the desired position. Thick trunks may take up to three years to set. If during that time the wire becomes tight (due to an increase in the trunk diameter) it should be removed before it damages the bark and the trunk rewired.

Small branches of other deciduous or coniferous trees are dealt with in a similar way only the wire used is thinner, and therefore easier to work with, and the branch will be set in anything from three months to a year depending on thickness and tree species. Wire is anchored by winding it around the trunk or branch from which the branch to be bent grows, then winding down this branch until the tip is reached. Excess wire is then trimmed off and the branch bent between finger and thumb. If on completion the result looks unattractive, the branch should be unwired and left in its original position for a season before rewiring and bending in another position; bending branches back and forth can kill them.

Some species of tree do not like bare wire next to their bark and for these, plastic-coated wire must be used. Most sensitive species are *Cryptomeria japonica* and the many members of the prunus or cherry family. Trees which are easily marked when wired include Japanese elm, the beech family, maples, crab apples, hornbeams and pines. Bonsai of these species should be regularly inspected when wired.

Potting and root pruning

One of the many areas of misunderstanding surrounding bonsai cultivation is in the potting and root pruning required. To understand why bonsai even need root pruning needs a little knowledge of tree roots. A tree growing in a field usually has a root system roughly equal in size to its branch and twig structure. This root system consists of one or several tap roots, which are thick and long and travel vertically downwards, acting as anchors for the big tree above and finding water for it, and a finer-branched feeding root system. This spreads horizontally and diagonally downwards and provides food for the tree in the form of dissolved salts in the soil. These roots grow ever outwards, roughly in proportion to the size of the crown of the tree because the only part of each root which can absorb the necessary salts is the growing tip, which is only about one inch long. The rest of the root acts as a hosepipe, carrying the salts to the tree itself. A tree growing in sandy or gritty soil will have a more finely-divided root system than one growing in

solid clay, because each time a root tip meets a particle of grit, it will tend to divide.

With a bonsai tree that has reached the desired proportions and is potted into a suitable sized container, the crown is maintained by pruning and pinching to remain roughly the same size. However, the roots are also growing and over a period of two or three years, the tree will become potbound. When this has happened, the tree would begin to starve unless it is attended to. As a larger container is not desired, the roots are pruned instead. This is a simple process. The tree has a pot-shaped rootball when removed from its pot. The outer and underneath parts of this should be loosened using a chopstick, household fork or similar object. Some roots may have wound round the pot, in which case these will hang down with other roots giving the rootball the appearance of having an untidy fringe all round. This fringe and any hanging roots should be cut off with a sharp pair of scissors or small secateurs, leaving 65 to 75 per cent of the rootball intact. The tree is then ready for repotting into its container.

The pot is prepared by washing and placing plastic mesh netting over the drainage holes. A layer of gritty pebbles should then cover the bottom of the pot to

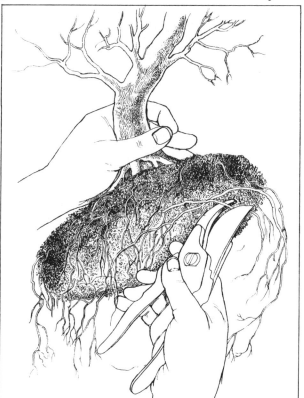

Root pruning Once the tree has reached its desired proportions, the root growth is checked by pruning away long and untidy roots

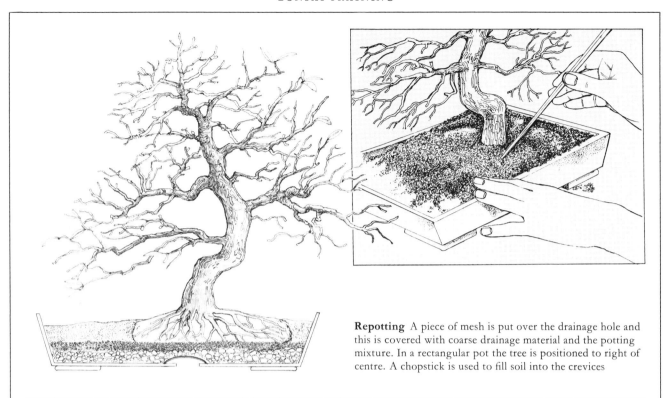

Repotting A piece of mesh is put over the drainage hole and this is covered with coarse drainage material and the potting mixture. In a rectangular pot the tree is positioned to right of centre. A chopstick is used to fill soil into the crevices

encourage good drainage. This is followed by a layer of coarse potting material (generally a mixture of equal parts loam, leafmould and sharp sand) followed by a little finer mixture. It is much easier to use if the mixture is bone dry.

The bonsai should now be positioned in the pot and checked to ensure it is at the right height. The base of trunk should be a little above the level of the pot rim so that, when completely potted, the soil will slope gently up to the trunk, giving the bonsai a more mature look.

The potting mixture is then added around the root-ball and eased in between roots using a chopstick rather than being pushed down with the thumbs as this breaks roots. Finally, when the soil contours are satisfactory, a very thin layer of good loam can be sieved over the surface, this encouraging the growth of mosses which give an attractive finish to the bonsai.

Once potted, the bonsai should be watered until water runs out of the drainage holes, using a can with a very fine rose. If it is a hardy tree it should then be placed in a sheltered spot out of the wind and with a little shade until established in its pot (four to six weeks later). If it is an indoor variety it should be placed in a light position out of direct sun. During this period it must not be fed. Where roots have been pruned, they will tend to divide, like pruned branches, thus giving a very efficient root system of many short

roots. A bonsai does not require a tap root, as it is not large enough to need an anchor and its moisture needs are provided for by its owner.

Root pruning and repotting of hardy trees is usually carried out in early spring, when buds are swelling but leaves are not yet appearing. This is generally February to April depending on species and location. Coniferous trees may also be treated in early autumn, roughly late August to October. Indoor bonsai, whether deciduous or evergreen, usually begin their period of summer growth in response to the longer summer days, house temperatures tending to be fairly stable. April is probably the best month for repotting these bonsai.

Young trees which are growing towards the required size will need little root pruning, as they will be potted on into a larger container. This is carried out in the same way as already described, but the larger pot provides the space that otherwise would be obtained by removing part of the rootball.

All compost used in bonsai potting should be free draining. The suggested mixture of loam, leafmould and grit or sharp sand can, with minor modifications, be used for almost any type of bonsai. Coniferous trees prefer a more open mixture so the sand and leafmould content can be increased, many indoor bonsai prefer a lime-free mixture, in which case lime-free loam (and leafmould) should be used and a little peat may be added.

Feeding and watering

The general care of bonsai, apart from potting, wiring and pruning already mentioned consists of feeding and watering. For the majority of bonsai grown only for foliage feeding is very simple. A liquid fertilizer such as those used for house plants may be given fortnightly once the tree is growing in spring, for about two months. The fertilizer should be diluted twice as much as the manufacturer recommends and used sparingly. From midsummer onwards, the fertilizer should be changed to one used for fruiting plants, such as tomato feed, and used in the same way with the same dilution, leaving off in the autumn before the tree drops its leaves.

This type of fertilizer contains more phosphate and potash and is more suitable for use at this time of year as it encourages the formation of ripe wood. Coniferous trees may be fed in a similar way but the feeding can start earlier in the year and the fertilizer should be even more dilute.

Trees that produce flowers or fruit require a different regime, which will depend on their season of flowering and fruiting. Generally speaking the tree can be lightly fed in spring once flower buds are formed, and until flowers are nearly open. Fertilizer should then be withheld for a period of about six to eight weeks, by which time flowers will have fallen and the fruit will be well formed. The tree may then be fed again, using a fertilizer for fruiting plants, until early autumn.

Watering of plants is a great art and the watering of bonsai is no exception. Many bonsai have for many years been wrongly watered, but a little thought and understanding can make conditions much better for them.

The correct way to water bonsai of most types (though there are one or two special exceptions which will be mentioned later) is to water them, preferably with rain water, until water runs through the drainage holes in the pot, then leave them until nearly all the water has been used by the tree (that is when soil is nearly dry but not bone dry), then water again. The frequency of watering is influenced by many factors, the amount of foliage the tree is carrying in proportion to its rootball size, whether it is recently potted or nearly potbound, the intensity of the sun, the temperature, the wind and rainfall to mention some of the more important. Watering must also relate to practicalities. Do not risk trees drying out on a hot day whilst you are at work, just because they were not dry enough to need watering before leaving in the morning. A fairly usual system adopted by most bonsai owners is as follows. During warmer weather, from April or May until September bonsai are checked each morning and watered unless they are fairly wet (as is often the case in the wet English climate). During very hot spells the bonsai are also checked in the evening. If they are still moist, they may be left until morning. In winter, the trees use far less water, the temperatures are lower and it rains frequently. Bonsai should be checked whenever there are three or four consecutive dry days but may not need watering for months.

The danger periods are spring and autumn. A tree leafing up in spring increases its water requirements dramatically and, the weather often being cold, it is not realized that it is drying out. During this period there are often winds which aggravate the situation. Conversely in September the bonsai is preparing for dormancy, the temperatures are dropping and heavy dews can occur. Geared to summer watering, the owner may, at this period, overwater the bonsai.

A fine specimen of pine grown in the twin-trunk style but on a piece of slate instead of in a pot

however, is a lack of humidity in the air around them. This is easily rectified by standing indoor trees on a shallow tray containing clean grit or sand. If this is kept moist, water will evaporate around the bonsai, giving them a humid microclimate.

Indoor bonsai should, whenever possible, be watered with rainwater. A supply of this should be kept in a dark place in the room where the bonsai are housed. In this way, the water will be at an acceptable temperature for the trees. However, if this water is stored in the light it will rapidly turn green due to algal growth.

Some exceptions to the watering rule have already been mentioned. These mainly concern those species of tree which would, in nature, grow in or close to water. Three of these, all well suited to training as bonsai, are willow, alder and swamp cypress. During the growing season, trees of these species trained as bonsai may be stood in water. This makes them very easy to care for, especially for the person who is often away from home for several days at a time. In winter, they need only be kept reasonably moist.

The reader may be feeling, at this stage, that bonsai are surprisingly easy and logical. This is in many ways true; bonsai are, after all, trees, and just because they are trained to be small and grow in pots does not change their inherent growth habits or needs. Bonsai can present problems, but these can usually be solved by thinking of the tree in its natural state, of its needs, likes and dislikes, and working out what is wrong in its present situation. This is as true of the more exotic varieties as of the hardy tree species.

The flowers of *Malus baccata* 'Mandshurica' are followed by bright red crab apples

Indoor bonsai are less of a problem in this respect. Like hardy trees they will need far more water in summer, both because of their active growth and because houses tend to be better ventilated and so more water is lost by evaporation. However, as the plants are near at hand, any drying out is usually noticed before it is too late. One problem such bonsai do have,

Pests and diseases

It follows that bonsai trees can occasionally be troubled with pests and diseases. Fortunately healthy trees rarely have many diseases, for these tend to attack sick or dying trees. Insects too are more often attracted to unhealthy trees though aphids are not so discriminating. Aphids appear in spring and early summer and feed on the sap contained in the young, soft shoots that are being produced at that time. A small tree can be much weakened by such sap loss and aphids should be removed when seen as their reproduction rate is extremely rapid. The most commonly affected bonsai species is the maple, especially *Acer palmatum* and its

cultivars, and these trees are sensitive to the use of insecticidal sprays. A suggested safe method to use is to hold the bonsai upside down and swill the crown and branches around in a bucket of water to which a dessertspoonful of washing up liquid has been added. If aphids have passed unnoticed for a few days, ants may have found them and be seen travelling up and down the trunk of the bonsai and in the soil in the pot. Ants milk aphids to feed their young and their presence on a bonsai is an almost certain indication that aphids or similar unwanted visitors are present. To remove both ants and aphids, add a spoonful of

A 100-year-old *Juniperus chinensis* grown in the semi-cascade style which requires a deeper than normal pot

Jeyes fluid to the washing up liquid and stand the tree and pot in the bucket for half an hour.

Woolly aphid sometimes affects bonsai trees, especially pines. It is well adapted to prevent removal with its cottonwool-like outer coating which is impervious to many sprays. It overwinters in bark crevices where it can be observed as tiny white spots. Bonsai pines can be sprayed with a suitable insecticide, used exactly according to manufacturers' instructions, and very localized infestations can be treated with a toothbrush and washing up liquid.

Slugs and snails eat the leaves of bonsai, and snails will bury themselves in rootballs. This problem is usually eliminated if bonsai are kept off the ground, on shelves or something similar where, in fact, they look better. Under special circumstances, as for instance with a newly-potted tree being placed in a semi-shady sheltered spot, slugs and snails should be watched for and removed when seen. Likewise in autumn,

falling leaves should be cleared away to ensure there are no hiding places for these pests.

Woodlice and earwigs are two more pests which thrive in gardens where debris is allowed to accumulate. Both can cause damage to roots and care should be taken to keep the area where bonsai are kept clear of leaves and any other debris.

The owners of indoor bonsai may, at this stage, be congratulating themselves as the aforementioned pests rarely trouble trees indoors. However, there are several pests which must be watched out for, two of which can also be a serious problem to outdoor trees. The first is red spider mite. This is not a spider and it is very hard to see but an affected broadleaf tree has mottled foliage and a conifer will look as though the sap has been sucked out of it (which is, in fact, what has happened). On both types of tree, the very fine webs can be seen on examination, especially if the tree is first sprayed with a fine spray of water.

Some varieties are especially susceptible, such as junipers and chamaecyparis amongst outdoor trees, and citrus, palms and many other indoor species. Affected trees must be sprayed with a systemic insecticide, with a second application two or three weeks later. However, prevention is relatively easy and far better than cure. Red spider mite thrives in hot dry conditions both indoors and out. If an area of humidity can be maintained around bonsai this pest is rarely seen. This is most easily achieved by standing trees on trays containing gravel, which can be watered at the same time as the bonsai.

Scale insect is another unpleasant visitor affecting many indoor and outdoor trees, including citrus, pomegranate, maple and elm. They appear as little limpets, firmly attached to bark or the underside of leaves. These are the females, who do not move around. Young scales are produced which undergo a 'crawler' stage, during which they move around until, having found a suitable location, they form the limpet cover. The best means of removal in a bonsai is by hand, using cottonwool buds dipped in methylated spirits or, with care, a lighted cigarette end. During this procedure, the soil in the pot should be covered to prevent falling scales lodging on the compost and producing more crawlers to reinfect the tree. Scale infestations should not be neglected because, like so many of these problems, it multiplies with great rapidity and weakens a bonsai seriously.

Mealy bug, well known to cactus enthusiasts, can affect some bonsai indoors. Young mealy bugs look like very small pale woodlice and they gather together in colonies protected by a white cottonwool-like substance. Treatment is by spraying with some caution. Sometimes, if the infestation is very slight it can be cleared by hand with cottonwool buds and methylated spirits.

The most commonly seen disease affecting bonsai is that of mildew, which looks like a chalky, powdery deposit on leaves. It is most prevalent during a wet summer and commonly affects oaks, hornbeams, hawthorns and crab apples. Affected trees should be sprayed with a suitable fungicide but for those people who grow their own bonsai from seed, this problem can be largely avoided by the simple process of growing plenty of seedlings of these varieties and discarding any that prove especially susceptible to mildew whilst they are young and relatively untrained.

Black spot is a less commonly seen disease affecting maples. Leaves will be covered with black spots. The best cure is to cut off all affected leaves when seen and in autumn, when leaves fall, to collect them all up and burn them, as the disease overwinters on fallen foliage and will otherwise reinfect the tree in spring.

Another disease confined to a single species is azalea gall, which appears like a white mould on azalea leaves. Affected leaves should be removed and burnt.

The conscientious bonsai grower is unlikely to be troubled by many of the pests and diseases mentioned, but, should any of them be seen, prompt action is important and, in the case of red spider mite most essential.

Traditional styles

The reader by now having a good idea of the procedures by which bonsai may be grown, potted, trained, pruned and generally cared for, may like to experiment at training his trees into a range of different styles, or group them together to form little forests. In Japan a number of different styles of trees are defined, all except the first being seen in large trees growing in natural circumstances and adapted from these.

THE FORMAL UPRIGHT

As the name denotes, this is a very formally shaped tree with an absolutely straight tapering trunk from which arise branches, each growing horizontally and radiating from the trunk in a predetermined pattern. Spacing is widest between the lower branches, be-

coming closer as one progresses up the trunk, and the branches also become shorter. Good examples are rarely seen in Britain. The most suitable varieties for this style of training are *Cryptomeria japonica*, pinus varieties and other evergreens.

INFORMAL UPRIGHT

This is the most popular style for bonsai and embraces a wide range of forms, from the typical tree growing in a field, to the gently sloping pines or junipers. Good examples should have greatest width on the lower branches and an attractive balanced appearance. A tapering trunk, which is essential for almost all bonsai, is a great advantage on trees of this style. Almost any species may be trained this way.

Formal upright

Twin trunk

Slanting trunk

SLOPING TRUNK

As the name implies this is a tree with a sloping trunk, but many practitioners neglect to observe that the position of the branches is very important to the balance of the tree. If branches are incorrect, the bonsai will look like an informal upright that has been potted crookedly by mistake. With this proviso, many species are suited to this style.

WINDSWEPT STYLE

Again the name is descriptive of the style which should give the impression of the tree growing in a windswept position. All the branches sweep in one direction and the bonsai should be potted to enhance the effect. Many of the bonsai trained in this way were originally wild trees whose initial trunk and branch shape was created by nature.

SEMI-CASCADE STYLE

In this infrequently seen, but very pretty style, the lower branches, or indeed the trunk, sweep sideways below the level of the top of the pot but remain above the level of the pot base. Again many of these bonsai had their origins in wild places, mountain sides or in areas where landslips occurred. Such bonsai are usually potted in deeper than normal pots for visual balance.

CASCADE STYLE

Sometimes described as upside-down trees, these bonsai have their trunk growing over the side of the pot downwards, ending below the bottom of the pot, which is always deep. They may or may not have a branch forming a crown above the pot, and the cascading part may be a single trunk, or several trunks or branches and may have undulating curves, or be straight. Although many trees can be trained this way, the style is perhaps most suited to pines, junipers and relatively fine foliaged evergreens.

TWIN-TRUNK STYLE

The most important aspect of this style is the relationship both in length and thickness between the main trunk and the subsidiary trunk, both of which have a common base. Many tree species can be trained this way, both coniferous and deciduous.

MULTI-TRUNK STYLE

Similar to the above but with numerous trunks, generally seven and always an uneven number. Few such trees are seen, it being an unusual form of growth, but yews and maples may be found growing in this manner.

RAFT STYLES

Superficially, trees trained in this way appear like group plantings, with a number of 'trunks' irregularly spaced to form a forest-like effect. They are, however, branches of a single tree, formed by the trunk which has been induced to root. Harder to create than a group planting due to the fact that each 'tree', being a branch attached to a trunk, cannot change its basic relationship to neighbouring 'trees'. However, they are great fun and if a suitable young tree is found, with most of its branches growing from one side of the trunk, there is a feeling of real achievement when looking at the results. Many species can be trained in this way, some such as pines, taking some years to grow the necessary roots, but all being worth the effort.

GROUP PLANTING

In this style, a number of trees are planted on a single container to give the effect of a forest, grove or spinney. Usually trees of a single species are grouped together and when groups of less than thirteen or fifteen trees are put together, an uneven number is always used, this being easier to balance visually.

ROOT-CLASPING-ROCK STYLE

Substantially different from all the previously mentioned styles in that the roots of the bonsai are trained over rock before going into the soil in the pot, giving the bonsai a very solid appearance. Almost all bonsai trained in this way are of the variety *Acer buergeranum*, these trees having the advantage of having roots that rapidly become massive and strong.

GROWING-IN-ROCK STYLE

Trees grown in this way are in fact growing in the selected rock rather than in a container. There may be one or several trees of the same or different species on a given piece of rock, and other plants such as ericas, dwarf rhododendrons may be included for effect.

LITERATI STYLE

This is a very strange style, bonsai trained this way having long, thin wandering trunks with a small crown of one or two branches. They are always potted in very small containers, having little foliage, the whole having a beautiful, if slightly unreal, appearance. The style was developed by scholars of the southern school of landscape painting who were stifled by the formality of life around them and used this means to seek their freedom. Literati trees are reminiscent of Japanese or Chinese calligraphy, itself an art form where the space surrounding the painted stroke achieves as much significance as the stroke itself. Literati bonsai are usually pines, though *Juniperus rigida* is also quite widely used, its needled foliage giving a similar effect.

BROOM STYLE

This is a very beautiful shape of bonsai where a slim tapering trunk gives way to a spreading multitude of branches and twiggy growth, somewhat reminiscent of an old-fashioned upturned birch broom. Radiating roots at the base of the trunk give balance to the crown of the broom-style bonsai which is almost always of the species *Zelkova serrata*, always beautiful but perhaps seen at its best during winter months when, bare of leaves, the silvery grey trunk and fine branch structure can show to best advantage.

Training

There are several other styles and categories into which bonsai could be grouped but the best known classifications have been included. All can be created by an interested amateur, some will give very good results in a single day, others take months or even years

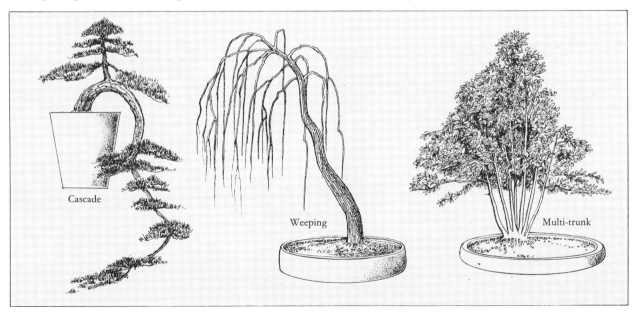

Cascade

Weeping

Multi-trunk

Pomegranates are well suited to growing indoors. This specimen shows the characteristic autumn brilliance

to show significant results. It is, therefore, recommended that the enthusiast try his hand at those whose appearance appeals to him, or for which he has material to hand. As time passes, moods change and others can then be experimented with until the collector has a very representative collection of bonsai.

UPRIGHT STYLE

As bonsai trees in the upright style are trained by the methods of pruning and wiring already outlined, these will not be repeated other than to give guidance on general proportions of trees before explaining the special cultivation requirements for other styles.

An average upright bonsai if its trunk is, say, 2 in in diameter will be six times as tall, i.e. 1 ft. It would normally be potted in a pot 2 in deep and 9 in long; that is three-quarters of the height of the tree. The lowest branch usually grows about one-third of the way up the trunk, that is 4 in from the base, and branches alternate each side of the tree and to the rear. Each branch becomes shorter and closer-spaced towards the apex, the foliage silhouette appearing as a lopsided triangle.

MULTI-TRUNK TREES

These are normally trained as a single tree.

GROUP PLANTING

After cultivating bonsai for a short period, the keen novice may have a number of young bonsai in pots which, whilst not immediately suggesting any particular style, are developing well into healthy young trees. An ideal use for these is to plant several of one species together on a shallow tray to form a group. The planting techniques are the same as for a single tree, the success or failure of such a group depends on the positioning of the trees in the tray and the way trees with special features, such as growth in one direction, or a bend in the trunk, are used.

A few simple guidelines should suffice to give a good idea of the route to success, and these, as with most other features of bonsai, can be observed in spinneys or woodlands. The trees in such areas are not all the same height. However, generally speaking, the taller trees have greater trunk girth than the smaller ones. Frequently a tall tree will be surrounded by trees of lesser stature, the smallest trees being furthest away from the big tree. In a small group of trees, these small trees will tend to grow and lean outwards, towards areas of greater light.

All these features should be present in a good group planting, in addition to which, to create a feeling of distance over the space of a few inches, the taller trees should be at the front of the planting, the smaller to the sides and rear. Trees rarely grow on flat land, so contouring of the soil will add realism to the planting.

RAFT STYLE

A raft planting as mentioned before can look similar to a group but the 'trees' are in fact the branches of a single tree, joined by its trunk which has rooted into the soil. To create this effect, a tree is needed that, through some accident of growth, has most of its branches growing from one side of the trunk. To

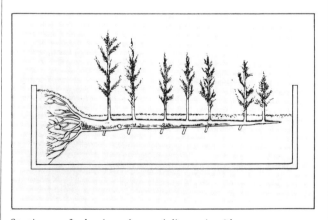

Starting a raft planting: the trunk lies on its side

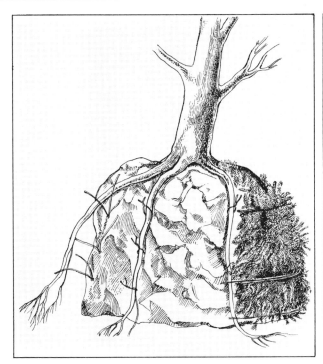

Mounting a root-clasping-rock style bonsai

prepare the tree first do preliminary wiring on the branches to be retained, then any branches on the other side of the trunk should be removed and sloping cuts made into the bark on that side. Rooting powder should be put into these cuts and the tree laid on its side (with retained branches uppermost) in a box deep enough and long enough to contain the rootball and the length of the trunk. The compost used should consist mainly of sharp sand and peat or leafmould to encourage rooting, and should cover the trunk by about one inch.

When the trunk has produced roots from the cut areas of bark on the underside of the trunk, a process that will take from one to five years depending on the species, the old rootball can be cut off. If this can be carried out while the rest of the raft remains undisturbed in the box, this is advantageous and a really good root system can be allowed to develop for a further year. The raft can then be potted into a long shallow tray. During the time taken for the trunk to root, training may be carried out on the branches, with the result that, when finally potted, the raft is very attractive.

ROOT-CLASPING-ROCK STYLE
Trees with their roots trained over rock are fascinating to see and fun to execute. If a bonsai of the species *Acer buergeranum* is selected, results can be achieved in a year

or two, though of course the bonsai and its roots will continue to improve for many years. This species can be easily grown from seed.

A tree should be selected that has a number of long roots. These can be induced by planting the bonsai in a deep flowerpot for a year or so. A rock should be selected, preferably dark in colour and hard in texture and large enough to take into account any increase in size planned for the bonsai. The tree should have the soil washed from its roots which must then be kept moist whilst the rock is prepared.

Lengths of thin wire 6 in long should be bent in half, then fixed by the use of epoxy resin to those parts of the rock where roots are planned to pass. A mixture of natural clay, peat and water should be prepared and applied to the rock. At this stage the bonsai can be placed on the rock and its roots draped over and fixed in position with the wires. More mixture should then be applied to the rock and roots and this should now be covered with moist sphagnum moss. This can be secured by tying the rock round with string. The bonsai on its rock can now be potted.

After a year or two, the moss can be carefully removed and the mixture washed off the rock. The bonsai is now ready for potting in an attractive shallow container.

Acer buergeranum grown in the root-clasping style which is a popular method of training for this species

Presentation of bonsai

When bonsai trees have been carefully trained they warrant the best possible means of presentation. This means not only the choice of pot and manner of potting but also the display of the bonsai whether inside or outside the home.

Most bonsai pots, as already mentioned, are shallow oval or rectangular containers, elevated on little feet and made of an unglazed type of clay which is both porous and frostproof. They are provided with drainage holes and elegant in appearance.

Trees in these attractive containers are normally potted so that the base of the tree is a little above the pot rim. Soil sloping gently from the rim to the tree gives a more mature look.

Bonsai, whether single, multi-trunk or groups, are never placed centrally in the pot, but to left or right of centre and behind a line drawn across the middle of the container. Exceptions to the rule are in the case of literati or cascade pots (the latter are quite deep) which are often seen in round, square or hexagonal shape. Bonsai are usually positioned centrally in such pots.

BONSAI DISPLAYED INDOORS

Care should be taken in choosing the position to display a bonsai at its best in the home. A hardy tree may have been brought in for an evening or two, whilst an indoor tree might be moved from its usual position to a point where it commands greater attention. A bonsai looks best when viewed at or near eye level so a shelf, as long as it is not directly over a source of heat, could be an ideal situation.

A simple but effective method of display is to stand the bonsai on a woven bamboo place mat, linen or a similar woven material also being appropriate. The bonsai can be further enhanced by placing a small attractive stone or a tiny pot containing grasses or bamboo nearby. Three trees of differing size could also be used.

BONSAI DISPLAYED OUTDOORS

Out of doors, bonsai are ideally suited to display on a patio or similar area close to the house. They should not be placed on the ground but elevated on low walls, a table or shelving. An interesting feature can be obtained by hanging a shelf from two brackets of the type used for hanging baskets. One or more bonsai can be placed on the shelf according to size.

This method may also be used on balconies, where a simple step arrangement can also be created at one end of the balcony to accommodate a number of bonsai. With a little imagination, bonsai, despite their superficially oriental look, can be successfully blended with any type of surrounding, from the ultra-modern to the period residence. Their maintenance is straightforward and the grower can be sure that they will, with simple care, give pleasure for many decades.

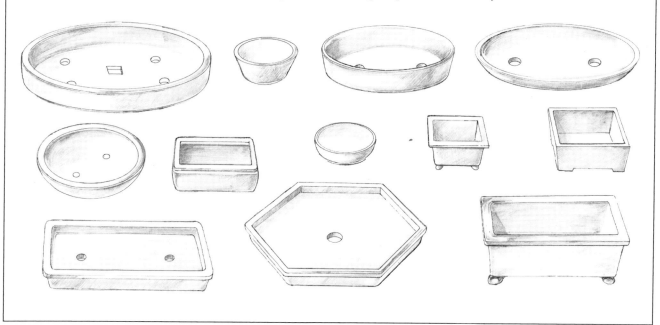

Index

Acknowledgements

Line drawings by Ron Hayward
Colour illustrations on pages 65, 74 and 78 by
Liz Pepperell; on pages 18 (bottom), 23 (top),
26 (bottom), 27 (top), 28 (bottom), 52 (bottom),
57 (bottom right) by June Baker. All other
colour illustrations by Henry Barnett.

The editor would like to thank Thompson and
Morgan (Ipswich) Ltd. and W. J. Unwin Ltd.

for their help in supplying references for
illustrations in chapter 5 – Vegetable and Fruit
Growing in Containers.

PHOTOGRAPHS
Pat Brindley, pages 73 (left), 82 (left and centre),
83; The Hamlyn Group, pages 6, 9; Jerry
Harpur, pages 135 (designed by Clifton
Nurseries Ltd.), 139 (designed by Victor

Shanley, 141 (designed by Clifton Nurseries
Ltd.), 145 (designed by Valery Stevenson), 147;
Paul Kemp, title page; John Lee, page 59;
Martin Rice, pages 85–128; The Harry Smith
Horticultural Photographic Collection, pages 82
(right), 129, 131, 142, 149, 169–188; Michael
Warren, pages 73 (right), 151.